Reassessing

Market, State

WILEY-
BLACKWELL

Reassessing
New Labour

Market, State and Society
under Blair and Brown

Edited by
Patrick Diamond
Michael Kenny

Wiley-Blackwell
In association with *The Political Quarterly*

Library of Congress Cataloging-in-Publication Data
Library of Congress Cataloging-in-Publication Data is available for this work.

A catalogue record for this book is available from the British Library.

ISBN 978-1-4443-5134-7

Set in 10.5/12pt Palatino by Anne Joshua & Associates, Oxford

Printed in the UK by the Charlesworth Group

1st edition 2011

Contents

CONTENTS

Section 4

Section 5

Acknowledgements

We are grateful to all of the participants and speakers at the *Political Quarterly* symposium which we organised in September 2010, and would particularly like to thank Emma Anderson for the considerable help she gave us with this event and the volume arising from it.

Notes on Contributors

Jessica Asato is a Councillor in the London Borough of Islington and Vice-Chair of the Fabian Society.

Vernon Bogdanor is Research Professor at the Institute for Contemporary History at King's College, London.

Dan Corry is at FTI Consulting. He was Senior Adviser on the Economy at Downing Street 2008-10.

John Curtice is Professor of Politics at Strathclyde University and a Research Consultant to the National Centre for Social Research.

John Denham is Shadow Secretary of State for Business, Innovation and Science.

Patrick Diamond is Senior Research Fellow at Policy Network and Nuffield College, Oxford.

Alan Finlayson is a Reader in the Department of Political and Cultural Studies, Swansea University.

Paul Gregg is Professor of Economics University of Bristol.

Tim Horton is Research Director of the Fabian Society.

Peter Kellner is President of YouGov and author of *Democracy: 1,000 years in pursuit of British Liberty*.

Michael Kenny is Professor of Politics at Queen Mary, University of London.

Francesca Klug is Professorial Research Fellow at the LSE and Director of the Human Rights Futures Project.

Guy Lodge is an Associate Director at the Institute for Public Policy Research and co-author (with Anthony Seldon) of *Brown at 10*.

Rick Muir is an Associate Director at the Institute for Public Policy Research.

James Purnell is Chair of the IPPR and former Secretary of State for Work and Pensions.

Kitty Ussher is Director of Demos.

Stuart White is a Fellow of Jesus College, Oxford.

Shirley Williams is a former Labour MP and minister who cofounded the Social Democratic party and has served as Leader of the Liberal Democrats in the House of Lords.

Tony Wright is joint editor of *The Political Quarterly* and Professorial Fellow in the Department of Politics at Birkbeck College, University of London.

Preface

IN ASSESSING Labour's time in office, it's maybe best to start at the end. Three images dominate my memory of the last election, and all are instructive about our successes and failures, and where Labour goes from here. First is the last debate. Gordon Brown had just had his worst 24 hours in politics, in the aftermath of his denunciation of Mrs Duffy. Yet the debate showcased one of his undoubted strengths—his pertinacity in a tough spot. Given what he was feeling, it was an extraordinarily dogged performance. However, it was a performance woven around the negative: gone was any pretence at defending Labour's record or offering an alternative. The message was simple: the Conservatives were a risk. The conventional explanation for why Labour had run out of steam by the election was that it had lost the courage to reform, and that is a good part of the truth.

But the second image, Mrs Duffy's original words in her conversation with Brown, pre-'bigot' if you will, perhaps teach us even more:

Look, the three main things that I had drummed in when I was a child was education, the health service and looking after people who are vulnerable. There are too many people now who aren't vulnerable who can claim, and people who are vulnerable who can't claim.

Mrs Duffy was the kind of voter that Tony Blair was supposed to have got back on-side. The rest of the exchange is just as instructive, in retrospect (http://www.timesonline.co.uk/tol/news/politics/article7110540.ece). She congratulates the local education system, hopes her grandchildren will go to university, but is worried that she has to pay tax on her widow's pension. Mrs Duffy stands for everything that Sedgefield was supposed to have taught New Labour—that we needed to be for aspiration, good public services and a concern for the most vulnerable. Yet, thirteen years on, despite recognising that Labour had delivered pretty much on those promises, Mrs Duffy still felt angry enough to upbraid the Prime Minister.

Why? Maurice Glasman, the creator of 'Blue Labour', argues that it was because of Labour's tradition of scientific materialism, or maybe that should be put as the elevation of technocracy over democracy. This tried to improve society from the centre, according to an exogenous standard—equality for Tony Crosland, a combination of economic growth and reducing poverty for New Labour. Much good was done with this method, as is catalogued in this important collection of essays. But it didn't work for Mrs Duffy. It operated outside her conception of fairness, and was too managerial. It was done to her, and wasn't what she'd asked for in the first place. This explains the chasm between Gordon Brown's recitation of Labour's achievements and what many Labour politicians would have experienced as a lack of gratitude from voters.

Published by Blackwell Publishing Ltd, 9600 Garsington Road, Oxford OX4 2DQ, UK and 350 Main Street, Malden, MA 02148, USA

There was an alternative to this tradition of scientific materialism. Indeed, it was in this current that Tony Blair first edged in to national consciousness. Before his Bulger speech, he was perhaps better known for having a mass membership party in Sedgefield, built on barbecues and social events rather than General Committee meetings. Blair did not follow through on this possibility of creating a bigger, more rooted party. However, this is a baton that has been picked up by this generation of Labour politicians. The Movement for Change (http://movementforchange.org.uk/), by bringing the disciplines of community organising back in to the Labour party, is actually reaching back to a much earlier Labour tradition.

Before Labour succeeded in taking control of the state, it achieved its goals through association. At the end of the nineteenth century, workers faced an obdurate capitalism, and organised to resist its worst defects. Labour grew out of that tradition, and could renew itself today by learning again from those practices. These would include reciprocity, mutualism and the consequent trust that grows out of people believing that if they contribute in to a system, whether in their community or through the welfare state, they will be protected in return. It is that conception of fairness that many Labour voters felt had been offended. To convince them of the alternative, it is no good showing an IFS (Institute for Fiscal Studies) graph demonstrating that Labour's tax and benefit changes benefited the poorest. It is an offence against relationships that has been committed: reciprocity and mutualism have broken down, and therefore trust has evaporated.

These are the lessons that 'Blue Labour' reaches for in the pre-1945 tradition. However, they are not enough. By themselves, or at least applied superficially, they tend to nostalgia—to an appearance of wanting to defend rather than create. As a number of contributors to this volume demonstrate, Labour's record was at its most successful when it was giving people power— giving cancer patients the power to control their care, or academy heads the power to turn around failing schools. New Labour's version of empowerment sounded good in the seminar, but it felt hollow on the doorstep. If we combine it with Blue Labour's reminder that our tradition has always been about protecting people from suffering, we can find fertile fields of policy renewal. In welfare, for example, it would lead us to ask how we can make the promise of protection true again. The 1945 settlement was Labour's bedrock for a generation because it genuinely protected people against the risks they worried about then—what happens if I get sick or old, how can I afford to have another baby?

Too often, New Labour sounded as if we no longer thought we could protect people. We could help them get their next job, but couldn't protect them against the threat to their current one. A new approach to welfare would ask what those risks are today, and how the welfare state can genuinely protect people against them. It might say that people want a guarantee of housing, work, wage protection, a pension, parental leave, and that they value less the universal benefits which are insufficient in times of need, but marginal when things are going well. Most of all, it would explore how that new covenant could be founded on a basis of reciprocity and trust.

The third image that dominates my memory of the campaign was Gordon Brown's speech at the Citizens UK civil society debate. Suddenly, he took rhetorical flight, and the audience went as close to wild as ever happens in modern politics. Brown reached back to his roots in Labour politics and thumped the proverbial tub. The audience was cohesive and delighted because they heard all the leaders that day endorsing their demand for progress on the living wage. This is the most important lesson of this vignette: that the content is not as important as the process—namely that ordinary people had come together through organising to develop a common interest and gather the power to make politicians listen.

As Eduard Bernstein, the founder of social democracy, said: '[T]he ideas are nothing, the movement everything.' Gordon Brown was in a room where the movement had given people power. Suddenly, empowerment had escaped the seminar. In that mixture of organising, practice and tradition lies the verdict of Labour's last term and the possibility of gaining its next one.

James Purnell

Introduction
Reviewing New Labour in Government: Progressive Dilemmas?

PATRICK DIAMOND and MICHAEL KENNY

Introduction

THE PRIMARY purpose of this collection is to bring together analysts, commentators and practitioners from a diversity of traditions on the centre-left to develop a balanced assessment of Labour's record in government, and to consider its future as a party of power in British politics. This involves looking back at what was achieved and what might have been during New Labour's thirteen years in office. The contributors to this volume each address the fundamental question of how the party ought to interpret its record after three unprecedented terms in government.

There is inevitably disagreement as to the impact and substance of New Labour's record across the policy agendas of government. However, the authors broadly agree that the party now faces fundamental strategic challenges which can only be met by marrying ideological clarity with political realism. They focus on the structural constraints that presently face centre-left parties across the world which were hardly discernible when Labour came to office in 1997. They also suggest that there is a powerful and compelling case for a new phase of critical rethinking, not just within Labour's ranks but among the diverse communities of centre-left scholarship and opinion in British society.

Evaluating Labour's period in power

Developing a properly contextualised account of New Labour's period in office is far from easy. Such an evaluation entails a subtle appreciation of the events and contingencies that confronted the Labour government, including the strategic aims of its leading protagonists, the policy options it chose not to pursue but might have been, and the constraints and obstacles New Labour perceived itself to have faced in power. By taking on these debates, this book intends to stimulate an extensive and nuanced process of revaluation. In delivering their verdicts on the most significant areas of domestic policy, our contributors shed additional light on the political space in which Labour operated that over time it helped to shape and redefine. They offer challenging and important reflections on the merits and limits of the governing

Published by Blackwell Publishing Ltd, 9600 Garsington Road, Oxford OX4 2DQ, UK and 350 Main Street, Malden, MA 02148, USA

philosophy that animated Labour's record. And they explore the underlying intellectual and ideological identity of the Blair and Brown governments.

After serious defeat, Labour now faces tough questions about its identity and purpose as a governing party. There has been relatively little systematic effort to understand the reasons why the party lost so much electoral support between 1997 and 2010. But Labour's capacity to reconnect with sceptical elements of the British electorate is contingent on a proper audit of its performance in office. The party needs to show that it understands where it went wrong, and which elements of its record ought to be built on if it is be entrusted with government ever again.

It should start by thinking harder about the underlying causes of defeat in 2010. Glib explanations alluding only to 'time for a change' and the unpopularity of Gordon Brown fail to grasp the enormity of Labour's strategic predicament. The memoirs and diaries that have pervaded post-election debate promote a distinctly agency-centred view, having a distorting effect by ignoring the wider structural context in which British politics is conducted. So engaging in a balanced and nuanced analytical assessment of the New Labour years remains an imperative.

This relates partly to Labour's model of governance. The party became associated with a style of governing—typically couched as centralist, statist and top-down—which proved to be a major barrier to the fulfilment of social justice and the public interest. This mode of centralist, lever-pulling statecraft was highly effective in certain respects, especially during Labour's first term (1997–2001). But over time the currency of that approach was rather devalued as fresh thinking, new ideas and reflexive criticism barely penetrated the New Labour citadel. For all the commitment to 'renewal' in the final years of the Labour government, there was little evidence that it was ever going to happen. In fact, the relentless rhetoric of political renovation became a substitute for concerted action.

Since the financial crisis, there is a widespread perception that Labour's statist instincts contributed to the familiar social democratic sin of financial profligacy in mismanaging the public finances, spending incontinently and contributing to the present fiscal crisis of the British state. While the causes of the crisis are inevitably far more complex, Labour continues to be damaged politically by the Coalition government's framing of the crisis, rooted in the levels of public debt accumulated by Labour. The damage done to the party's reputation for economic competence has been considerable, and may well prove long-lasting.

In order to construct a viable alternative, Labour must be prepared to admit candidly that errors were made both in relation to the deregulation of the financial system, and the inadequacy of the United Kingdom's tax base. At the same time, the party has to defend its economic record, which did, after all, result in forty consecutive periods of growth, with unemployment reaching its lowest ever recorded level. This was the first Labour government in history that had not been blown off course by an early economic crisis. Additional investment in scientific and technological research brought new jobs and industries to Britain in niche sectors such as pharmaceuticals, biosciences and advanced manufacturing. Sustained investment in cities and public infrastructure helped to narrow the regional economic divide, as well as bolstering Britain's high-value service and creative industries. Neither should it be forgotten that—as the Nobel prize-winning economist Paul Krugman observed—Gordon Brown's government excelled in its handling of the 2008–09 crisis, providing leadership to safeguard the global economy, staving off the worst meltdown in the financial system for more than eighty years.

The second rationale for a sustained assessment of the New Labour record is that there has been a marked shift within the party's ranks during the early phase of opposition against the agendas most associated with the Blair era of British governance. Nonetheless, learning lessons from the various approaches and strategies that the party adopted throughout its time in government will provide a vital store of governing know-how in years to come.

The third rationale for a serious audit of New Labour's record relates to a question of foundational significance for the centre-left: whether the current plight of progressive parties throughout Europe indicates that the core proposition underlying social democracy is no longer viable. Labour has to address fundamental questions about its purpose and prospects as a potential party of government. Can the marriage of social justice and economic efficiency that New Labour advocated plausibly be re-established in the wake of the economic melt-down of 2008–09? It has to carefully consider whether the waning of confidence in the notion of the state as an agent that is able to protect and promote the public interest is now reversible, or whether unqualified statism has been tested to destruction and the era of 'big' government is over. These are profound and important debates, which the centre-left cannot avoid if it wants to govern again with a sense of purpose and confidence.

Labour has an electoral mountain to climb

The scale of Labour's defeat in 2010 and the precarious nature of its current predicament have yet to be confronted. The party achieved the second lowest share of the vote in a national election since universal suffrage. It lost ground among all constituencies and classes, suffering a dramatic collapse in support among C1 and C2 voters on middle and lower incomes. More generally, Labour lost over five million votes since the landslide of 1997, and its support is now geographically concentrated in Scotland, Wales and northern England. Only 49 out of 302 seats in the Midlands and the South outside London are still held by Labour. And almost a third of working-class voters, many of whom previously voted Labour, chose not to vote at all.

Indeed Labour's claim to be a national party capable of representing a range of interests and institutions across society looks increasingly threadbare. The Conservatives are now the dominant party in England, although they are a long way from establishing themselves as a nationwide force. Coalition with the Liberal Democrats ensures that the government has adequate representation in Scotland and Wales, but it retains a predominantly English face.

Labour's electoral quandary is even starker because the Coalition is intent on reducing the number of parliamentary constituencies in a drive to equalise the number of voters. Under the current first-past-the-post system for elections to the Westminster Parliament, there is an increasing likelihood of hung parliaments and a decreasing prospect of overall parliamentary majorities for any single party. This trend has been accentuated by the rise in support for parties other than Labour and the Conservatives across the United Kingdom. The era of 'winner takes all' politics may well be drawing to a close. This means that Labour now faces a double challenge in electoral terms. It has to regain the significant support it lost in 2005 and 2010, especially in southern England where it was almost wiped out as a political force. At the same time, the party has to signal that it grasps that a new era of plural, multiparty politics is unfolding in Britain.

Change and contingency in British politics

The tensions besetting the Coalition government mean that the current political situation remains fluid and may change dramatically. Many familiar landmarks in British politics have been uprooted, leading to new ideological alignments cutting across the traditional ideological boundaries of left and right. The apparent predilection for avoidable administrative blunders by the current government has given many in Labour hope of short-term political revival. Fear of the Conservatives as the party of inherited wealth and the privileged sections of society still haunts large segments of the British electorate, and voters remain sceptical as to whether the fiscal austerity programme initiated by Cameron and Osborne represents a fair distribution of the costs and burdens imposed by the global financial crisis.

Nonetheless, denied an absolute majority in the aftermath of the 2010 election, Cameron seized the opportunity to remake the identity of his party, forging an historic coalition with the Liberal Democrats. In so doing the new Prime Minister took possession of two prized assets in British politics: the mantle of the 'new politics', and the holder of the title deeds to 'the future'. By working comfortably with a rival party and apparently eschewing short-term party interests, it was the Conservatives who appeared most in tune with the political zeitgeist. It is far from clear that Labour has settled on a style of opposition politics that signals its ease with this new political landscape, or that it has the capacity to operate as a dynamic and progressive force for the future.

For all the invective directed against the Blair and Brown governments, 1997–2010 could easily be judged the most successful period of Labour government since the Attlee administration in the 1940s. New Labour secured three successive election victories and initiated a host of constitutional and social reforms that historians will regard as socially and politically transformative. One important measure of genuinely radical governments concerns their impact on their political opponents, and whether the latter are pulled towards the parameters and forms of 'common sense' associated with the party in power: attributes that are commonly associated with the Thatcher administration. New Labour helped to forge a new political settlement framed around constitutional renewal, substantial investment in public services, the restoration of the National Health Service to a central position in British national life, and a programme of social liberalisation which has significantly strengthened individual rights. The Cameron-led coalition government continues to be judged by the extent to which it consolidates or seeks to break out of the pathways and trajectories established by the Blair and Brown governments after 1997.

But just as New Labour may have had a mesmeric effect on its political opponents, the government was also characterised by the range and depth of opposition it elicited, particularly during the second (2001–05) and third (2005–10) terms. At times it appeared that the party had united almost every strand of progressive opinion against it. This stemmed in part from the deep schism created by the Iraq War, and Britain's compliance with President Bush's quest for regime change in the Middle East. But its unpopularity arose too from the palpable sense of disenchantment with the centralism and statism that were a hallmark of Labour's model of governance, and the limitations of its model of political economy which struggled to address intractable inequalities of wealth and income in British society.

New Labour's travails also arose from tensions concerning its political strategy as a modern centre-left party. This conception of statecraft was based around the notion of dominating the centre-ground, rejecting ideological doctrines that had made the party increasingly off-putting to centrist voters. It sought to construct the widest electoral coalition imaginable, but in so doing weakened Labour's ability to pursue a more 'conviction-orientated' politics. All governments confront sectional interests standing in the way of progressive reform, and New Labour was certainly no exception. Despite three record-breaking majorities, however, Labour in government remained oddly reticent about taking on powerful interests. Among the two most obvious examples are the police force in England and Wales despite serious concerns about its performance and efficiency, and the banks whose risky and irresponsible practices in financial markets threatened the long-term stability of the British economy. Labour weakened its own moral standing by appearing more than willing to take on benefit claimants and the excluded, while ignoring irresponsible and 'anti-social behaviour' at the very top of society.

An intimidating charge sheet has been assembled by the Labour government's critics making the development of a more dispassionate and reasoned judgement of New Labour's performance all the harder. This is another reason why senior figures within the party—notably during the leadership contest that followed the election—have been reluctant to clarify their own stance in relation to key aspects of Labour's period in government, also reflecting the persistent hangover of the divisions and conflicts associated with the Blair–Brown era. The temptation to consign the entire period to the past and move on as quickly as possible is quite understandable, but in politics it is hard to move forward without an extended phase of rethinking drawing on a measured evaluation of past successes and failings.

A separate challenge facing any rigorous evaluation of the New Labour years is that the yardstick against which the government's performance ought to be assessed is heavily contested. There are a range of historically informed accounts that compare the Blair and Brown administrations unfavourably with the postwar Labour governments of Attlee, Bevin, Morrison and Bevan. There are others which tend to interpret Blair as a more contemporary version of Harold Wilson, swept to office with high hopes of radical social reforms but failing to meet the expectations of his supporters, and becoming immersed in endless scandals and squalid compromises. Such judgements often rest on implicit and unstated normative assumptions which can distort as much as illuminate political life. In addition, there is a persistent tendency to overstate the radicalism of Labour's past, diminishing its more recent governing achievements. All postwar Labour governments embraced markets and competition as the driving force of a modern industrial economy. At the same time, New Labour's programme was often highly redistributive, particularly in its first two terms in office. Too often understanding of Labour's historical development as a governing party has been subject to deliberate misinterpretation.

Among the more problematic interpretations of New Labour in government are to be found among those who erect an 'ideal-type' model of social democracy, against which Labour's period in government is inevitably found wanting. The leadership is lambasted for failing to tackle 'structural' and 'systemic' challenges, refusing to deliver long-cherished radical goals such as reversing entrenched patterns of economic inequality in British society. These judgements often overlook the fact that the political project enunciated by New Labour explicitly repudiated more familiar social democratic objectives.

This disagreement about the plausibility and implications of ethical values and the shift in 'ends' is quite legitimate, but *a priori* negative judgements which presume the eternal superiority of particular values are a different matter. As well as leading to faulty historical judgements, such approaches ignore the most pressing contemporary issue: how to develop an identity for Labour enabling it to leave behind the era of Blair and Brown without losing sight of the strategic insights on which New Labour's electoral and ideological appeal was founded.

Modernisers and traditionalists

The most potent and far-reaching debates within the party continue to be framed by the frustrations and alignments of those long years in office. On the one hand, the 'Blairite' New Labour wing continue to argue that the party will only successfully compete for office where it resumes its role as a modernising centrist force, articulating support for lower levels of income tax, further reform of public services, stronger emphasis on conditionality in the welfare state, a punitive approach to law and order, and sustaining Britain's robust military alliance with the United States. This worldview regards Britain as an essentially conservative country which has little instinctive sympathy with social democratic values. The future for Labour is that of a party that is willing and able to shift further from its roots, resuming the reforming zeal of the New Labour era.

On the other hand, there is the 'soft left' wing which looks back favourably to the leadership of Neil Kinnock and John Smith, and regards much of the New Labour period as an unfortunate aberration in the party's history. Accordingly, Blair and Brown abandoned the party's historic mission to advance social justice and eradicate human misery and suffering by tackling poverty and deprivation. The Blair government in particular became entranced by the wealthy and privileged to the detriment of the party's core supporters. And while the Brown premiership appeared to offer the hope of rediscovering ideological purpose, such hopes were dashed by Brown's evident fallibilities as a holder of prime ministerial office, and his manifest inability to forge a post-Blair agenda.

Both the 'Blairite' and 'soft left' narratives are marred by their sectarian origins, and are unhelpful starting-points for a credible re-examination of the party's record in government. Neither is sufficiently nuanced to confront the key issue facing centre-left politics in Britain, highlighted above. Is social democracy still politically viable and if so, what does a social democratic programme now entail? With centre-left politics in disarray in almost every major industrialised country, the abject unwillingness to confront this question is telling indeed.

Social liberalism and social democracy

Labour has historically drawn from both liberalism and social democracy as a progressive party committed to the promotion of social welfare and equality, alleviating the injustices arising from an unstable and unregulated market economy. The link between liberty and equality is fundamental to the party's identity. Progressive politics in Britain has advanced through a conjunction between the broad lineage of social liberalism and historical labourism. It has gained strength from the emphasis of liberalism on liberty and constitutional freedom, while drawing on communitarian and collectivist commitments at the core of the British socialist tradition. This has resulted in a nexus of overlapping and mutually supporting arguments and narratives through which social liberals and liberal social democrats have enunciated their ideational commitments.

The Attlee government would have been immeasurably weaker without the contribution of William Beverage and J. M. Keynes, just as the pioneering social reforms of the 1960s and 1970s depended on the liberal zeal of Roy Jenkins. Throughout Labour's history, the party has drawn on the synthesis of equality and liberty associated with the conception of positive freedom espoused by T. H. Green, J. A. Hobson and Leonard Hobhouse in order to justify the enabling and interventionist role of the state. At the same time, fashioning a broad electoral coalition has always required the party to reach beyond its working-class base—one reason why it has always been home to such a wide range of progressive opinion.

Without a wider revival of centre-left progressivism in Britain, it is hard to envisage a majoritarian social democratic project in the foreseeable future. In the meantime the participation of the Liberal Democrats in the current coalition, alongside long-term structural change such as the fragmentation and pluralisation of progressive opinion, make any conception of the 'progressive alliance' that shaped the mind-set of leading commentators and politicians until the Blair–Brown era increasingly irrelevant. The very idea of a 'progressive alliance' needs to be fundamentally reimagined given the contemporary conjecture of British politics. Such an endeavour is umbilically tied to a fundamental reassessment of the social democratic project after the demise of New Labour.

The revisionist spirit that Labour now needs ought to be rooted in an appraisal of its recent historical past as a governing party, as much as the current vogue for reaching back towards the early labour movement of the mid-nineteenth century. This perspective is a reminder that the British left has undertaken a fundamental reassessment of its ideological direction and programmatic commitments every thirty years or so. The last major bout of sustained revisionism erupted during the long years of Thatcherism. The journal *Marxism Today* enraged and stimulated with its distinctive mixture of theoretically informed iconoclasm and affinity for the modernity that was emerging from the wreckage of the 1980s. Thirty years previously, intellectuals and artists had flocked to the unconventional and eclectic New Left movement. They sought to pose fundamental questions about the meaning of socialism in an era of affluence, advertising and the H-Bomb. The new left shared with Labour's more conventional revisionist thinkers such as Anthony Crosland an appreciation that Labour was likely to succeed when it projected itself as the party most attuned to the popular mood, equipped to seize the title deeds to Britain's future.

In the 1950s and the 1980s, it took more than one heavy defeat for the penny to drop that Labour was facing a crisis of ideology and identity, and not merely short-term unpopularity. If history is not to repeat itself three decades on, ideological renewal and revisionist reappraisal of orthodoxy has to take precedence. Labour must act as the incubator for sustained rethinking, and use the policy review process as the catalyst for a more fundamental process of reappraisal.

The revisionist impulse necessitates far greater sociological curiosity about the experiences and identities of Britain's places and communities: Labour has to reacquaint itself with the insecurities and aspirations of an increasingly complex and heterogeneous electorate. That means posing challenging questions about what terms like 'community' now mean, and where people gain their sense of belonging and affiliation in twenty-first-century Britain? Is it possible to combine the values of 'community' and 'aspiration', still routinely invoked by Labour politicians, into a coherent ideological framework? Does equality remain the abiding normative value of social democratic politics, or should the notion of 'fairness' endure despite its contested meaning and implications? Given the implosion of the British economic model founded on high levels of household debt, unsustainable consumer spending and speculative asset bubbles, how does Labour now frame and project a new conception of well-being and personal self-fulfilment?

Embracing a new revisionism requires these aspirational and ethical concerns to be assessed alongside key contemporary dilemmas. Can Labour credibly remake itself as a political force that speaks imaginatively to young people at the sharp end of the growing intergenerational divide? Is the party able to speak coherently across deep cleavages of political identity and geography given the new found fragility of the British state? And will Labour break with its historical mind-set and learn to accept the implications of electoral competition in a multitiered polity? In Britain, power in Vernon Bogdanor's words has been 'cut up' and dispersed to elites across the United Kingdom, including the judiciary and devolved institutions, challenging the long-cherished social democratic dream of seizing power at the centre and administering change, uniformly, from above.

This is closely connected to the putative shift towards a more community-focused model of political organisation which has recently achieved prominence. The key strategic question that needs to be debated among advocates of community organising is how to sustain a plural, organic and community-engaged movement, *and* retain the focus to challenge for power given the realities of modern electoral politics in Britain? As well as investing in training community leaders, Labour needs to consider how best to deal with a political culture that is still tailored towards a centralised, and disciplined approach reinforced by an adversarial and antiquated tribalism. The pool of political representation in Britain has become too stagnant, and politicians have been too keen to manipulate rather than reform a culture that has closed off routes for those from working-class backgrounds, while undermining the relationship between voters and their elected representatives.

Finally, Labour has to think more expansively about the international best practice from which it draws ethical and practical inspiration. New Labour was forged in the early 1990s, drawing heavily on its links with the Democrats in the United States. It was impressed by reforms initiated by the Clinton administration—notably the Earned Income Tax credit, welfare reform and the expansion of the 'Head Start' programme to alleviate early childhood disadvantage. But Labour paid far too little attention to models of success in continental Europe—notably the Netherlands and the Nordic countries, which have historically combined high levels of growth and equity. There are national models of success on which Labour can now draw, including the Danish conception of 'flexicurity' in the labour market, and the German model of high productivity, partnership-orientated 'stakeholder' capitalism. There are inevitably limits to policy replication given divergent national contexts and political traditions. Those who seek a more interventionist role for government in the economy following the global financial crisis need to accept it will not be generated overnight given the constraints and obstacles associated with the political culture and institutions of the British state. Nonetheless, it would be foolhardy not to learn from policies and practices which have been tried and tested by others.

Contents

These themes are elaborated in the thematically focused essays that comprise this volume. In Section I, the contributors assess New Labour's performance in relation to the welfare state, labour market reform and social policy. **Paul Gregg** contends that Labour made substantial progress in reducing relative poverty among children and pensioners. Nonetheless, it had lost momentum by the third term, bequeathing a legacy of rising income inequality measured by the United Kingdom Gini coefficient. **Tim Horton** similarly highlights the mixed success of Labour's record, suggesting that the government struggled to translate multiple initiatives and programmes into a coherent set of institutions that would sustain cross-class support for a modern welfare state. **John Denham** argues that Labour has to reconsider the strengths and limitations of the welfare model which was developed during those years in the light of new concerns about reciprocity and social fairness.

Section II explores New Labour's record on constitutional reform and the new politics. **Vernon Bogdanor** shows how Labour's reforms altered the nature of the British state, but effectively redistributed power to elites rather than engaging popular energies. **John Curtice** draws attention to how Labour's reforms have coincided with the fragmentation and pluralisation of British politics, providing a critical assessment of New Labour's repeated claims to have transformed the relationship between people and politicians in the name of a new politics. **Francesca Klug** interrogates New Labour's legacy in relation to civil liberties, addressing the paradox that a party which introduced the Human Rights Act and a host of new social freedoms developed such a poor reputation on civil liberties. Klug connects these concerns about the precariousness of civil liberties to the emergence of a heavy-handed and centralising bureaucratic state in Britain. Finally, **Guy Lodge** and **Rick Muir** consider the cautious and limited nature of New Labour's initiatives to pass back power and responsibility to local communities and local government.

Section III examines New Labour's conception of economic policy and political economy. As **Kitty Ussher's** contribution makes clear, Labour's record on the economy prior to the 2008–09 financial crises was unprecedented, ensuring more than a decade of rising growth, productivity and living standards, and sharing the gains across the income distribution. This was shattered by the crisis and the onset of the most severe global economic recession since the 1920s. Ussher argues that Labour's culpability needs to be carefully qualified, and that public debt when the global shocks hit the United Kingdom was not abnormally large. **Dan Corry** suggests that even with the benefit of hindsight it is far from clear that an alternative conception of economic management existed given the constraints operating on any social democratic government in Britain. Corry maintains that the Labour government did seek to adapt and alter the underlying trajectory of the British economy, but inherited a state which palpably lacked the capacity for strategic intervention and modernisation. **Stuart White** concludes by reflecting on the missed opportunities to enact new models of stakeholding and popular ownership. Labour had the opportunity to establish a new model of sustainable capitalism, undertaking a wide-ranging redistribution of assets and opportunities in British society. But political caution meant that momentum after the 1997 and 2001 victories was quickly lost.

In Section IV, the authors reflect on the historical legacy and wider impact of New Labour, focusing particularly on issues of class, community and the public realm. **Peter Kellner** suggests that New Labour's legacy has been to demonstrate that the traditional model of redistributive 'tax and spend' social democracy is no longer tenable given the intensity of technological and demographic change. **Alan Finlayson** also reflects critically on the problems created by New Labour's ambiguity concerning the politics of class. The failure to acknowledge the continuing relevance of class weakened its electoral appeal, blinding New Labour to a host of emerging social and cultural cleavages. Finally, **Jessica Asato** assesses New Labour's record on public services, where the impact of substantial investment in the public sphere was blunted by structural changes which alienated the public and professionals despite the overall improvement in NHS and school performance.

The fifth and final section offers personal reflections on the politics and impact of the New Labour years. **Shirley Williams**, in conversation with the former Labour parliamentarian **Tony Wright** considers the challenges currently facing social democratic politics. She depicts Tony Blair as a figure cut from the cloth of Christian Democracy struggling to come to terms with epochal change, and explains why a revitalised social democracy has a crucial part to play in Britain's future. **Brian Brivati** provides an historically informed analysis of New Labour, arguing that the party only broke the spell of the Thatcherite consensus in the aftermath of the global financial crisis. Nonetheless, Brivati maintains that the Blair and Brown governments will be viewed in a more positive light by future historians given that they have helped Britain to finally escape from a long period of relative economic decline.

This volume does not seek to address New Labour's legacy in foreign affairs, particularly the conflicts in Afghanistan and Iraq to which British armed forces have been committed. We acknowledge their significance in assessing Labour's record in government, and hope that such events will be analysed fully in the burgeoning literature on British foreign policy under New Labour. The book ends with a brief 'afterword' from the editors, **Patrick Diamond** and **Michael Kenny**, in which they bring together major themes and arguments elaborated in the essays, proposing a forward-looking prospectus for Labour as it seeks to resume its role as a serious contender for power in British politics.

New Labour and Inequality

PAUL GREGG

Introduction

THE TRAUMATIC experience of the 1992 election defeat led New Labour to adopt a hostile position towards the imposition of higher income tax rates, especially for the affluent. Yet, while the phrase 'redistribution' was largely avoided, considerable efforts were made to tackle relative income poverty among families with children and pensioners. The tension in New Labour's strategy was encapsulated by Tony Blair's now notorious interview with Jeremy Paxman in the 2001 election campaign. Despite repeated attempts by Paxman to pin down the former Prime Minister on where he stood in relation to inequality, Blair made the significant distinction of caring about the income gap between the poorest Britons and the bulk of society (that is, relative income poverty), while making clear he was unconcerned about the gap between the affluent and those in the middle of the distribution.

This relatively nuanced position meant that Labour oversaw a period of falling poverty but rising inequality in the United Kingdom, primarily driven by a continuation of very rapid income growth among the highest earning 2 per cent of people in Britain. However, redistributive policies in the form of changes to tax and benefits were not the major driver of inequality in Britain over that period, or, indeed, during the preceding Conservative administration. Rising inequality came primarily from changes in the pretax distribution of wages and work across households. This does not mean that inequality is not and cannot be influenced by government policy. Rather it implies that the government's macroeconomic and microeconomic policy making, including agendas such as tackling unemployment or increasing the supply of skills, are at the heart of any drive to reduce inequality and, indeed, poverty in the United Kingdom. It is in these domains as much as through redistribution that the government achieved relatively modest improvements in poverty, and failed to address inequality.

At its heart New Labour sought to adopt, even champion, the post-Thatcher liberal economic model while ameliorating its harder edges and adverse social consequences. The amelioration was undertaken through a mix of redistribution (tax credits, etc.) and 'economic' policy, such as tackling worklessness, community deprivation and significant labour market-based interventions such as the National Minimum Wage. But the overall picture that emerges of Labour's performance is that many of the policies adopted were moderately successful, but simply too small-scale to overturn the underlying macroeconomic and microeconomic forces driving inequality.

Labour inherited a country where inequality had risen rapidly in the 1980s and 1990s, with the Gini coefficient—the share of income that would need to

Published by Blackwell Publishing Ltd, 9600 Garsington Road, Oxford OX4 2DQ, UK and 350 Main Street, Malden, MA 02148, USA

be redistributed from the rich to the poor to create a fully equalised income distribution—rising from around 25 per cent in 1979 to 34 per cent in 1997, although the picture had been broadly flat since 1990. The reasons behind the increased inequality have been widely discussed, with the major forces at work falling into three main areas. Mrs Thatcher was elected with a clear intention to refashion the economic and institutional fabric of Britain. She sought to build the incentives and ability of management and investors to operate outside the institutional constraints built up in the postwar period. The most obvious area with respect to inequality was the tax and welfare system. It is widely but mistakenly believed that Mrs Thatcher cut taxes, when in fact the tax burden in the economy actually rose under her steward-ship. In 1979 around 38 per cent of GDP was taken in government revenues; it was very similar when the Conservatives left office in 1997 but, in the depth of the 1980s recession, it rose to 44 per cent. What did occur was an overall rebalancing of the tax structure away from income tax, especially for higher earners, and towards consumption taxes—mainly VAT. This made the tax and benefits system much less redistributive toward the poorest groups.

The generosity of welfare benefits was reduced dramatically for those out of work, including pensioners and working families. Child benefit, for example, sometimes rose even less than prices, rather than the prior norm of rising with earnings. There is a paradox here nonetheless. Any given tax and welfare system will have to work harder to redistribute from the rich to the poor when inequality is greater. In 1980 inequality in original income, before taxes and benefits, was about 43 per cent and after taxes and benefits around 25 per cent. So the tax and welfare system was levelling out inequality at approximately 18 per cent of national income. By the mid-1990s this redistribution was almost identical. This was driven primarily by two off-setting factors: inequality in original income was rising, while the existing tax and benefit system would have reduced inequality by far more than 18 per cent of national income had it remained in place. However, changes in taxation and welfare which shifted resources toward the affluent occurred at the same time.[1] So as inequality in original incomes rose, the tax and benefit system would naturally work harder to offset this. The Thatcher government's reforms prevented this from happening, leaving the extent of redistribution at a similar level.

The significant rise in inequality of original income (pretax and benefits) was a combination of rising wage inequality and growing worklessness, offset only by rising occupational pension incomes. The rise in wage inequality was closely related to Mrs Thatcher's deregulatory agenda. A central plank of her economic strategy was to abolish a sweep of government regulations in the economy, including wage, exchange and credit controls. The incomes policies of previous Labour governments had squeezed wage inequality with a series of fixed percentage wage rises, alongside minimum nominal pay rises for the lowest paid. The early period of rising wage inequality can be directly related to the withdrawal of incomes policy. Furthermore, the successive curbs on industrial strike action restricted the ability of the trade unions to influence pay levels in the private sector. Machin suggests this made a substantial contribution to rising inequality in the 1980s.[2]

Probably more important, however, is what has been described by Goldin and Katz as the 'race' between education and technology.[3] Their argument, shared by many other studies of rising wage inequality, is that new technology over the last thirty years or so including mobile communications and the computer have increased the demand for highly educated workers. If the supply of well-educated staff rises relatively slowly, as only a small proportion of the workforce is leaving education in any year, then this leads to a growing shortage of well-educated workers and a surplus of the less educated. This drives wage inequality and unemployment among the lower skilled rapidly upwards. It should be noted that this skill-biased technological change does not lead inevitably to rising wage inequality. Countering it requires a better educated workforce, including raising average attainment levels among young people. It requires a growing proportion of young people to attend university, take up apprenticeships and pursue training opportunities. The ending of the industry-based training levies (a move to reduce the regulatory burden on business) led to a sharp decline in the number of young people achieving valuable higher level apprenticeships such as plumbers, metal workers and electricians. The numbers attending university in a period when it was free for students, there was generous funding for universities and many students received grants did not rise in the austerity period of the early 1980s. An expansion of student numbers was underway by the mid-1980s. Yet by the time the expansion was leading to increased numbers of graduates, the rise in earnings inequality was virtually over. This of course, may not be a coincidence. The expansion of graduate numbers may well have contributed to the halting of the rise in the wage gap between degree holders and other workers. It is very noticeable that the rise in inequality has been most marked in the United States where student numbers have barely moved since the early 1970s, when they were artificially boosted by the Vietnam War, and by far less in other developed countries with steadily increasing graduate numbers.

Table 1 shows how in the 1970s, wage inequality measures across the full distribution—the 90:10 earnings ratio and the ratios between the top and middle (90:50) and middle to bottom (50:10)—were flat for men and falling for women. In the 1980s, the overall gaps widened by about 2 per cent per year; wages grew by 2 per cent a year faster for the people at the highest paid than the lowest paid. This was evenly split between the top and middle and the middle and bottom. In the 1990s, this increasing inequality ran at about half the pace of the 1980s.

The changes described above were largely deliberate acts of the Conservative government with the shifts in taxation and welfare and the broad strategy of deregulation and reducing union power being at the core of the neoliberal economic agenda that was being pursued. The third major driver was in all

Table 1: Trends in United Kingdom full-time weekly earnings inequality indices (annualised percentage points)

	1970–1980	1980–1990	1990–2000	2000–2009
Men				
90:10 ratio	0.0	2.4	1.1	0.7
90:50 ratio	0.1	1.2	0.6	0.6
50:10 ratio	−0.1	1.2	0.5	0.1
25:10 ratio	0.0	0.6	0.2	0.0
Women				
90:10 ratio	−0.8	1.9	1.0	0.3
90:50 ratio	−0.5	1.0	0.3	0.3
50:10 ratio	−0.3	0.9	0.7	0.0
25:10 ratio	−0.1	0.3	0.4	−0.2

Source: S. Machin, 'Changes in UK wage inequality over the last forty years', in P. Gregg and J. Wadsworth, eds, *The Labour Market in Winter: State of Working Britain 2010*, Oxford, Oxford University Press, 2011.

likelihood unintended, but came about as a by-product of the economic dislocation that followed in the two major recessions, and the closure of so much heavy industry in the United Kingdom. This was the rise of worklessness.

As Figure 1 makes clear, this was due not only to rising levels of unemployment, but to an increase in the numbers claiming one of three major workless benefits: unemployment benefit, income support for lone parents, and sickness and disability benefits. Between 1979 and 1993, the number of claims for the three major workless benefits tripled. This rise dwarfed the cost reductions from freezing or cutting benefit levels and the net cost was a doubling in spending on working age and child welfare from just over 2 per cent of GDP to 5 per cent. This huge economic failure was one of the major reasons that the Conservatives failed to reduce overall government spending and taxation levels after 1979. This rise in worklessness was particularly focused on families with children. In 1979, just 6 per cent of children grew up in a family where no one was working. By 1995 this had risen to just below 20 per cent—the worst in any Western industrialised country by a large margin.

Labour's response

Labour in opposition made a set of deliberate choices in seeking to combine the post-Thatcher liberal economic model with an ambitious agenda to ameliorate its adverse effects on the poor. In this sense Labour sought to match the perceived economic efficiency of a deregulated economy, but

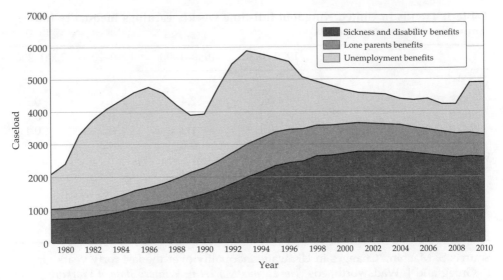

Figure 1: Welfare reliance: numbers of claims major workless benefits.
Sources: ONS Employment and Labour Market Review Table (Web publication, Chapter 2: Selected Labour Market Statistics, Table 2.30, May 2011), for 2009–10; P. Gregg, *Realising Potential: A Vision for Personalised Conditionality and Support—An Independent Report to the Department of Work and Pensions*, London, Department of Work and Pensions, 2008, for 2008 and before.

without the growing inequality that occurred under its predecessor. In short it sought to marry efficiency and equity. So Tony Blair publically committed to not raising taxes, especially income taxes for the wealthy, and to not considering any direct attempt to restrain pay at the top. This was a political choice driven by the negative experience of the 1992 election and the fear that presenting the success of the wealthy in disparaging tones made Labour appear 'anti-aspirational'. Furthermore, there was no attempt to reintroduce the regulatory arrangements that had been in place prior to the Thatcher governments, and certainly not to substantially reverse the employment relations legislation that had curbed the power of the trades unions. However, Labour did develop a clear economic agenda aimed at dealing with the legacy of failure left by the Conservatives, including high worklessness and low wages, which were biting hard for the poorest. This was a deliberate attempt to address one side of the inequality agenda: the gap between the poorest and the middle. This strategy also, to a degree, included an attempt to reduce the economic pressures that were driving up the pay of highly educated workers. In substantive terms, Labour sought to use market forces to reduce inequality rather than to overturn market outcomes through regulation and redistribution.

New Labour's strategy can be characterised as relying upon four main drivers: direct redistribution; tackling the causes of worklessness; improving take-home pay for low-wage work; and seeking to reduce social exclusion—namely the factors that leave long-term scars on people's lives including teenage parenthood, low educational attainment, long-term worklessness and income poverty itself.

Redistribution

While the government did not pursue tax rises for high earners, there was a large-scale redistribution toward the poorest groups in the early years of the Labour government. The well-known target to eliminate child poverty in a generation was backed by large-scale investment in rates of child support in benefits and tax credits (so both in and out of work), and adult elements in tax credits (largely available only to those with children). Less well known perhaps was a similar drive on pensioner poverty with the Pension Credit, and reductions in tax and national insurance (NI) for those on low wages in the form of the 10 pence rate of income tax and aligning the tax free element of NI and income tax which reduced contributions for the low paid.

Overall, this redistribution amounted to around 1.5 per cent of GDP by 2008, approximately £22 billion in real terms. This huge cost was managed in three ways: initially, it was substantially met by falling spending on workless benefits as strong growth resulted in fewer benefit claims. Reductions in the numbers of lone parents claiming income support also made a sizable contribution as their employment rate rose as a result of the welfare reform programme described in the next section. At the same time, as adult out-of-work support continued to rise only in line with prices rather than earnings, this also released resources. Welfare and tax credits for those of working age and children hovered at around 5 per cent of GDP throughout Labour's time in office, somewhat below that of peak spending at the end of the 1990s recession. Labour oversaw a reduction in the number of workless benefit claims, which fell from six million in 1993 to four million by 2008, and switched resources to more generous support for families with children and poorer pensioners. However, when the economy began to slow and Labour tried to increase spending significantly on education and health, something had to give. As a result, the increase in the generosity of child support payments was halted for two years, despite the 2004–5 target date to reduce child poverty by a quarter. This resulted in some of the good work being undone. Taxes also went up in the form of Council tax, fuel, alcohol and tobacco duties, while tax allowances did not keep up with earnings: as a result, low waged workers paid more in tax. Tax rises in this period were strongly regressive—the abolition of the 10 pence tax band being the most striking example. The obsession with not raising income tax rates which are strongly progressive meant that tax income was increased through highly regressive 'stealth' taxes: part of the reduction in inequality and poverty from tax credits and benefit changes was lost and, for low waged workers without children, real incomes barely grew and actually fell after 2005.

Tackling worklessness and raising take-home pay

Labour developed a twin track approach to tackling worklessness in its early years and developed a third, more aggressive approach after 2006. The twin track approach consisted of improving the financial rewards to working through tax credits and the early tax and NI changes described above. This phase was clearly marked up until 2004, after which no substantive efforts to increase take-home pay were attempted, except the proposal to extend free school meals to tax credit recipients right at the very death—a move the new Conservative-led government didn't follow through. This was buttressed by Labour's one major attempt to reregulate the labour market: the National Minimum Wage (NMW).

Minimum wages rarely affect more than 7–8 per cent of the working population (France being an exception) and the two dominant groups on the NMW are the young and those working part time (often second earners). So the effect on incentives for members of workless families to move into work was relative modest. Most adults starting a new job will secure wages above the NMW. In terms of income inequality, the minimum wage has little overall affect as those receiving it do not typically reside in the poorest families, as they are second earners or young people in working families. However, this broad approach directly bears on inequality by raising take-home pay for low waged work through minimum wages, tax credits and the 10 pence tax rate.

The minimum wage initially came in at a low rate affecting no more than 3 per cent of the workforce, but was progressively raised between 1999 and 2007 above average earnings, leading to a sharp push on wages at the bottom end. Figure 2 shows how earnings growth prior to the introduction of the NMW was slowest for the lowest paid at 10 per cent below the median and highest for the best paid and 10 per cent above the median. After the introduction of the NMW, pay for the lowest paid rose by 30 per cent above the median but by the 5th percentile this was just 5 per cent, illustrating the narrow range of its impact. Top pay continued to grow rapidly much as before.

The second approach was the development of 'back to work' support programmes under the New Deal. For the unemployed, participation in the New Deal was compulsory, but for lone parents, the sick and the disabled, it remained voluntary. Hence in the early phase of welfare reform under New Labour, welfare conditionality was not that much in evidence. The New Deal for Young People (NDYP) was evaluated astutely by Van Reenan.[4] He showed that it made a moderate difference to subsequent employment chances and easily paid for itself. Evaluations of the New Deal as a whole were generally positive, but for lone parents and the sick and disabled, take up remained low as it was only a voluntary requirement. From 2001 lone parents were subject to the relatively minor condition of attending a job centre and discussing their return to work through Work Focused Interviews, this

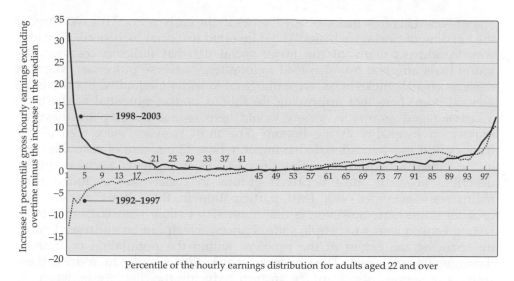

Figure 2: Wage growth relative to median earnings growth at different points of the earning distribution 1992–97 and 1997–2003. Median (50th percentile is the base and hence zero).
Source: Low Pay Commission.

substantially raised participation in the New Deal for Lone Parents with no reduction in employment entry rates—in fact, around 50 per cent moved into work within six months.

For those on disability benefits, no behavioural conditions were attached. In this area, policy making ground to a halt from 2004 to 2006 as Blair wrestled control of this policy agenda. A rapid turnover in Secretaries of State followed, with Alan Johnson, David Blunkett and then John Hutton all being appointed within eighteen months. More aggressive reform followed with the Freud Review recommending the lone parents with their youngest child aged over six should be moved on to Job Seeker's Allowance (JSA).[5] This meant they were treated the same as regular unemployed claimants in relation to job search conditionality, while disabled people were switched to the Employment Support Allowance (ESA) instead of disability benefits. The ESA switch occurred only for new claims for disability benefits until April 2011, since when those with 2.5 years or more on Incapacity Benefit are being retested under the new Work Capability Assessment. It remains highly controversial with a very large number of complaints and appeals.

Social exclusion

The other significant agenda to tackle poverty and inequality among the lowest paid was to address the circumstances that are known to damage people's employment and earnings potential in the labour market. This was one of New Labour's major policy themes in the early years. This went under the heading of 'Social Exclusion' (later inverted to 'Social Inclusion'). The idea was to address many of the major social ills that inflicted costs on the individuals affected, but also lead to long-term adverse outcomes. Many of these, such as homelessness, were marginal to wider inequality, but there is a general point here that improving the labour market potential of the most disadvantaged groups in society would help reduce poverty and have an impact on inequality at the bottom. The most relevant were teen births, truancy and low educational attainment, where 12 per cent of school leavers in the United Kingdom are without five GCSEs of any level. Social exclusion describes how the most deprived groups in society are excluded from mainstream activities—not least participation in the labour market. The broader point here, however, is that these states come with large and long-lasting consequences to people's life chances, which can be addressed either by reducing the extent of the problem within the population or limiting damage after the event. The government was thus seeking to address these sources of serious disadvantage, in turn reducing the distance between the marginalised and the rest of society.

Labour market response

These were the most salient areas of policy development, but there was also an expectation that by addressing many of these issues, the underlying level of unemployment (referred to elsewhere as the sustainable rate of unemployment or 'NAIRU') could be reduced, and many of the forces shaping the huge levels of wage inequality would be reversed. The argument was that the concentration of unemployment on the most disadvantaged groups in society had driven down wages in low-skilled sectors, since there was such low demand for unskilled labour. In turn, there was higher demand for well-educated workers, leading to strong wage growth in the United Kingdom economy. The tightening labour market would begin to reduce the massive surplus of unemployed less educated workers, and as a result wages would start to recover. Likewise a major expansion of educational attainment, fewer people leaving school early with no qualifications and a sharp expansion of the number of graduates would start to reduce wage pressures at the top. Hence the tighter labour market and the improved educational performance of the workforce would put downward pressure on inequality, especially the gap between the poor and the middle, without recourse to large-scale redistribution. Labour was in essence trying to work with market forces to tackle inequality and this broader strategy was at least partly in a series of Treasury documents in the early years of Labour's term.[6]

Labour's record

To assess Labour's record on inequality, after considering the observed outcomes, it is necessary to consider what Labour did not do as much as what it did, and consider how successful it was in achieving its aims. The picture we observe is that Labour came to office with the Gini coefficient at 34 per cent; according to ONS HBAI data in 2009–10 it was 36 per cent.[7] The record shows that inequality grew a little in the early years of Labour's term in office and then fell back until 2005, since when its rise has been more sustained.

As Labour set its sights more on tackling low incomes rather than reducing overall inequality, it is worth looking at income growth across the distribution. This is shown in Figure 3, which reveals income growth for the Labour and preceding Conservative years. The picture is interesting: income growth was strongest for those on incomes just above the poorest groups, in the 20th to 30th percentiles. Indeed, between the 20th and 80th percentiles inequality clearly fell. Inequality, however, was driven upward by the tails, with both rapid income growth among the top few percentiles and very slow income growth in the bottom 10 per cent.

Compared to the years of Conservative government this picture is benign: overall income growth was almost exactly the same at just under 2 per cent per year, but was notably faster in the bottom half and slower in the top half. As was made clear in Table 1 and Figure 2, wage inequality did rise at the top and this no doubt contributed to rising inequality: top pay for the very few paid in excess of £100,000 or so grew rapidly. At the top, rising profitability, share options and other bonus payments to top management were major factors, highlighted by the current focus on banker's remuneration and bonuses. However, wage inequality at the bottom end actually fell a little, and so did the extent of worklessness up until the recession. So here the story is more subtle: those with the lowest reported incomes now are the self-employed and those not working who do not have children; among these groups there have been no rises in the value of benefits. The move to ESA from Incapacity benefits has also resulted in lower value welfare benefits for some in this demographic. Labour's poverty reduction successes were for those with children and pensioners, but poverty rose among low-income families without children.

Another point to note here is that in its first two terms, Labour did reduce inequality but in the third term the rise was as rapid as occurred in the long Conservative years. After 2005, Gordon Brown felt unable to continue tackling pensioner and child poverty. This period also witnessed the introduction of regressive tax rises such as the abolition of the 10 pence tax band. In the first two terms, Labour was at least actively addressing one side of the inequality issue—namely the gap between the poor and the rest, even if it was less worried about the top. After 2005 it gave this up as well until towards the end of its time in government, when Alistair Darling was Chancellor. The

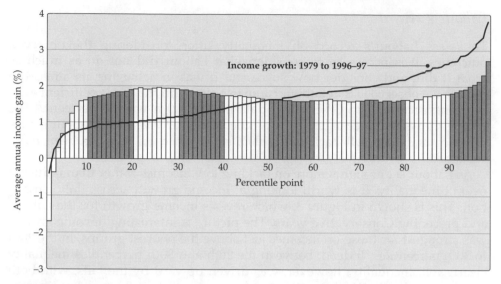

Figure 3: Real income growth by percentile point, 1996–97 to 2008–9 (GB) (Source: Institute for Fiscal Studies).

Notes: The change in income at the 1st percentile is not shown on this graph. Incomes have been measured before housing costs have been deducted. The differently shaded bars refer to decile groups.

Source: Author's calculations using Family Expenditure Survey and Family Resources Survey, various years.

pressure on the public finances meant that this area became a lower priority when compared to investment in health and education. The period also witnessed rising worklessness and large-scale immigration which may have suppressed wage growth at the bottom end, although the academic literature has not yet found such effects.

So, looking at inequality rather mechanically, Labour achieved three positive outcomes: (1) a rise in real wages for the lowest paid 10 per cent that was faster than the average, as a result of the NMW; (2) a fall in the number of households without an earner, although this was largely undone during the subsequent recession; and (3) a redistribution of resources toward families with children. It should be noted, however, though that the first of these three points had relatively little impact on overall inequality as the lowest paid are rarely in the poorest families. On the other hand, there were three major forces driving inequality upwards under Labour: (1) rapid earnings growth at the top among those who are also in the most affluent households; (2) some low income groups, particularly working age people without children, having benefits frozen in real terms; and (3) a series of regressive taxation measures after 2002.

It is worth assessing the success of what Labour implemented before discussing the limitations of the broad strategy Labour adopted. Redistribution during this period was successful in reducing child and pensioner poverty significantly. Dickens assesses whether this was driven by benefits and tax credits or work and earnings.[8] He suggests that work and earnings made a contribution, but were offset by a growing number of lone parents and a worsening of the labour market potential of lone mothers who had lower educational qualifications relative to the population as a whole. This meant that benefits and tax credits were the major driver of poverty reduction in the United Kingdom. The strategy of reducing worklessness yielded major gains until the recession. Yet even after the present downturn, the deepest since the Second World War, the number of claims for the major workless benefits stands at five million—down from six million after the 1990s recession (see Figure 1). The loss of employment in the recession was relatively modest and there is no doubt that the emergency measures from the Bank of England and the Treasury helped. But the welfare-to-work programmes that Labour put in place also made a significant contribution: tax credits, for example, made part-time work more viable relative to benefits.

Gregg and Wadsworth calculate the excess of households who have no work, given the available work and family size.[9] Although welfare systems can influence overall employment levels and indeed people's choices to be in couples or remain single, these side effects are small. So the 'excess' is a reasonable measure of the performance of the welfare system and supporting institutions such as the NMW in getting families into work. In 1979 there was no excess; by 1995 this peaked at 6.7 per cent of households—about 1.4 million more without work than there should have been. By 2009 this had fallen to 5 per cent, or 1 million.

So Labour reversed about a third of the increased worklessness that emerged under the Conservatives, but was too slow in developing new approaches for the sick and disabled. Outcomes for this section of the workless were a major disappointment, with very little progress in raising employment levels. The picture for lone parents, however, was impressive with the employment rate rising from 45 to 57 per cent. The NMW was successful in raising the wages of the lowest paid (see Figure 3), but this only affected the bottom 5 per cent or so. The rest of the wage distribution did not really respond to the combination of tightening in the labour market, and an increase in the supply of graduates, which reduced wage premiums and inequalities. An examination of the regional pattern suggests that when labour markets get very tight with an employment rate of over 75 per cent, wage inequality often falls. But too few regions got to this figure, and their achievement was often short-lived. The labour market was only sufficiently tight for long enough to halt the rise in wage inequality, rather than reversing it.

Thus Labour's strategy had some success in its own terms, reducing child poverty, worklessness and long-term unemployment and wage inequality at the bottom end. But the same period saw an increase in poverty among those without children, and a rise in the number of NEETs (that is, those not in education, employment or training). The reduction in available funds from economic growth and a growing shift in spending priorities saw the poverty agenda downgraded after 2004, and increased use of regressive tax changes, such as the abolition of the 10 pence rate. Although there was an attempt to resuscitate it from 2008, this meant that Labour was successful in reducing inequality at the bottom up to 2005 but then saw rising inequality as severe as under the Conservatives in the last term in office. So even on its own terms, New Labour had mixed results with several programmes achieving only moderate success, and the broad redistributive strategy for the poorest up to 2005 being partially undermined during the third term of the New Labour government.

Labour and the neoliberal economic model

What is perhaps more telling, however, is what New Labour did not do—it governed, having largely adopted the Thatcherite neoliberal economic model. There was also a wider failure to renew policy and to revisit assumptions in the light of experience and events. Developments in Denmark and Holland, often described as 'flexicurity', were widely discussed but never acted upon as an alternative model. This failure to reassess as economic problems emerged had both a macroeconomic and a microeconomic component. Through its period in office it boasted of the success of this model, built on a deregulated labour market, low business regulation (particularly in the City) to deliver jobs, rising living standards, low inflation and economic stability. Labour's belief in its own rhetoric meant that worrying signs of the 'hollowing-out' of manufacturing, a large trade deficit, high levels of consumer debt and a house price explosion were ignored. Obviously this was a significant error in hindsight, although it would have been very difficult to predict the financial crisis of 2008–9. Labour's period in office saw a consistently overvalued currency, largely as a result of the City's success in attracting overseas funds. This lay behind the United Kingdom's dismal manufacturing performance, as well as persistently low inflation. The large available funds in the banking system were funnelled into consumer debt and housing rather than productive investment. Attempts to control the housing price explosion and consumer borrowing would have allowed lower interest rates, a lower exchange rate and more productive investment. And at the macroeconomic level there was no attempt to develop a coherent industrial policy to seek what is now being called the 'rebalancing' of the British economy. This inability to reassess the need for a rebalancing of the economy, so evidently needed now, came sandwiched between some clearly successful macroeconomic policy making, giving the Bank of England independence in 1997, which produced significant advances and again the crisis in 2008–9 where rapid action prevented the complete seizure of the British finance system.

In the more microeconomic arena, Britain's labour market is characterised by high job turnover and very low incidence of training among low-wage workers. Furthermore, there are no agreed wage steps for qualifications at the industry level, which are common on the Continent and Australia. Labour never sought to address the 'hire and fire' model that operates in the United Kingdom's low-wage sectors, which could have led to higher productivity and improved wage rewards. This is essential for the functioning of the flexicurity model of the Netherlands and Scandinavia. A natural place to start would have been the more regulated sectors such as childcare and care for elderly or infirm. And, of course, Labour never sought to restrain the excessive bonus culture of top management that was linked to excessive risk taking and the financial collapse. The unwillingness to raise income tax or the burden of taxation on the better off saw widespread use of more regressive revenue raising via consumption taxes, Council tax, fiscal drag in income taxes, increased NI and the bizarre abolition of the 10 pence tax rate. Even if it was reluctant to raise tax rates, it could have initiated a major drive against tax avoidance by capping how much wealthy people can avoid taxes via pension contributions, ISA style savings, capital gains and more complex tax avoidance schemes.

Conclusion

New Labour sought an accommodation with the neoliberal economic model applied most in the Anglo-Saxon countries, especially the United Kingdom and the United States. In Britain, there were very limited controls on the operation of market forces, but there was an attempt to compensate for low wages and job instability with redistribution through tax credits and child-related benefits. As such, New Labour sought to address poverty and to invest in public services, rather than tackling inequality per se. On these terms, New Labour had considerable success up to 2005 as strong growth produced the revenues required to meet these goals. When growth slowed, the circle could be squared only by reducing attempts to address several major spending priorities simultaneously, but poverty reduction was the main loser. Broader attempts to reduce worklessness and wage inequality through incentives, back-to-work programmes and more investment in the supply of graduate labour were only moderately successful even in the years with a tight labour market.

Arguably, the best of Labour's policy making was in the first four years when a raft of ideas and decisions were implemented effectively, such as giving the Bank of England independence which produced significant advances. Again the crisis in 2008–9 removed some of the ideological taboos and led to a speed and scale of response, and a shift in thinking, that remains impressive. Even then, however, Labour after the crisis did not undertake a fundamental rethink of the model of British capitalism within which United Kingdom policy makers had operated. This remains a significant lacuna of the New Labour years.

Notes

1 P. Johnson and S. Webb, 'Explaining the growth in UK income inequality, 1979–88', *Economic Journal*, vol. 103, no. 417, 1993, pp. 429–35.

2 S. Machin, 'The decline of labour market institutions and the rise in wage inequality in Britain', *European Economic Review* (Conference Volume), vol. 41, 1997, pp. 647–58.

3 C. Goldin and L. Katz, *The Race between Education and Technology*, Cambridge, MA, Harvard University Press, 2008.

4 J. Van Reenen, 'Active labour market policies and the British new deal for unemployed youth in context', in R. Blundell, D. Card and R. Freeman, eds, *Seeking a Premier Economy*, Chicago, IL, University of Chicago Press, 2004, pp. 461–96.

5 D. Freud, *Reducing Dependency, Increasing Opportunity: Options for the Future of Welfare to Work*. Independent report to the Department for Work and Pensions, London, 2007.

6 HM Treasury, *The Modernisation of Britain's Tax and Benefit System. Number 1: Pre-budget Publication*, London, The Stationery Office, November 1997, and later follow ups.

7 Department of Work and Pensions, *Households below Average Income*. http://research.dwp.gov.uk/asd/index.php?page=hbai

8 R. Dickens, 'Child poverty in Britain: did work work?', in P. Gregg and J. Wadsworth, eds, *The Labour Market in Winter: State of Working Britain 2010*, Oxford, Oxford University Press, Oxford, 2011, pp. 240–54.

9 P. Gregg and J. Wadsworth, 'Workless households and the recovery', in P. Gregg and J. Wadsworth, eds, *The Labour Market in Winter: State of Working Britain 2010*, Oxford, Oxford University Press, 2011, pp. 72–83.

Solidarity Lost? Labour and the Politics of the Welfare State

TIM HORTON

Introduction

THROUGHOUT its period in office, an often-heard charge against the Labour government from the left was one of *timidity*: when it came to welfare and redistribution, Labour too often saw the attitudes of middle-class voters as a veto on the ambitions of progressive politics. If true, this would represent an important strategic failure—though, ironically, not in the way that these left-wing critics imagined. By arguing that Labour should simply ignore *Daily Mail* readers and 'show leadership', these critics in fact accepted exactly the same fatalistic viewpoint as those on Labour's right—namely that middle-class attitudes are somehow fundamentally irreconcilable with a generous welfare state.

In fact, designing policy in ways that can gain middle-class support for redistribution is critical to the success of anti-poverty programmes since sustaining generous welfare over long timescales requires the support of electorates. The sorry fate of some of Bill Clinton's progressive reforms—subsequently undone by the Republicans with little public outcry—provides a salutary warning of the dangers of not taking the public with you and provides a lesson for these left-wing critics that real leadership is not about acting in spite of public opinion, but requires building support for your policy.

This chapter looks at the extent to which Labour succeeded in entrenching its progressive advances on welfare and public services by creating popular support for them. Did its policy designs seek to harness middle-class attitudes? Or were these attitudes simply viewed as constraints to be worked within, if necessary, by 'stealth'?

There are perhaps two basic routes by which one might seek to build middle-class support for welfare and services. One is to ensure middle-class households gain directly from a programme by including them within it. This involves concerns about the coverage of policy—the extent to which it is targeted or universal. Where a programme does not, or cannot, include middle-class households, a second route is to ensure they nevertheless see expenditure on poorer or needier groups as legitimate and fair. The key question here is the nature of the 'social contract' involved in targeting welfare—in particular, whether those receiving benefits and services are seen to be contributing back to society.

Below I look at the extent to which Labour succeeded or failed in building support for the welfare state via each of these two routes.

Published by Blackwell Publishing Ltd, 9600 Garsington Road, Oxford OX4 2DQ, UK and 350 Main Street, Malden, MA 02148, USA

Labour's approach to targeting and universalism

Through decisions about the coverage of policy, policy makers can align or counterpose the interests and identities of low- and middle-income groups. In doing so, they have tremendous power to shape public attitudes to policy—including willingness to pay for it. Policies with wide coverage will secure the self-interested support of middle-income groups, who have historically been important in defending key aspects of the welfare state against retrenchment,[1] while policies restricted to those on low incomes will create trade-offs between the interests of low- and middle-income groups. For example, the reason why Scandinavian countries have generally low rates of poverty is not because their citizens are altruistic saints, but rather because their welfare states have successfully aligned the interests of middle-class and working-class voters; these are welfare states in which middle-class voters feel they have a stake.

Public perceptions of fairness are also important here: many studies of public attitudes show that, while people are often supportive of policies that give more to those on lower incomes, they feel uneasy about policies that are restricted only to those on low incomes. Here, perceptions can also be affected by another aspect of narrow targeting—namely that dividing people into groups of recipients and non-recipients can, if done insensitively, create a sense of 'them and us' in which a politics of grievance can flourish. None of this is to say that targeting is not necessary in welfare policy, especially when certain social groups have very distinct needs. But in many cases it is the inclusion of middle that determines the politics of the possible.

What approach did Labour take to targeting and universalism? Almost every type of policy design can be seen in the new benefits and services created by Labour, as well as in the extensions to, and reforms of, existing benefits and services. Classic flat-rate universalism was used in the creation of an entitlement to free early years education for all three and four year-olds (currently 15 hours a week for 38 weeks a year). It was also a distinguishing feature of some of the new support introduced for pensioners—most notably the Winter Fuel Payment and the entitlement to free bus travel.[2] At the other end of the spectrum, Labour introduced several new policies that were restricted in coverage to low-income households, especially cash transfers such as the Working Tax Credit (an in-work payment for those with low earnings) and the Pension Credit (an income-tested top-up for pensioner households), as well as Educational Maintenance Allowances (an incentive payment for young people from low-income households to stay on in education after the age of 16). In the domain of asset-based welfare, the Saving Gateway was a matched-saving programme specifically for low-income households.

However, to the extent that Labour had a distinctive 'philosophy' of policy design it was *progressive universalism*—combining wide coverage with variable levels of entitlement, such that those on low incomes received more than those on high incomes (in Labour's phrase: 'Help for all; most help for those who need it most'). This was a feature of the Child Trust Fund (an asset for every child that could be accessed at age 18), where the initial investment for each child was £250, but those from low-income households had a further £250 invested for them. It was also, to some extent, a feature of Sure Start, which was initially conceived as an intervention for disadvantaged families, but was later extended into a universal programme in which disadvantaged families would nevertheless be able to access a more intensive package of support.

Perhaps the paradigmatic example of progressive universalism under Labour was the creation of a near-universal system of tax credits to support families with children. Income-tested financial support for low-income families with children has been a feature of the United Kingdom tax and benefits system since the early 1970s (via the Family Income Supplement and then the Family Credit). Labour's tax credits—initially the Working Families Tax Credit, and then the Child Tax Credit from 2003—widened these into a system of financial support for which 90 per cent of families were eligible (up to a household income level of around £58,000).

To put this in historical context, Figure 1 shows how the profile of income-related financial support for families has evolved since the 1970s.[3] As can be seen, the introduction of Labour's tax credits substantially widened the coverage of this type of support. The trend illustrated in the graph corroborates the thesis sketched out above: that creating middle-class buy-in enables

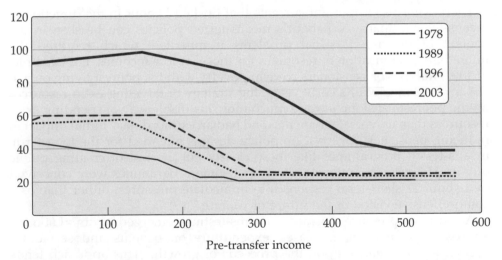

Figure 1: How the value of income-related financial support for families with children (y-axis) has varied with pretransfer household income (x-axis) since the 1970s. Figures expressed as £ per week.

Note: This shows the profile of all child support, including child benefit (which is responsible for the plateau above the È20 level at high incomes). However, most of the changing shape of the profile is due to changes in the system of income-related child support.

Source: S. Adam and M. Brewer, *Supporting Families: The Financial Costs and Benefits of Children since 1975*, London, Policy Press, 2004.

increases in expenditure on programmes. Increases in the value of support for low-income families correspond with moments where the coverage of programmes was widened.

To what extent did progressive universalism or any of the other policy designs described here represent an explicit strategy in relation to welfare and public services? Labour's approach in government is perhaps best understood as the interaction of several different dynamics and approaches. Labour certainly recognised the importance of a majoritarian welfare state not just as a way of extending support to middle-class families, but also as a way of giving a majority of taxpayers a stake in major welfare state initiatives. For example, Labour clearly saw the provision of tax credits and Sure Start to middle-class families as a key part of its electoral offer, and as a way of popularising increases in provision for low-income families.[4] Similarly, moves to reform the financing and provision of care services just before Labour left office were in part driven by popular discontent over the existing means-tested regime.

Labour also recognised the practical advantages of inclusion within programmes as a way of eliminating stigma and improving take-up. For example, the decision to include an extra payment to disabled workers within the tax credit system, rather than as a separate benefit explicitly recognised that disabled people wanted to claim extra support as part of the same system as everyone else.[5]

There were also important currents that pushed Labour in the direction of means-testing. Many of Labour's means-tested policies can be seen in the context of the urgent social problems it inherited, which required the immediate prioritisation of resources for those on low incomes. For example, in 1997, millions of pensioners were in poverty with the poorest living on just £69 a week. In Labour's early years, the strategy of targeting extra resources on the poorest pensioners was a much more justifiable way of spending extra resources than universal payments (and had an extraordinary initial impact in reducing pensioner poverty). As policy designs intended for the long term, means-tested programmes like these clearly fail the test of creating public buy-in. However, it appears that at least some programmes were conceived by Labour as short-term responses to immediate pressures, rather than as a comprehensive vision of the future of welfare.[6]

A second pressure towards means-testing emerged from Labour's approach to financing increased expenditure on benefits and services—specifically its reliance upon the proceeds of growth.[7] This approach tends to militate against large-scale institutional restructuring, instead placing a focus on how many additional resources are raised each year and how best to spend the marginal pound. And in the context of targets for reducing poverty, this marginal pound strategy very often tends to result in targeting extra resources on those on low incomes.

An evaluation of Labour's approach

What were the consequences of these policy strategies, and what will be their legacy? By and large, Labour's universal programmes, or extensions to the coverage of existing programmes, such as Sure Start, tax credits, and universal pensioner support (such as free television licences, the Winter Fuel Payment and free bus passes), have been highly popular and show signs of becoming entrenched as enduring institutions.

In the 1997–2001 Parliament, Conservative plans to scrap free television licences and the Winter Fuel Payment and invest the resources in the basic state pension met with fierce resistance from pensioners, and were abandoned. And in the run-up to the 2010 election, Conservative plans to cut tax credits for middle-income families met with vocal opposition, including from the *Daily Mail*, which declared the plans to be a 'Tory Tax War on the Middle Classes' (27 July 2009). This illustrates precisely the power of majoritarian welfare: the mobilisation of middle-class constituencies to defend anti-poverty policies.[8]

It is therefore no surprise that, to the extent the Coalition has been able to attack these universal programmes, they have started to do so by restricting their coverage, such as lowering the household income limit for tax credits and announcing their intention to 'refocus' Sure Start once again on low-income families. They have also taken an initial step on restricting the coverage of Child Benefit by removing it from households with a higher rate taxpayer from 2013. Whilst presented as deficit-cutting measures, these moves are deeply strategic: the Conservatives know that gradually taking the middle classes out of these benefits and services will fundamentally change their nature, and make their future expansion much less likely.

Labour's targeted programmes sometimes aroused more public opposition, although by no means consistently so. Perhaps the initiative that aroused most public concern was the Pension Credit. By the end of its term in office, Labour had committed to relinking the basic state pension to earnings as part of a gradual rebalancing of support away from means-tested provision.[9]

Since the change of government in May 2010, Labour's targeted programmes have not fared well, with Educational Maintenance Allowances and the Savings Gateway scrapped, the Working Tax Credit cut, and support with childcare costs through the Working Tax Credit cut significantly. It could well be that the targeted nature of these programmes has been an important element in their vulnerability. The exception to this pattern is the abolition of the universal Child Trust Fund (CTF)—although the main change here has been to prevent new entrants from joining the scheme, rather than clawing back investments already made. The fact that the first assets through this scheme will not become available to young people until 2020 may also inhibit any political fall-out.

Perhaps the most vulnerable forms of provision are those where Labour allowed competing modes of provision to develop for those on low- and middle-incomes. Examples include:

- On support with childcare costs, Labour created one policy primarily of benefit to lower income households (the childcare element of the Working Tax Credit) and another primarily of benefit to middle-class households (tax relief on childcare vouchers). A common programme of support for all income groups would have created a far more entrenched and popular system.
- On housing, policy remained far too based on tenure distinctions, with programmes often focused on one group or another, whether social tenants, the rental sector as a whole, or homeowners. While different tenures naturally give rise to different policy challenges, there are significant commonalities across housing problems that could have supported policies that spanned groups in different tenures (for example, a programme supporting low-income homeowners as well as low-income renters).
- On savings, Labour continued with a hugely inequitable system of pension tax relief to provide incentives for most of the population, while creating a very good but narrow programme (the Saving Gateway) for low-income households. Far more effective would have been to replace these two different systems with a universal system of matched savings, which would not only have united people within a single programme, but would have delivered a far fairer distribution of resources and incentives.

A key conclusion from these and other areas is that Labour did not put enough work into institutional restructuring to align the interests of different groups. Had it done so, it could have transformed the politics of the welfare state, rather than merely managing it.

Welfare for 'others': did Labour succeed in building public confidence in selective welfare?

Of course, it is often necessary to target benefits and services on particular groups. This tends to create political challenges not only of maintaining public support for spending on these benefits and services, but of how to ensure that they are perceived as legitimate in the first place. Selective welfare tends to open up questions about who 'deserves' to receive support, placing added demands on policy makers to ensure that policies are seen as fair.[10]

Research shows that a sense of *reciprocity* is key to people's perceptions of fairness in welfare.[11] Specifically, people need to feel that those who are taking out of the system are also putting something back in, especially when a policy is targeted at distinct social groups. The perception that recipients are 'freeloaders' reduces voters' willingness to contribute through taxation and can lead to support for welfare retrenchment.[12]

To what extent did Labour succeed in fostering a sense of legitimacy when it came to selective welfare for the poor and the unemployed? The evidence suggests that it did not. There has been a substantial deterioration in sympathy for the poor and the unemployed since the mid-1990s (see Figure

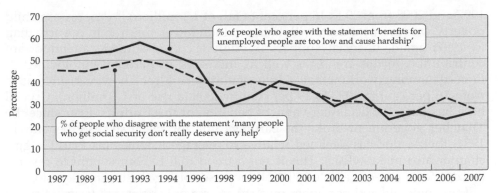

Figure 2: The decline in support for welfare over the last two decades.
Source: Data from NatCen's British Social Attitudes Survey. http://www.natcen.ac.uk/series/
british-social-attitudes/

2). Public support for redistribution also fell during this period—for example, the numbers agreeing that 'government should spend more money on welfare benefits for the poor, even if it leads to higher taxes' fell from 50–60 per cent through the 1980s and early/mid-1990s to just 32 per cent in 2007.[13]

In this context, it is perhaps no surprise that Labour's most publicised efforts in tackling poverty (as well as the anti-poverty campaigns of non-governmental organisations) tended to be focused on children and pensioners—both seen as relatively 'deserving' of help.[14] Spending on these groups tends to rank relatively high in terms of public support (probably because many can easily imagine the ways in which children and pensioners in poverty are not fully responsible for their situation). By contrast, attitudes to working-age adults in poverty are harsher; workless adults, in particular, are still often seen as the 'undeserving poor' (see Table 1). And attitudes towards provision for these different groups became more polarised during Labour's time in office: when asked to pick their first or second priority for spending on benefits, those selecting the unemployed fell from 26 per cent in 1997 to just 7 per cent in 2005, while those picking pensions or child benefits rose from 71 to 80 per cent and from 30 to 39 per cent, respectively.[15]

Labour's progress on tackling poverty reflected these priorities. Thanks to increased financial support, pensioner poverty fell very significantly between

Table 1: Percentage choosing these benefits as first or second priority for extra spending

	1996	2005
Retirement pensions	71	80
Child benefits	30	39
Benefits for the unemployed	26	7

Source: NatCen's British Social Attitudes Survey.

1997 and 2008 from 29 to 16 per cent (a fall of 1.1 million).[16] Progress on child poverty was more modest, with half a million fewer children in poverty than in 1997; again, financial support through tax credits made an important contribution to this trend, as well as increases in parental employment.[17] Poverty among working-age adults without children, however, increased from 16 per cent in 1997 to 19 per cent in 2008 (a rise of 1.1 million). Crucial here has been the declining value of benefits for these adults. Ever since the Thatcher government broke the earnings link for social security benefits in 1981, their value has declined relative to average incomes (as Paul Gregg's chapter also makes clear). This is not a trend that Labour sought to reverse (except for a one-off, above-inflation increase during the recent recession).

Tackling child and pensioner poverty are major concerns in terms of social justice, and Labour's progress here is to be celebrated. Even modest falls in child poverty stand in stark contrast to the trend between 1979 and 1997, when it more than doubled. However, adult poverty was very much an 'unspoken subject' of Labour's time in office, with welfare for working-age adults increasingly beset by a legitimacy problem.[18]

Tackling public anxieties or stoking them? Conditionality, fraud and welfare narratives

At the centre of this legitimacy problem stood out-of-work benefits. The erosion since the 1980s of the contributory basis of unemployment benefits has created a gradual shift from a system based on reciprocity to one based on need. Few now see entitlement as something built up through National Insurance payments; rather, unemployment benefits are increasingly viewed as transfers to 'the unemployed'. Understandably, as this has occurred, questions about how deserving recipients are have become more and more salient in public consciousness.

The legitimacy of out-of-work benefits thus posed an important political challenge for Labour when it came into power. One option might have been to rejuvenate the contributory basis of unemployment benefits by rebuilding the notion of social insurance—an approach rejected by Labour early on (see the government's response to the Social Security Select Committee's 2000 report on the contributory principle).[19]

Labour instead tried to deal with the 'legitimacy' issue by introducing a stronger framework of conditionality, and by telling the public that it was policing the system to eliminate fraud.[20] This enabled Labour to claim it was strengthening reciprocity within the system—that welfare would again be a 'something-for-something' culture.

Labour's approach to active labour market policy not only provided welcome extra support for claimants, but could also have been used to restore public confidence in the system and foster greater support for welfare. Sadly, by narrating its policy in a 'get-tough' style, with the language of 'welfare

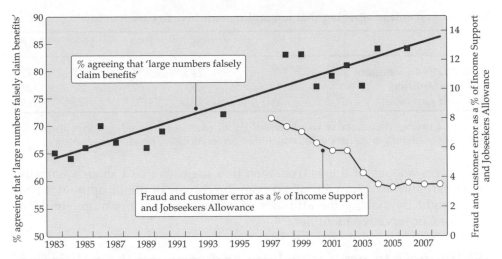

Figure 3: How fears about benefit fraud have increased as the level of benefit fraud has fallen.
Note: Fraud and customer error across all benefits account for just 1.3 per cent of expenditure, and have followed a similar trend to that in Income Support and Jobseeker's Allowance given here.
Sources: *Fraud and Error in the Benefit System: October 2007 to September 2008*, London, Department for Work and Pensions, 2009.

crackdowns' and 'targeting benefit thieves', the effect was to *reinforce* people's concerns about the integrity of the system: as Figure 3 shows, while benefit fraud more than halved under Labour, anxiety about fraud shot up, with 85 per cent now thinking that 'large numbers falsely claim benefits'.

Earlier we noted that an insistence on reciprocity in welfare is important for ensuring public support, but this strategy will only be successful if implemented in a way that fosters more positive perceptions of claimants. Narratives about 'scroungers' and 'crackdowns' have the opposite effect, stoking anxieties about whether or not people deserve support, and creating a vicious circle, with added political pressure for further crackdowns, and so on.

Further disturbing evidence that Labour's narrative has been a cause of increasing opposition to welfare, rather than simply a response to it, emerges if we consider which groups in the population have changed their attitudes to welfare. This reveals that, first, the big drop-off in support for welfare came just after 1994, when Labour's narrative on welfare changed to emphasise the responsibilities of benefit recipients; and, second that the biggest fall in support for welfare has been among Labour's own supporters.[21] Table 2, taken from a recent study by John Curtice,[26] shows this change in attitudes among Labour identifiers relative to Conservative identifiers with respect to one of the series illustrated in Figure 2.

Prominent theories of public opinion suggest that a party's supporters often rely on statements from its leadership as a cue to the opinions they should

Table 2: Percentage agreeing that unemployment benefits are 'too low'

	1986	1994	1998	2008
Conservative identifiers	24	34	15	12
Labour identifiers	63	67	37	28
Con–Lab gap	−39	−32	−23	−16

Source: J. Curtice, 'Thermostat or weathervane? Public reactions to spending and redistribution under New Labour', in A. Park et al., eds, *British Social Attitudes*, London, Sage, 2010.

themselves adopt.[23] If this is true, then this suggests that Labour's narrative on welfare may have unwittingly driven the climate of public opinion further to the right by making the attitudes of its own supporters more similar to those of Conservative identifiers.[24]

Willingness to pay for welfare and services: the politics of tax and spending

One way of assessing Labour's success at creating middle-class buy-in to the welfare state is to look at people's willingness to pay for it through taxation (Table 3). Presumably, a greater attachment to welfare institutions—whether for reasons of self-interest, fairness or anything else—will be reflected in a greater willingness to pay, and vice versa.

At first glance, the trend in public attitudes towards tax and spending over the last fifteen years does not look positive for Labour. The number saying we should 'increase taxes and spend more on health, education and social benefits' fell from 62 per cent in 1997 to 39 per cent in 2008, while the number saying we should either 'reduce taxes and spend less on health, education and social benefits' or 'keep taxes and spending on these services at the same level as now' rose from 34 per cent in 1997 to 58 per cent in 2008.[22] The media interpretation of this trend has been that people have become more right wing in their attitudes.[26]

Some care is needed before concluding that people have turned against the state, however. In fact, the numbers saying we should 'reduce taxes and spend less on health, education and social benefits' stands at just 8 per cent (a very small component of the 58 per cent figure cited above). What has altered

Table 3: Attitudes to tax and spending (percentages)

	1997	2008
Increase taxes/spend more	62	39
Keep taxes/spending same	31	50
Reduce taxes/spend less	3	8

Source: NatCen's British Social Attitudes Survey.

is that those wanting to keep tax and spending the same has risen to 50 per cent—something that could be interpreted as broad satisfaction with the status quo, and a sign that Labour got the balance about right.

Public attitudes to tax and spending have become an important part of the debate within Labour about its future political direction, especially over the extent to which state spending should be central to its policy agenda. Some prominent figures on Labour's right argue that the public have turned against tax and spending to such an extent that Labour must fundamentally revise its own approach.

Of course, there are many possible reasons why it is now timely for Labour to reassess its approach to the state, and many future challenges that might recommend a less statist approach. But we should also be careful about overestimating the extent to which public attitudes pose a constraint here. Former Foreign Secretary David Miliband has recently suggested that parties of the left across Europe are losing elections because of public distaste for tax and spending.[27] Perhaps this is true, but we should note, too, the extent to which parties of the right have felt the need to adopt social democratic commitments to the welfare state prior to those elections.[28] This is especially true within the United Kingdom, where David Cameron promised not to cut frontline services just prior to the 2010 election.[29] Polling conducted straight after the 2010 general election suggested he had been right to do so, with more people worried the government would go too far in cutting spending than not going far enough.[30]

And beyond questions on deficit reduction, public attitudes are not especially conducive to a Conservative agenda either. In the same post-election poll, only 30 per cent agreed that 'It is time to cut taxes', compared to 66 per cent who disagreed; 71 per cent thought 'This is a time for government to get more involved', while just 22 per cent thought that 'This is a time to depend more on markets'. This is why strategists within today's Conservative party correctly regard public support for spending on the welfare state to be their key electoral problem.

Abstract notions of 'willingness to pay' are perhaps less politically useful than looking at support for particular programmes. People tend to support or oppose particular benefits and services, rather than 'the welfare state' as a whole. And public attitudes towards different planks of the welfare state vary considerably. For example, when asked recently which areas should be *exempt* from spending cuts, 67 per cent picked the NHS, but only 11 per cent picked benefits for people of working age.[31] And while the Coalition government is increasingly anxious about the perception that it is cutting spending on the NHS, it is aware that the proposed cuts to Housing Benefit currently command wide public support.[32]

And this brings us back to our key point about policy design: those policies that include a majority, or that are perceived as fair and legitimate, will command far more support that those which do not. In taking forward the debate about the role of the state, it is crucial for the Labour party to recognise the extent to which public attitudes to tax and spending are not fixed and immutable, but can be strongly influenced by how governments shape and structure social programmes themselves.

Conclusions

So to what extent did Labour succeed in entrenching its vision of the welfare state by creating popular support for programmes? The picture presented here is mixed. On the one hand, especially in the area of child welfare, Labour created a set of institutions (tax credits, Sure Start, the free early years' entitlement) that command broad support amongst the electorate and seem relatively resistant to attack from the right. Indeed, the transformation of support for children—particularly for less advantaged children—will surely be seen as Labour's key social policy legacy in decades to come. Yet in other areas, there was a failure to build public support for Labour's policies— particularly in the areas of asset-based welfare, social housing and housing benefit, Educational Maintenance Allowances, skills programmes, and, per- haps most strikingly, benefits for working-age adults.

What lessons can be drawn for politicians and campaigners who want to see a generous welfare settlement entrenched in the United Kingdom? First, we need to understand the importance of majoritarian welfare and services in generating public support for anti-poverty programmes. In the short term, the challenge must be to defend existing universalism in a climate where there is enormous pressure to target provision more narrowly to save money. History shows us that nothing could be worse for the long-term interests of the poorest than taking middle-class households out of the benefits and services they rely on. This would set us on a path to a residualised set of 'sink services' with a deeply segregating effect on society.

Over the long term, this agenda will involve shifting away from the culture of targeting that pervades some areas of the welfare state to building broad- based coalitions in support of social provision. For example, the debate over the creation of a National Care Service that Labour was starting as it left office recognised that meeting the challenge of financing care services for our future population will involve shifting to a less targeted system of support. More generally, we should avoid policy designs that pit the interests of low- and middle-income families against one another, in which a politics of grievance can flourish.

Second, when it comes to selective welfare, Labour needs to take the demands of reciprocity seriously, reframing welfare not simply as a response to need, but as recognition of the importance of social contribution. This will challenge those on the left committed to a paradigm of 'welfare rights'; though, as we have seen, if public support is necessary to sustain generous welfare, then policies actually do their beneficiaries a great disservice if they fail to cultivate the perception that recipients are contributing back to society. It is also a challenge to the approach taken by Labour in office which was to retain a need-based system policed in a 'get-tough' style. Compared to a system of social insurance—where it is understood that people have already contributed to their benefits, or that they will go on to pay them off—conditionality by itself is a very 'thin' form of social contract, which may not be capable of carrying the weight of public concerns over entitlement. From out-of-work benefits, to social housing, to immigration, a deeper and more positive notion of earned entitlement will be necessary if Labour is to transform the politics of welfare.

Finally, a lesson that emerges from looking at the deterioration in public support for out-of-work benefits is that what governments say matters. Before it won power in 1997 Labour seemed to think that shifting its own narrative to emphasise responsibilities and tackling fraud were a necessary response to satisfy an existing climate of public opinion. In fact, it seems that Labour's narratives have played a role in *changing* public opinion (primarily through changing the attitudes of its own supporters), shifting it further to the right in a way Margaret Thatcher never achieved. In doing so, it has made the political climate much more hostile to achieving progressive ends while legitimising an approach in which Labour will never be able to out-bid the Conservatives. To get out of this Dutch auction on welfare, a new narrative will be needed—one that seeks to challenge negative stereotypes of benefit claimants, rather than confirming them.

Whether through the design of its policies or the construction of its narratives, perhaps the biggest failing of Labour's period in office stemmed from the lack of confidence in its own ability to change and harness public attitudes, rather than be a hostage to them. This is a lesson that the next generation of Labour politicians must learn.

Notes

1 See R. Goodin and J. Le Grand, *Not only the Poor*, London, Allen . A good example here is when the Thatcher government froze child benefit in 1987; the ensuing disquiet ensured it was un-frozen again by the early 1990s.

2 There were also some existing benefits and services that Labour planned to expand in coverage. Before it left office, Labour had set out plans to extend free school meals to a wider range of low-income households than those currently entitled, along with hints at an eventual ambition of universal free school meals. Similarly, on care services, it had begun a debate on the creation of a National Care Service to extend the coverage of free services beyond those with critical needs. The financial crisis from 2008 onwards and the subsequent change of government prevented either of these goals from being realised.

3 Data from S. Adam and M. Brewer, *Supporting Families: The Financial Costs and Benefits of Children since 1975*, London, Policy Press, 2004.

4 For example, these were important elements of Labour's 2005 election 'pledge card'.

5 This issue was also one of the reforming thrusts behind ambitions for universal free school meals, where—even though the administration of free meals within schools

has improved markedly within recent years (with far fewer schools requiring children on free school meals to publicly identify themselves when claiming them)—around a third of children entitled to them still do not take them up.

6 It is worth adding that not all means testing is the same. Much depends on one's motivation for means-testing, which has profound effects on the character of a programme and the experiences of those using it. There is a legitimate distinction to be made between means testing to cut expenditure (which we often see under governments of the right) and means testing to ensure that *increases* in expenditure are targeted on those that need them most. The former is more likely to result in strategies of restricting coverage and will create a system where the ethos is to discourage claiming (with unfriendly and intrusive administration). The latter—of which the Pension Credit is an important example—is more likely to create a system where the ethos is to encourage claiming (Labour even had a Public Services Agreement target to increase take-up).

7 This was basically the strategy recommended by Tony Crosland (A. Crosland, *The Future of Socialism*, London, Robinson, 2006).

8 These pressures from middle-class opinion have also been in evidence as the Conservatives have attempted to trim back important programmes in government; for example, opposition to their plans to cut back on Child Benefit for high earners united Netmums, the *Daily Telegraph* and the Child Poverty Action Group.

9 In government, Labour sometimes went to great lengths to present means-tested cash transfers as part of the same system as more universal guarantees (often through the language of 'minimum income guarantees'). For example, the Pension Credit was often described as a complement to the basic state pension, the Child Tax Credit as a complement to Child Benefit, and (more tenuously) the Working Tax Credit as a complement to the National Minimum Wage.

10 See, for example, W. van Oorschot, 'Who should get what and why? On deserving criteria and the conditionality of solidarity among the public', *Policy and Politics*, vol. 28, 2000, pp. 33–48.

11 See, for example, T. Sefton, 'Give and take: attitudes towards redistribution', in A. Park, J. Curtice and T. Sefton, eds, *British Social Attitudes*, London, Sage, 2005; L. Bamfield and T. Horton, *Understanding Attitudes to Tackling Economic Inequality*, York, Joseph Rowntree Foundation, 2009.

12 See, for example, I. Aizen, L. Rosenthal and T. Brown, 'Effects of perceived fairness on willingness to pay', *Journal of Applied Social Psychology*, vol. 30, no. 12, 2000, pp. 2439–50.

13 Figures from the British Social Attitudes Survey , http://www.natcen.ac.uk/series/british-social-attitudes/. See J. Curtice, 'Thermostat or weathervane? Public reactions to spending and redistribution under New Labour', in A. Park et al., eds, *British Social Attitudes*, London, Sage, 2010.

14 See, for example, W. van Oorschot, 'Making the difference in social Europe: deservingness perceptions amongst citizens of European welfare states', *Journal of European Social Policy*, vol. 16, no. 1, 2006, pp. 23-42.

15 See, for example, P. Taylor-Gooby and R. Martin, 'Sympathy for the poor, or why New Labour does good by stealth', in A. Park et al., eds, *British Social Attitudes*, London, Sage, 2008.

16 All poverty figures cited here from Department for Work and Pensions (DWP), Households below Average Income: An Analysis of the Income Distribution 1994/95–2008/09, London, Stationery Office, 2010. This fall has been historically

unprecedented during a time of strong economic growth (when pensioner poverty tends to increase). Ironically, if Labour had committed to similar targets on eradicating pensioner poverty as it did for child poverty, then it would have met the first target to cut it by a quarter in 2005, and be close to meeting the target to halve it by 2010.

17 Child poverty fell more substantially up until 2005, then rose again for three years, before starting to fall again in Labour's last two years in office. But with much smaller increases in financial support announced in Budget 2009 than were needed to meet the 2010 target, it seems likely that the government will fall well short of it.

18 It was perhaps only with the abolition of the 10 pence income tax rate that the welfare of working-age adults without children received major political attention.

19 *Report on the Contributory Principle: Reply by the Government to the Fifth Report of the Select Committee on Social Security, Session 1999–2000*, London, Department of Social Security, September 2000.

20 This included both a stronger conditionality regime for jobseekers, as well as a new work-focused interview regime for lone parents and new incapacity benefit claimants. Additionally, reforms announced during Labour's final years in office placed requirements on lone parents of older children to look for work.

21 T. Sefton, 'Moving in the right direction? Public attitudes to poverty, inequality and redistribution', in J. Hills, T. Sefton and K. Stewart, eds, *Towards a More Equal Society? Poverty, Inequality and Policy since 1997*, Bristol, Policy Press, 2009; Curtice, 'Thermostat or weathervane?'

22 Curtice, 'Thermostat or weathervane?'

23 See, for example, J. Zaller, *The Nature and Origins of Mass Opinion*, Cambridge, Cambridge University Press, 1992.

24 As John Curtice puts it: 'In repositioning itself ideologically, New Labour helped ensure that the ideological terrain of British public opinion acquired a more conservative character. . . . The wind of change blown by New Labour has proven to be very powerful indeed' (Curtice, 'Thermostat or weathervane?').

25 Figures from the British Social Attitudes Survey. See Curtice, 'Thermostat or weathervane?'

26 See, for example, 'Britain has grown more Conservative under Labour', *Daily Telegraph*, 26 January 2010.

27 'Why is the European Left losing elections?', *The Political Quarterly* lecture, David Miliband, 8 March 2011.

28 There is good evidence from across the OECD that public attitudes are constraining governments—of left or right—from cutting public spending. Since the 1980s, most OECD countries have increased their overall welfare spending as a proportion of national income, while nearly all of the others have maintained it. Recent analysis by Clem Brooks and Jeff Manza suggests that voter attitudes have been the key driver of increased spending and the key force preventing cuts (B. Brooks and J. Manza, *Why Welfare States Persist: The Importance of Public Opinion in Democracies*, Chicago, IL, University of Chicago Press, 2007).

29 The Andrew Marr Show, *BBC One*, 29 April 2011.

30 Polling on 6–7 May 2010 by Greenberg Rosner Quinlan for the Royal Society for the Encouragement of Arts (RSA). See *The Change Election: What Voters were Really Saying*, May 2010, RSA.

31 YouGov/*Sunday Times* poll, 11 June 2010.

32 YouGov/*Sunday Times* poll, 31 October 2010.

Reappraising New Labour's Political Economy

JOHN DENHAM

I ALWAYS think that if there is a unifying pathology of Labour party members, it is to live in a perpetual state of dissatisfaction and disappointment. This tends to mean that we carry on working to change the world, but we also tend to go overboard in our analyses of election defeats—a focus that fits with our generally pessimistic frame of mind.

Critical evaluation of New Labour tends to begin with what we might have done better. However, let me start with what I have said at every Labour party members' meeting I have attended since the general election: we should never lose pride in what we actually achieved in government. These include forming the longest ever Labour government, the transformation of public services, the changing of the nature of political debate and the constitutional reforms we introduced. So our critique of what we did should not be dominated by a sense of failure because we lost at the end. Instead, the nagging questions are 'could we have still been there?' and 'could we have done more?'.

What is clear is that in the 1990s we pulled together an unprecedented electoral coalition in terms of its absolute size and breadth. That coalition steadily eroded, losing four million votes between 1997 and 2005 and another million by 2010. Uncomfortably, part of the explanation of our longevity in power is that the electoral system enabled us to do that, even though we were becoming unpopular, just as Mrs Thatcher was in power for much longer than was warranted because of our electoral system.

Within our postelection debates there are quite a few different stories about why we lost. There is a story that says 'well, it was ok until the last couple of years'. People either then blame the recession or Gordon Brown. But actually we had lost an awful lot of votes before the last couple of years. There is a different story which says that it was all pretty good until the second term, but then we lost our way. Again people repeat this either because they think that we retreated from radical public service reforms at that point, or because we invaded Iraq. On these views, everything was going ok until about 2003. And then there is a view that we became a tired government and the public wanted a change.

The argument I want to make is different to these, although none of them are entirely wrong. I want to focus upon the nature of our model of political and social change. The way we thought that we were trying to change the world, which lay at the core of New Labour, was bound to run into trouble.

Published by Blackwell Publishing Ltd, 9600 Garsington Road, Oxford OX4 2DQ, UK and 350 Main Street, Malden, MA 02148, USA

The very things that enabled us to achieve real success had the seeds of their own downfall inside them.

There are a few areas we need to look at carefully. The first is the political economy of New Labour. The vision of this was fairly clear, and explicitly set out around 2001 in one of Gordon's party conference speeches. It said that you can allow the private market, the free market, to operate with a great deal of freedom, and it will produce a considerable amount of wealth that you can redirect, either in terms of raising family incomes or funding public services. This was set out explicitly as an economic and political philosophy for government.

A second precept was about globalisation: that it was not only inevitable (it is), but that it was essentially a benign, if challenging, opportunity if only we responded to it appropriately. And part of that appropriateness consisted of a pro-business stance, tax regulation, flexible labour markets and being positive towards legal migration into the country. For a considerable period of time that approach to the economy worked pretty well. We had much more impressive job creation than most other similar Western European economies. We got huge wealth in, which enabled us to transform the levels of funding of public services and we were able, despite the effect of what was happening at the top of the income level, to make significant changes to the gaps between the poorest families and those on middle incomes.

What became increasingly apparent was that that this approach had its own in-built problems. Our decision not to really have an active industrial policy until the last few years of the Labour government helped produce an economy that was over reliant on the banks and that made us particularly vulnerable when the crisis arose. Labour market flexibility was helpful in job creation and this approach fitted with the decision to continue to extend much of the public service to market competition. Together, these policies helped generate a group of many millions of people for whom living standards had stalled long before the global recession came along. These people benefited from improved public services, but wages soon stagnated, working conditions were often less than secure and pension rights diminished. These developments formed the background to the complaints that 'no one speaks for us or understands the way our lives are' that we heard in the election. These were not misunderstandings of what was going on. Such claims had real roots in people's actual experiences of labour markets.

There is a wonderful quotation by Tony Blair from around the time of the 1997 election in which he said that: 'If you work hard, and pay your taxes, you should be able to expect a decent standard of living, provide a good home for your family, a good future for your kids and have a secure retirement.' That was almost the core New Labour deal. Actually, while that was true for many people right up to 2010, for many others, it was not. And this deal further weakened by other changes in welfare and the state.

The early targeting of pension credits for the poorest pensioners was absolutely right, but the wholesale move away from the traditional Labour support of earned entitlements towards means testing gradually eroded the sense that playing by the rules was rewarded. The loss of occupational pensions was perceived as punishment for savings. Policies like the provision of free computers to families on benefits had a clear social objective, but exacerbated the sense that Labour had lost touch with the common sense fairness of British people. So while Labour talked a lot about fairness because this came up all the time in the focus groups, we never got to grips with what was causing the underlying problems.

I was one of the first to warn in writing about the political impact of Polish migration and to document its local and public service effects. I can say with absolute even-handedness that neither Tony nor Gordon wanted to do anything about this issue. The debate about migration and culture is very complex and there are many strands to it. But if you wanted to track Labour's problems with migration down to a core issue, it was the failure to understand how in a rapidly changing society, which was already deeply unequal, where family and personal security varied enormously, where class still mattered, and where community and cultural identity was not only important, but one of the key things people held onto in a changing world, migration on the scale we had was bound to challenge deeply held notions of fairness, entitlement and obligation.

One issue ended up defining many of our debates. This was public service reform, and its twin sister—the extent to which the state can be an instrument of social change. It is telling that we left government with no settled consensus on either of those issues; on the role of the state and how to do public service reform. Yet these are crucial areas for the future.

We did of course bring about big changes and improvements. My son broke his collarbone on Monday and I know that his experience of going to a specialist paediatric A&E department and being home again within two hours is utterly different to what would have happened fifteen years ago. So we didn't fail; we achieved a great deal. But, we wandered about a bit on public service reform. We had periods of stressing top-down target reform. We had a period in which we seemed to believe that user choice and provider competition would improve public services in the same way that markets worked in the private sector.

We valued very highly a certain breed of progressive public sector manager in education, health and policing; but, perhaps from our historic fear of being seen as a producer party, largely dismissed the views of others who worked in public services. We had a great deal of confidence in the ability of the state to bring about social change through, for example, the construction of massive children's databases. And we were pretty negligent until recent years of the democratic potential of elected local government, tending to see this as a secondary player in our models of change. Ed Miliband has talked about the casualness with which we treat civil liberties. I think we can add to that a casualness about the way in which we treated the views of those who provided public services, on the best ways of providing public services.

In our tendency to focus always on how the state could be an instrument of social change, we neglected the debate about why people behave the way they do. And this, despite the fact that many of the real preoccupations of government from obesity to anti-social behaviour, from school achievement to parental support and aspiration, ultimately depended on why people behave the way they do. We never really developed our political thinking here. Quite a considerable volume of work was done in government—not least in the various policy units in Downing Street—about behavioural change, very little of which got traction in the way in which we designed policy.

Why did these problems arise in New Labour's period in power? The first answer to this question concerns the way we developed our electoral strategy after 1997, and the unnecessary way we changed our idea of what our political appeal was going to be. In the 1990s New Labour was based very heavily on an inclusive, deeply values-based appeal to the electorate. This was made up of clear value statements: 'the many, not the few', 'rights and responsibilities', 'economic efficiency and social justice', 'we can all do better if we look after each other'. Put together, these told an inclusive, collective story about where our country was going which had a broad appeal. It enabled us to reach out to the middle ground voters that were a key target for us in the 1990s and who we hadn't reached previously. But—crucially—this was not achieved by designing a separate appeal to those voters, but by bringing together the values they shared in common with a more traditional working-class vote. We told a clear story about our country and where it might go if Labour was successful in power.

One of my major criticisms of New Labour in government is that almost from the day we took office we abandoned that values-based inclusive way of telling the story about what we were up to in favour of a much more segmented approach. There was a focus on those parts of the media who were seen to be read by the middle ground voters we had gained at the previous election. Yet instead of maintaining our values-based appeal to their readers, we adjusted to the agenda promoted by those parts of the media, as though they knew better than we what values we should reflect. That focus turned us away from key issues, it dulled our sensitivity to some of the things that were happening in the real world—and happening to other people who had bought into the New Labour promise.

The second problem was that we adopted something we criticised our predecessors for: a tendency to believe that whatever people thought about policies, we were right! The problem must have been our inability to explain to them why we were right, not that we might be wrong. This characterised the way in which we talked about globalisation, about flexible labour markets or the way we responded to migration. In opposition, we worked very hard to understand those whom we wanted to vote for us. In government, we wanted to explain to them why we were right. Mrs Duffy is, I suspect, going to be forever connected with Gordon Brown, but she was talking about a deaf ear that was much more widespread across the Labour party.

We first put community cohesion into the political language after the northern riots in 2001 gave us the evidence we needed about the real divisions that were taking place in our communities. At that time, Tony Blair was insistent that we only had a problem with the Muslim community and there was no wider problem. So what was happening to an alienated and disenfranchised white working class was never actually grasped by government because we didn't take the opportunity that was presented to us. That inability to listen came rather too quickly in government and probably says something about how the Labour party had learned to operate.

As we all know, Tony and Gordon had tensions and they had disagreements. Funnily enough, where they had real tussles, they were often resolved with pretty effective outcomes. If you look at the financing of higher education, although their package was not sustainable in the long term, we came up with something that enabled better funded higher education to offer more places to more students without any slowing of the increase in participation by students from poorer backgrounds. That's not a bad public policy outcome. The real cost of these personality tensions was that issues that neither of them were interested in did not get anywhere near the political agenda. That was a real problem. You could say that issues like the way that welfare worked in alienating a key section of voters never got into the political debate. We talked and acted tough on benefits, but never reflected the deeper concerns about fairness that voters were talking about. The real need for investment in social housing never got into the debates. These were not on the radar of either of the two key personalities of New Labour.

Looking to the future, we are going to have to change our thinking on our basic model of political economy. This idea of a separation between the way we look at how to run the productive, profit-making, wealth-creating part of the economy and how the public sector spends that money will not last us in a new era. What happens at work is key to voters and so too are questions of fairness, rewards and the overall structure of the economy.

We have some building blocks for our new thinking. We began some really serious work on an active industrial policy in the last two or three years of Labour government, which particularly accelerated after Peter Mandelson came back from Brussels, having seen what was happening in some of the other European countries. There is a renewed interest in fairness in the labour market itself with the number of people in the 2010 leadership campaign endorsing the living wage. There is a sense that there has to be a new balance between flexibility and fairness. There is a great deal of work to be done on this question.

There is recognition that a globalised world may be inescapable, but it is not inherently benign. Indeed most of the global forces from capital to manufacturing, industrial organisation to climate change, all have a tendency to make us more insecure and unequal.

Part of the response to the future is going to be the assertion of collective responses—collective resilience and collective security alongside the individual resilience and security that we have tended to focus on in the past. We are going to have to start a new debate about the types of institutions we want to create. The loss of trustee-led benefit pension schemes illustrates something of great importance to us politically on the centre-left. The existence of collective institutions which operated in a space created by the state but were not synonymous with the state, and in which people had a sense of ownership, was a key part of the postwar environment in this country. We are going to have to look again at what that environment will look like in the twenty-first century. One of the reasons is that the fragility of the advancements we made through direct state provision is going to become increasingly obvious. You could not have had a bolder Pensions Minister than Barbara Castle in the 1970s Labour government. Yet the ease with which Norman Fowler and Peter Lilly took apart the state-based pension system that she had put into place in the 1980s is extraordinary. We will, I fear, fight the next election with many of the advances that we made in the last government taken apart by the Liberal Democrats and the Tories. It is a moot point whether the simple proposition 'let's go back round and do it again' is going to convince people that this is how we secure the future that they want.

This is not about government versus no government, or state versus no state. Active government will be core to us in the future as it has been for the past thirteen years. Looking around, there is a new revival in mutualism around Lambeth Council and this has become contested political territory. We have to make sure it is not lost to us. Yet none of this is going to work unless our thinking is based on a clear and united set of values. A segmented electoral strategy will not work. We need to identify the things that have the greatest support and the greatest reasons for optimism for the centre-left in this country. Our deep sense of fairness chimes with a robust and hard-headed notion of reciprocal fairness that is widely held across this country. This implies a wholesale rethinking of our approach to redistribution, rights and entitlements. We must also tell a story not just about values, but about where we want to go as a country and as a society and be more sensitive to how people are changing. Some of the policies that we had—the Licensing Act, the closure of post offices, dare one say it, a warmth to Tescos that we never showed to local shops—made people feel that we had no understanding of their communities.

Being clear about how we can encourage and shape the way people behave as well as committing to doing things through the state is going to be critical. We will have to tell a story about where our country and society are going and not just what our values and policies are. We came across as a party insensitive to questions of identity, place and community. One such example is that while you are allowed to be Scottish Labour, Welsh Labour, or be part of British Labour, you cannot join the English Labour party at a time when English national identity is growing. So our response to all of that has got to be more than good policy, more than reinforcing our values, and more than taking greater care to make sure that things like welfare policy reflect them.

JOHN DENHAM

What we are going to have to do is develop a story about where we as a country go, and that story will be one that is patriotic, national, but progressive as well.

This chapter is based upon a speech delivered by John Denham at The Political Quarterly *annual conference 'Auditing New Labour', September 2010.*

An Era of Constitutional Reform

VERNON BOGDANOR

I

TONY BLAIR was notoriously uninterested in constitutional reform. His approach was perhaps best summed up in an altercation with the Liberal Democrat leader, Paddy Ashdown, in 1999, when the Scottish Liberal Democrats were pressing for a more generous policy on student support than was being implemented in England.

'You can't have Scotland doing something different from the rest of Britain,' Blair complained.

'Then you shouldn't have given the Scots devolution,' Ashdown retorted, 'specifically, the power to be different on this issue. You put yourself in a ridiculous position if, having produced the legislation to give power to the Scottish Parliament, you then say it is a matter of principle they can't use it.'

Tony Blair (laughing), 'Yes, that is a problem. I am beginning to see the defects in all this devolution stuff.'[1]

In an exchange with Henry Porter in the *Observer* newspaper on 23 April 2006, Blair insisted that the Human Rights Act gave the judges power to strike down government legislation, which is precisely what it does not do.

It is a paradox, then, that Blair's government will be primarily remembered for the massive and radical constitutional changes it introduced—changes which are, almost certainly, irreversible, and which have permanently altered the way that Britain is governed. It is worth listing the main reforms:

- The independence of the Bank of England from government in monetary policy.
- Referendums, under the Referendum (Scotland and Wales) Act, 1997, on devolution to Scotland and Wales.
- The Scotland Act, 1998, providing for a directly elected Scottish Parliament, and with a Scottish Executive responsible to it on devolved matters.
- The Government of Wales Act, 1998, providing for a directly elected National Assembly in Wales.
- The Northern Ireland Act, 1998, providing for a referendum on a partnership form of government and devolution in Northern Ireland.
- The establishment, under the Northern Ireland Act, 1998, following the successful outcome of the referendum, of a directly elected Assembly in Northern Ireland.

Published by Blackwell Publishing Ltd, 9600 Garsington Road, Oxford OX4 2DQ, UK and 350 Main Street, Malden, MA 02148, USA

- A referendum, under the Greater London Authority (Referendum) Act, 1998, on a directly elected mayor and assembly for London.
- The introduction of proportional representation for the elections to the devolved bodies in Scotland, Wales, Northern Ireland and the London assembly.
- The European Parliamentary Elections Act, 1998, providing for the introduction of proportional representation for elections to the European Parliament.
- The Local Government Act, 2000, requiring local authorities to abandon the committee system and providing for directly elected mayors, following referendums.
- The Human Rights Act, 1998, requiring government and all other public bodies to comply with the provisions of the European Convention of Human Rights.
- The House of Lords Act, 1999, providing for the removal of all but 92 of the hereditary peers from the House of Lords, and intended as the first phase of a wider reform of the Lords.
- The Freedom of Information Act, 2000, providing for a statutory right of access to government information.
- The Political Parties, Elections and Referendums Act, 2000, requiring the registration of political parties, controlling donations to political parties and national campaign expenditure and providing for the establishment of an Electoral Commission to oversee elections and to advise on improvements in electoral procedure.
- The Constitutional Reform Act, 2005, providing for the Lord Chief Justice, rather than the Lord Chancellor, to become head of the judiciary, depriving the Lord Chancellor of his role as presiding officer of the House of Lords, and establishing a new Supreme Court, whose members, unlike the law lords, will not be members of the House of Lords.

This is a formidable list. It is scarcely an exaggeration to suggest that, under the Blair government, a new constitution was being created.[2] But, because the reforms were introduced in a piecemeal, unplanned and pragmatic way, rather than in one fell swoop, the extent of the change was hardly noticed. Nevertheless, the years 1997–2007 can be regarded as an era of constitutional reform comparable to that of the years of the Great Reform Act of 1832 or the years before 1914.

Two features of the reforms are worth underlining. The first is that many of them were validated by referendum. That is remarkable, for, until 1975, when Britain held its first national referendum (the second occurred in May 2011 on whether to adopt the alternative vote electoral system) this instrument was widely held to be unconstitutional. In 1964 a standard work on British government remarked: 'It has occasionally been proposed that a referendum might be held on a particular issue, but the proposals do not ever appear to have been taken seriously.'[3] Yet there can now be little doubt that the referendum has become accepted as a method of validating legislation and that the people have become, at last, a part of the British constitution.

A second hardly noticed but momentous feature of the reforms is that it has now come to be accepted that elections to any body other than the House of Commons or a local authority should be by proportional representation. There was hardly any dispute that the devolved bodies in Scotland, Wales and Northern Ireland should be elected by proportional representation. In 2004, a referendum was held in the northeast of England on whether there should be a directly elected regional authority in the region. This was a controversial proposal, and it was defeated by a margin of four to one. Yet hardly anyone disputed that a regional authority, were one to be created, should be elected by proportional representation.

This broad acceptance of proportional representation is a quite unexpected development. Until the 1970s, it was generally assumed that the plurality or first-past-the-post electoral system was the natural one for Britain to use. Opposition to it was largely confined to the Liberal party, whose arguments could easily be dismissed as special pleading. Yet by the end of Labour's period in office in 2010, there were no fewer than four electoral systems in operation in Britain in addition to first-past-the-post. There would have been a fifth if the alternative vote had been endorsed in the referendum held in May 2011. These four systems are:

- The single transferable vote method of proportional representation used for all elections in Northern Ireland, except elections to the House of Commons, and for elections to local authorities in Scotland.
- A system of proportional representation based on the German method of voting, sometimes called the 'additional member' system, used for elections to the Scottish Parliament, the National Assembly of Wales and the Greater London Assembly.
- The regional list method of proportional representation used for elections to the European Parliament.
- The supplementary vote used in elections for all directly elected mayors, including the mayor of London.[4]

At the beginning of the twentieth century, Britain enjoyed a uniform electoral system, the plurality or the first-past-the-post system, but a diversified franchise, there being no fewer than seven different ways in which a man could qualify for the vote.[5] By the end of the twentieth century, by contrast, the qualification for the franchise was uniform, but there were a wide variety of electoral systems. An elector in London would use four different electoral systems. In voting for a Member of Parliament, she would use first-past- the-post; in voting for a mayor of London, she would use the supplementary vote; in voting for the Greater London Assembly, she would use a variant of the German system of proportional representation; and in voting for the European Parliament, she would use regional list proportional representation.

II

The main consequence of the constitutional reforms of the Blair era, together with Britain's entry in 1973 into the European Communities, as the European Union then was, has been to limit the power of government and Parliament. In his Dimbleby lecture of 1976, Lord Hailsham famously suggested that government in Britain was approaching the condition of an 'elective dictatorship'. That would no longer be an accurate description. A government now has to surmount no fewer than six hurdles if it is to secure its legislation. The first is the law of the European Union. If legislation is not consistent with EU law, it can be disapplied by the courts, as the second *Factortame* case[6] and later judgements show.

Second, the government must ensure that its proposed legislation does not breach the conventions of the devolution legislation, which created a quasi-federal system of government in Britain.[7] If the legislation deals with domestic affairs in Scotland, Wales or Northern Ireland, then, by convention, it lies outwith the government's powers. So, if a government wishes to reform the National Health Service, raise student fees or create 'free schools', then that legislation can, by convention, apply only to England. In 1997, Tony Blair produced five pledges. Two of them, the proposals to reduce class sizes and hospital waiting lists, became in practice pledges for England, not for the United Kingdom as a whole. For matters such as education, health and transport, Westminster has become an English parliament. It is no longer a parliament for the whole of the United Kingdom.

The third hurdle facing a government was created not by legislation, but by gradual changes in the habits of MPs. Much journalistic comment contrasts the supposed sheep-like behaviour of MPs today with a mythical 'golden age' when they were, supposedly, genuinely independent. In fact, the truth is the opposite. During the 1950s and 1960s, party cohesion was so near 100 per cent that there was little point in measuring it. From the 1970s, however, as has been shown by students of Parliament such as Philip Norton and Philip Cowley, back bench rebellions have become frequent.[8] In consequence, the Blair government faced particular problems with its backbenchers on votes on, for example, National Health Service foundation hospitals, top-up fees for universities and 42 days detention. A government can no longer take the support of back bench MPs for granted.

If legislation has passed the Commons, there is then a fourth hurdle: the House of Lords. Before 1999, the Lords had a permanent Conservative majority, composed primarily of hereditary peers who constituted two-thirds of the House. A permanent one-party house was regarded by many as offensive as a permanent one-party state. Because it lacked legitimacy, the Lords were generally careful not to dispute government legislation. However, following the House of Lords Act, 1999, the principle came to be accepted that no single party should ever again enjoy an overall majority in the Lords.[9] From 1999 to 2010, the outcome of votes in the Lords depended primarily on the stance taken by the Liberal Democrats and the crossbenchers, the two groups which held the balance of power. The crossbenchers are of course beyond the reach of any party whip. The reformed Lords, being composed primarily of professional politicians and experts rather than hereditary peers has become more assertive and self-confident, more willing to challenge government legislation. To secure their legislation, ministers now have to win the argument in the House of Lords as well as in the Commons. They cannot secure a majority from the government benches alone.

There is then a fifth hurdle: the judges. The Human Rights Act, admittedly, does not give judges the power to strike down legislation. All that the judges can do if they are unable to construe legislation so as to make it compatible with the European Convention of Human Rights is to issue a declaration of incompatibility, a statement without legal effect. Nevertheless, the Human Rights Act provides a fast-track procedure by which an offending statute or part of a statute can be amended or repealed; and so far, all legislation which has been declared incompatible with the Convention has been so amended or repealed. Thus the Human Rights Act gave the judges in effect, though not in form, a new weapon: the power of judicial review of legislation.

The sixth hurdle is the people. Now that the referendum has become part of the constitution, it has become more difficult for a government to secure passage of measures of constitutional importance. A government seeking to alter the electoral system, to join the eurozone or to devolve power to the English regions now needs the support of the people as well as that of Parliament. The Coalition government has extended the role of the referendum through the European Union bill, which provides that approval by the people in a referendum is necessary before a government can agree to any treaty amendments or transfer of powers to the EU. The people, therefore, are now, albeit on a very limited number of issues, part of the lawmaking process.

As a consequence of these changes, the description of British government as an 'elective dictatorship' is no longer appropriate. Such a description was becoming out of date even when it was first made by Lord Hailsham in 1976 since MPs were already becoming more willing to vote against the whip, and judges were becoming more assertive against the executive. Despite journalistic descriptions of the Blair government as being 'presidential' and 'dictatorial', no British government since the Second World War has dispersed power to the same extent.

The era of constitutional reform emphasised the separation of powers in the British constitution and gave it a wholly new importance. That, perhaps, is the central leitmotif of the various reforms. The change in emphasis has been so great as to amount to a change in quality. Liberty, it may be argued, is power cut into pieces. In Britain, constitutional reform has cut power into pieces, and, in particular, it has cut the power of the executive into pieces. Parliament, both Commons and Lords, has more power over the executive; so do the judiciary and, to a limited extent, the people. The British constitution is now characterised less by the sovereignty of Parliament and a concentration of power at the centre than by a separation of powers at the centre and a quasi-federal territorial separation of powers between Parliament, the EU and the devolved bodies. Britain is in the process of becoming a constitutional state, marked by checks and balances between the different organs of government, and a state in which the judiciary now has a crucial role to play in the determination of individual rights and the proper scope of government. It is the transformation of Britain into a constitutional state that forms the deepest significance of the era of constitutional reform.

III

In modernising the constitution, the Blair government departed significantly from the goals of social democracy, which had always presupposed a strong and centralised state. That was why devolution had been opposed by leading figures on Labour's left, such as Aneurin Bevan, who, when establishing the National Health Service, rigorously set his face against any separate Welsh, Scottish or Northern Irish Health Service. It was to be a *National* Health Service, and its benefits would be provided on the basis of need, and not of geography. As a young man working in a South Wales colliery, Bevan declared that he was concerned with just one practical question: 'Where does power lie in this particular state of Great Britain and how can it be attained by the workers?' The answer, he believed, was that 'power meant the use of collective action designed to transform society and so lift all of us together'.[10] Such collective action could best be undertaken by central government. The needs of the South Wales working class were no different from those of the Scottish working class and the English working class. They could be met only by a strong Labour government, representing the interests of the working class in the United Kingdom as a whole, at Westminster. 'My colleagues,' Bevan insisted, 'have no special solution for the Welsh coal industry which is not a solution for the whole of the mining industry of Great Britain. There is no Welsh problem'.[11] Bevan, like most socialists of his day, insisted that the welfare state required that benefits and burdens be distributed according to need and not according to geography. It would be wrong for a sick person in Ebbw Vale to receive a different standard of care from that offered to a sick person in the north of England just because Wales had a devolved body that could press for higher standards while the north did not.

Bevan's aspiration has not, of course, been achieved, and there remain widely different standards of care today in different parts of the country. Yet the aim of a Labour government, he believed, was to help remove such inequalities—not perpetuate them through devolution. Devolution, by fragmenting the state, would merely weaken the socialist response to the depredations of capitalism. In the 1970s, Neil Kinnock, who regarded himself as Bevan's disciple, opposed devolution for similar reasons, declaring in 1976 that it 'could be an obituary notice for this movement'.[12] 'We shall,' Kinnock argued in 1978, 'be introducing into all political considerations an argument that has barely figured at all in British political dialogues and discussions. . . . We have had divisions on a class basis, but not on a geographic or nationalistic basis.'[13]

For social democrats, only a strong centralised state could evaluate the needs of different social groups and ensure that redistribution was effective. However, devolution would fragment the power of the centralised state and cut it into pieces. There could not, in the ideology of social democracy, be a separate Scottish or Welsh political will, for the problem of securing equality in Scotland or in Wales was no different in nature from the problem of securing it in England. These problems should be resolved not by establishing toytown parliaments in Edinburgh and Cardiff, but only by a strong social democratic government at Westminster.

The consequences, less than a decade after the Scottish Parliament and the National Assembly of Wales have been established, would have confirmed Aneurin Bevan's worst fears. In a number of areas of public policy, including residential care for the elderly, the cost of prescriptions, student support, city academies, foundation hospitals, the dispensation in Scotland and Wales is quite different from that in England. The Scottish and Welsh devolved bodies have chosen to be more generous than Westminster; they have decided not to adopt city academies, foundation hospitals or top-up fees; they have been, it might be said, Old Labour rather than New Labour. Devolution therefore runs counter to social democracy as traditionally understood, and even to the New Liberalism of the early twentieth century, which also sought to equalise welfare opportunities between those living in different parts of the country. It has more in common with the Old Liberalism of Gladstone, who was a devolutionist, but a strong opponent of all forms of social democracy, redistribution and state action in the economy, which he slightingly termed 'construction'.[14]

The Conservative argument against devolution had been that by undermining the sovereignty of Parliament, it would lead to the break-up of the kingdom. The Labour case against it was somewhat different. It was that devolution would deprive Westminster not so much of sovereignty, as of power: the power to correct territorial disparities. Only a strong Labour government at Westminster could secure the socialist values of equity and territorial justice. In a Fabian pamphlet entitled *The Third Way*, Tony Blair claimed that the main aim of social democracy was the promotion of 'social justice with the state as its main agent'.[15] It is difficult, however, to see how the state can promote social justice if it has been fragmented and cut into pieces by devolution.

IV

The main weakness of the constitutional reforms of the Blair era is that despite the commitment to referendums on major constitutional issues, they did so little to open up the political system to the people. They did little to meet popular aspirations in what David Cameron has called a 'post-bureaucratic age'. If one were to visualise an average voter living in England, who does not seek devolution for England in the form either of English regional government or an English parliament; who thinks that the Human Rights Act is a useful reform, but hopes never to have to consult lawyers or to appear in the courts; and who asks 'what difference has constitutional reform actually made to me?', it would be difficult to frame a convincing answer.

The constitutional reforms of the Blair era redistributed power, but they redistributed power between elites rather than between elites and the people. They redistributed power 'downwards' to politicians in Edinburgh, Cardiff, Belfast and London, 'sideways' to the life peers in the House of Lords and 'sideways' to the judges interpreting the Human Rights Act. But they did not redistribute power to the voter. They did not shift power from the politicians to the people. That is the central reason why they have not achieved the aim of regenerating democracy or even of countering disenchantment with the political process.

In a perceptive Fabian pamphlet written as long ago as 1992, entitled *Making Mass Membership Work*, Gordon Brown argued that: 'In the past, people interested in change have joined the Labour Party largely to elect agents of change. Today they want to be agents of change themselves.'[16] He instanced as agents of popular participation such bodies as tenants associations, residents groups, school governing bodies and community groups. Neither the Blair nor the Brown governments did much to empower people 'to be agents of change themselves'. For this reason the constitutional reforms of the Blair era need to be complemented with reforms that seek to open up the political system to popular participation. Such reforms, involving a much greater degree of direct democracy, will supplement, though they will not of course replace, the traditional machinery of representative government. Reform, therefore, will have to move beyond the new British constitution created in the Blair era.

The next stage of constitutional reform, and a far more difficult one, must be a redistribution of power not from one part of the elite to another, but from the elite to the people. Such a shift was heralded in the Green Paper entitled *The Governance of Britain* issued by Gordon Brown's government in the summer of 2007. Together with a series of reforms designed to make government more accountable, by, for example, rendering the war-making power accountable to Parliament, it contained a short but important section entitled 'Improving direct democracy'.[17]

In the past, individuals and communities have tended to be seen as passive recipients of services provided by the state. However, in recent years people have demonstrated that they are willing to take a more active role, and that this can help improve services and create stronger communities.[18]

The government proposed, therefore, to begin a consultation process on such matters as the introduction of citizens juries and on giving citizens the power to ballot (that is, call for referendums) on local spending decisions. The Brown government was moving, however tentatively, into a new area of constitutional reform: the introduction of elements of direct democracy into the British political system.

Sadly, the Brown government, faced with economic crisis, was not able to enact these reforms. However, the proposals, limited though perhaps they were, recognised that the era of pure representative democracy, as it was understood for much of the twentieth century, is now coming to an end. During the era of pure representative democracy, the people, though enfranchised, exercised power only on relatively infrequent occasions at general elections. Between general elections, they trusted their elected representatives to act on their behalf. There was some degree of deference towards elected politicians and, in any case, in an era when educational standards were lower than they are now, few voters believed that they had the political competence to make decisions for themselves. In the late 1940s, for example, the level of political knowledge was pitiable. Just 49 per cent could name a single British colony, while, in a sample survey in Greenwich during the 1950 general election, barely half could name the party of their local MP.[19] Voting tended to be tribal and instinctive, based largely on an inherited viewpoint derived from parental attitudes and social class. That, however, was bound to be a transitional stage in the development of democracy. It would take time before universal adult suffrage, introduced as recently as 1928, came to be taken for granted, and its implications for popular empowerment fully understood.

The model of representative democracy (perhaps 'guided democracy' would be a better term) that was acceptable during the first years of universal suffrage is no longer adequate. The exercise of a modicum of power at relatively infrequent general elections is seen by many as insufficient. Voters wish to exert influence between elections as well as at them. Deference has largely disappeared, and it is no longer accepted that political decisions should be made only by politicians. Elected politicians, therefore, are no longer accepted as the sole source of power and authority. Few now believe that the system of pure representative democracy is sufficient to enfranchise them, and this feeling of disengagement seems most pronounced amongst the young. It is one of the main reasons why turnout has fallen so precipitously amongst the 18–24 age group. In addition, many voters, better educated than those of their parents' generation, find themselves empowered in other areas of their lives, while the collective organisations, and in particular the trade unions, have lost much of their authority.

Margaret Thatcher responded to these developments by opening up the economic system, by restricting the powers of the trade unions and by her policy of privatisation. There are now more shareholders in Britain than there are trade unionists. John Major's response was to open up the public services so that their customers were encouraged to expect the same standards as from the private sector, and to complain if these standards were not achieved. Part of the purpose of public service reform has been to give individuals more power over their lives. Yet, in politics they are still expected to remain passive and deferential. The political system has not yet responded to the new individualism. But it is hardly possible to bifurcate human beings, hardly possible to expect someone who is expected to be independent and self-reliant in his or her economic dealings and in his or her dealings with the public services not also to demand a more active role in the political system. There is a striking contrast between the empowered consumer and the passive citizen. The reforms of the Blair government were an insufficient response to the popular and radical forces which had put constitutional change onto the political agenda. They may have begun the task of transforming Britain into a constitutional state. They did not begin the task of transforming Britain into a popular constitutional state.

V

The constitutional reforms proposed by the coalition government which came to office in 2010 will do little to remedy the deficiencies of the Blair reforms.[20] Their overall effect, indeed, could be small in comparison with the sound and fury that they have aroused. The Fixed-term Parliaments Act might make less difference than either its proponents or its opponents imagine since, despite its title, it offers two possibilities for an early dissolution of Parliament: a vote of no-confidence or a two-thirds majority for dissolution. The alternative vote would have made less difference than either its proponents or its opponents imagine if, as would have been likely, many voters decided to plump rather than use their preferences to the full. Certainly the reforms will do little to assist in the further opening up of the political system. Insofar as they do exert an effect, they could even put the process into reverse by serving to insulate Parliament from the people. The Fixed-term Parliaments Act, if it makes it more difficult for a prime minister to dissolve in order to break a parliamentary deadlock, or to appeal to the country on a clear-cut issue dividing government from opposition, might serve to entrench a weak government in power; while if a party knows that it can switch coalition partners with impunity because it will not have to face the voters for five years, there could be changes of government between elections without the voters being consulted.

Reform of the House of Lords, transforming it into a directly elected upper house, would appear at first sight to be a step towards opening up the political system. A more likely outcome, however, is conflict between the two houses leading to deadlock. If disputes between the two houses require some new mechanism to resolve them, such as joint sittings on the Australian model, that will render the political system even more remote from the people. Finally, the alternative vote, if it had been endorsed in the referendum, would have made hung parliaments more likely since it would have probably increased support for the Liberal Democrats, the second-choice party for many Conservative and Labour voters.

A series of hung parliaments will do little to open up the political system. The danger is that decisions about government formation will be taken after the votes have been counted, and, with dissolution becoming more difficult, the government so formed may become less accountable to the people. Westminster could become even more of a house without windows than the public thought it was in 2009 during the expenses scandal. Parliament would come to be characterised by what the French call *'la politique politicienne'*: manoeuvring which excites the political class but alienates the voter.

If the constitutional reforms of the Coalition government, together with regular hung parliaments, do have the effect of further insulating the political system from the people, it would be an unfortunate paradox. The aim of the constitutional reform movement was to strengthen accountability and increase participation, not to give political leaders and parliamentarians more autonomy and enable them to become more distant from the people.

The British constitution must come to reflect what the Prime Minister, among others, has labelled the 'post-bureaucratic age'. The essence of a post-bureaucratic society is fluidity. Whereas the characteristic instrument of the immediate postwar age was the class-based political party, in the post-bureaucratic age it is the individual, and its characteristic purpose is the enhancement of individual choice and individual aspiration. If it is to be congruent with a society which has become fluid, the politics of a post-bureaucratic age must also become fluid, more open to the voters, more open to popular control. The constitutional reforms of the Coalition need, therefore, to be counterbalanced by reforms designed to open up the political system, not further to insulate it. That counterbalance is best secured through the instruments of direct democracy.

It is, of course, impossible either to predict the end-point of the process of constitutional reform initiated by the Blair government or the precise contours of the new British constitution, but the constitutional changes proposed by the Coalition will not end the era of reform which began with the Blair government. That era will come to an end only when our political system has come to be congruent with the public philosophy of the post-bureaucratic age whose watchword is fluidity, and whose leitmotif is the sovereignty of the people, the only sure foundation for a new British constitution.

When Welsh devolution was being implemented, the Welsh Secretary, Ron Davies, declared that it was a process rather than an event. The same is true of constitutional reform. A major task of social democracy is to complete the unfinished business of the Blair era, to transcend the constitutional state and convert it into a popular constitutional state.

Notes

1 *The Ashdown Diaries*, vol. 2, 1997–1999, London, Allen Lane/Penguin Press, 2001, p. 446: entry for 7 May 1999.
2 That was the main theme of V. Bogdanor, *The New British Constitution*, Oxford, Hart, 2009.
3 A. H. Birch, *Representative and Responsible Government: An Essay on the British Constitution*, London, Allen & Unwin, 1964, p. 227.
4 For short descriptions of these various systems, see Chapter 3 of V. Bogdanor, *Power and the People: A Guide to Constitutional Reform*, London, Victor Gollancz, 1997.
5 See J. Curtice, 'The electoral system', in V. Bogdanor, ed., *The British Constitution in the Twentieth Century*, Oxford, Oxford University Press, 2003, esp. pp. 484–6.
6 *R v. Secretary of State for Transport, ex p. Factortame* (No 2) [1991] 1 All ER 70; [1991] 1 AC 603.
7 See V. Bogdanor, *Devolution in the United Kingdom*, Oxford, Oxford University Press, 1999, esp. the final chapter.
8 See, for example, P. Norton, *Conservative Dissidents: Dissent within the Parliamentary Conservative Party, 1970–1974*, London, Temple Smith, 1978; P. Cowley, *Revolts and Rebellions: Parliamentary Voting under Blair*, London, Politico's, 2002.
9 Problems arise, of course, when the government is a coalition. Critics have accused the 2010 coalition of seeking, through the large-scale creation of peers, to acquire a majority for itself in the Lords.
10 A. Bevan, *In Place of Fear*, London, Heinemann, 1952, pp. 1, 2.
11 House of Commons Debates, 5th series, vol. 403, col. 2312, 10 October 1944.
12 Labour Party Conference, 1976, cited in M. Taylor, 'Labour and the constitution', in D. Tanner, P. Thane and N. Tiratsoo, eds, *Labour's First Century*, Cambridge, Cambridge University Press, 2000, p. 180.
13 House of Commons Debates, 5th series, vol. 941, col. 1540, 10 January 1978.
14 See Bogdanor, *Devolution in the United Kingdom*, passim.
15 A. Blair, *The Third Way*, London, Fabian Society, 1998, p. 1.
16 Quoted in L. Byrne, 'Powered by politics: reforming parties from the inside', *Parliamentary Affairs*, vol. 58, 2005, p. 620.
17 Paras. 157–79.
18 Para. 169.
19 D. Kynaston, *Austerity Britain, 1945–51*, London, Bloomsbury, 2007, p. 382.
20 See, for a more detailed discussion, V. Bogdanor, *The Coalition and the Constitution*, Oxford, Hart, 2011.

Rebuilding the Bonds of Trust and Confidence? Labour's Constitutional Reform Programme

JOHN CURTICE

THE NEW Labour governments of 1997–2010 arguably rewrote the British constitution to a greater extent than any previous administration had done since 1922, when most of the island of Ireland left the United Kingdom. Separately, elected devolved institutions were introduced in Scotland and Wales, and restored in Northern Ireland. London acquired a directly elected Mayor, as did a number of other towns and cities. New electoral systems were introduced both in elections to the new devolved bodies and in elections to the European Parliament. Government information and decision making were exposed to far greater public scrutiny via freedom of information legislation. Legislation passed by Parliament became subject to a degree of domestic judicial review following the passage of the Human Rights Act. Finally, political parties were made subject to far greater regulation, not least in respect of their financial affairs.

There was, of course, more than one purpose behind this programme of reform. Devolution to Scotland and Wales was primarily a reaction to the apparent threat of nationalism to Labour's electoral prospects and ultimately to the continuation of the Union. The demand for freedom of information was given impetus by the BSE scandal, in which fears about the safety of British beef were allegedly hidden from public view by the then Major government. Tighter regulation of political parties' financial affairs was in part motivated by a wish to deny the Conservatives the ability to raise money from abroad. However, there was also a key common leitmotif running through the various arguments that were put forward in favour of reform in the years and months leading up to Labour's victory in 1997: a desire to restore the bonds of trust and confidence between politicians and the public—bonds that had been damaged during the tenure of John Major's Conservative administration between 1992 and 1997, not least as a result of the allegations of 'sleaze'.

For example, in their influential presentation of the case for New Labour published a year before the party came to power, Peter Mandelson and Roger Liddle argued that Britain needed 'a new constitutional settlement and a new relationship of trust between politicians and the people'.[1] The report of the joint consultative committee on constitutional reform that Labour formed together with the Liberal Democrats immediately prior to the 1997 election stated that one of the key purposes of reform was 'to renew the relationship

Published by Blackwell Publishing Ltd, 9600 Garsington Road, Oxford OX4 2DQ, UK and 350 Main Street, Malden, MA 02148, USA

between politics and the people'.[2] In its 1997 manifesto, Labour itself stated that: 'Our mission in politics is to rebuild this bond of trust between government and the people.'[3] And in his triumphant speech made outside the Royal Festival Hall as dawn was breaking on the day after his 1997 election victory, Tony Blair declared that the new government would be one 'that seeks to restore politics in this country, that decentralises it, that gives people hope again that politics is, and should be always, about the service of the public'.[4]

It is not difficult to see why restoring the bond of trust between politicians and the public should have become a key theme behind Labour's programme of reform. Devolution was intended to ensure that demand for separatism were assuaged, and thus the bonds that tied the people of Scotland and Wales to the Union repaired and strengthened. If government information were made more easily available to the public, public suspicion that vital information was being withheld would be less likely to grow. Meanwhile, opening up to public view the sources of money given to political parties would help assuage concern that money bought influence inside political parties. After the difficulties that had befallen John Major's administration, such arguments had a clear resonance.

So in assessing New Labour's programme of constitutional reform, one central question to ask is how successful it proved to be in strengthening the bond between Britain's political system and its people? If that assessment is to be a positive one, then first of all, the constitutional changes made by Labour should have been acceptable to the British public. In particular, where new institutions were created, those institutions should have been accepted by the public as legitimate sources of decision making. If they were not, then rather than helping to restore the links between public and politicians, the new institutions might have become potential sources of discontent.

Still, avoiding that pitfall would only be a start. To be a success not only did the new institutions and reforms need to be backed by the public, but the changes should also have engendered increased levels of trust and confidence in politics and politicians. After all, people might have wanted a Scottish Parliament or a Welsh Assembly, but still regarded those who occupied those institutions as untrustworthy. And, as we have seen, increasing the public's trust in politics was at the heart of the rhetoric behind New Labour's programme of reform.

Yet on its own even that might be regarded as only of limited benefit. However much the public might trust those in power, the bonds between public and politicians might still be considered weak if the public are not willing to participate in the political process, including, above all, at election time. So the final part of our assessment should be to explore what happened to electoral turnout in the wake of Labour's programme of constitutional reform, both in the new institutions that were created, and in elections more generally.

Legitimacy

Arguably the most significant of the changes introduced by Labour, and certainly the one that required the creation of new institutions, was the introduction of devolution in Scotland and Wales. So we clearly need to establish whether the new institutions had public support within their respective jurisdictions of the United Kingdom. However, one of the most striking features of New Labour's devolution reforms was that England was largely left out of the picture—a feature that critics suggested would lead to discontent in the English regions. We should therefore also examine whether giving a measure of self-rule to Scotland and Wales has fostered a 'backlash' within England.

New Labour did, of course, try to ensure that there was a tide of public support behind the new institutions by first seeking approval for their creation in referendums held in Scotland and Wales in 1997. In Scotland, the response appeared unequivocal. Nearly three-quarters of those who voted backed the new Parliament in a contest that attracted a 60 per cent turnout. But in Wales, just over half voted in favour in a ballot where the turnout was only just over 50 per cent. The latter result suggested that the new Assembly might simply be a source of controversy and division, while in Scotland there was no guarantee that people might not come to have second thoughts.

In practice, however, neither scenario came to fruition. In Scotland, despite controversy about the expense and delays in completing a new building for the Parliament, there was little sign that the public wanted to get rid of the institution itself. By the time the Parliament was up and running in 1999, the Scottish Social Attitudes survey found that just 9 per cent did not want any kind of Scottish Parliament at all. A decade later that figure was still just 8 per cent.[5] In Wales, meanwhile, public support for the new Assembly soon grew in the wake of the initially very narrow referendum result. In the years immediately after its creation, only around one in five did not want an assembly at all, and by 2009 opposition had fallen to 14 per cent.[6] It seems that once the Assembly had become a reality, it quickly secured public acceptance—a mood that by 2006 helped persuade Labour that the Assembly should be granted some of the primary legislative powers which it had initially been denied.

This, however, raises the larger question as to whether people in Scotland and Wales wished to remain in the United Kingdom at all. Some of its critics argued that devolution would prove to be a 'slippery slope' to independence.[7] Such fears seemed to be confirmed when in 2007 the Scottish National party secured power in Edinburgh, while in Cardiff, Labour found itself forced to enter into a coalition deal with Plaid Cymru. However, it appears that independence remains a minority cause in both parts of the United Kingdom. In 1999, 27 per cent of people in Scotland were in favour of independence; ten years later that figure was still only 28 per cent.[8] When devolution was first introduced in Wales, just 10 per cent wanted independence, and only 8 per cent wanted it in 2008.[9]

What of England: was she unhappy at being left out of the devolution process? For the most part, it seems not. The British Social Attitudes survey consistently found that despite the advent of devolution elsewhere in the United Kingdom, somewhere over half of people in England felt that the laws for England should still be made by the Parliament at Westminster— though there were some signs towards the end of Labour's time in power that that mood might be beginning to change.[10] Meanwhile, those who wanted some form of devolution were divided between those who favoured a regional assembly and those that wanted an English parliament. This mood helped ensure that when Labour did attempt to introduce a form of regional devolution in the North East of England, the proposal was roundly defeated in a referendum held in the region in November 2004. Little more was heard thereafter about extending devolution to all or parts of England.[11]

Still, that did not necessarily mean that resentment about some of the apparent anomalies thrown up by the asymmetric nature of Labour's devolution settlement was entirely absent in England. The most obvious source of discontent was the infamous 'West Lothian question', which highlights the anomaly whereby English MPs no longer had any say in laws pertaining to devolved matters such as health and education in Scotland, whereas Scottish MPs continued to vote on the fate of equivalent legislation about the same matters in England. Consistently around 60 per cent of the public in England said that Scottish MPs should not now be able to vote on English laws.[12]

A second potential source of resentment was the fact that public spending per head is higher in Scotland than in England—and to a greater degree than would likely be justified by any form of needs analysis.[13] This difference existed before devolution, but debate about its merits became more salient now that England no longer had any direct influence over how much of that money was actually spent. However, the extent to which this was a source of resentment is far from clear. Certainly when opinion pollsters pointed out to their respondents that spending per head was some 20 per cent higher than that in England, those respondents indicated that they thought that this was unfair.[14] But in the absence of such prompting, only between a quarter and two-fifths indicated that Scotland received more than its fair share of public spending—albeit there were signs towards the end of Labour's time in power that this proportion was increasing.[15]

Although for the most part devolution largely passed England by, London did secure a new directly elected Mayor who was answerable to a new city-wide Assembly. This move, too, was only implemented following a referendum held at the same time as the London borough elections in May 2000. Nearly three-quarters of those voting backed the idea, but only just over one in three actually voted at all. Still, survey evidence collected at the time suggests that there was initially relatively little opposition to—if not necessarily wild enthusiasm for—the idea of a directly elected Mayor, or indeed the

London Assembly.[16] Certainly both institutions now appear to have secured a firm place in the running of the capital's affairs.

However, the idea of directly elected mayors has not caught on more widely, despite encouragement from Labour ministers who believed that a vote focused on one individual rather than a body of councillors would help revive public interest in local government and help to ensure it was more accountable. As in London, a directly elected Mayor was only introduced elsewhere if the idea secured public backing in a referendum. A total of 37 referendums were held in various parts of England and Wales, but only in a dozen cases did a majority vote in favour. In one instance (Stoke), a subsequent referendum resulted in the abolition of the city's Mayor. Among the concerns that have been expressed about the system is that too much day-to-day power is vested in one person whose decisions cannot be easily overturned by the council, the body to whom the Mayor is meant to be answerable.

Not only did devolution and the restoration of capital-wide government result in new institutions being created, but they also saw new electoral systems introduced into some public elections in Great Britain for the first time since 1945. A system of proportional representation was introduced in elections to the European Parliament, though a promise to hold a referendum on changing the electoral system for the House of Commons remained on the backburner until, shortly before the 2010 election, the party committed itself to holding a referendum on introducing the Alternative Vote. For the most part, the use of proportional representation in devolved elections appears to have been met with substantial, if not uncritical, approval; around three in five people in both Scotland and Wales appear to have backed the idea, both in 1999 and again in 2003, with support even higher amongst those who actually voted in the first devolved elections.[17] However, it is far from clear that the public across the United Kingdom as a whole would have preferred Labour to have made further progress on changing the system for the House of Commons too.[18]

While Labour may have done nothing to change how MPs secured election to the House of Commons, it did, of course, bring about significant change to the House of Lords with the near removal of the hereditary peerage. There seems little doubt that the public felt that the upper chamber was ripe for reform, but that that change should have gone further. In the 1999 British Social Attitudes survey, nearly two-thirds of respondents thought some kind of change should be made to the Lords, with the majority favouring reform rather than abolition. At the same time, however, subsequent surveys in the same series found that no more than 7 per cent wanted a second chamber that was wholly or mainly appointed. Most wanted a body where the number of elected members was at least equal to the number of appointees.

In contrast to the reforms considered so far, neither freedom of information nor the Human Rights Act involved the creation of new legislative or executive bodies or a major change to the composition of an existing one.

Thus the degree of public support for these two measures is arguably less of an issue. In fact, little systematic research has been undertaken on attitudes towards freedom of information. Perhaps not surprisingly, one survey that did tackle the subject found that the public had an appetite for openness and Labour's legislation was not regarded as 'doing enough to meet public demands to reduce government secrecy'.[19] Meanwhile, repeated analysis by the State of the Nation surveys on attitudes towards human rights legislation found near universal support for the principle of a 'Bill of Rights to protect the liberty of the individual', though it might be noted that the same survey series also found that a majority backed detention without charge for up to sixty days.[20]

So for the most part it would appear that the changes instituted by Labour had public support. The new institutions that Labour created had a wide degree of legitimacy. In part, this was the case because many of the changes were only introduced after they had secured endorsement in a referendum, the widespread use of which device was itself another constitutional innovation. Indeed, its use ensured that some of Labour's other constitutional reform proposals—regional government in England and the widespread introduction of directly elected mayors—in fact ground to a halt. Even where a narrow referendum result did raise questions about whether a new institution would take root, as happened in the case of the Welsh Assembly, in practice it did. True, some of the anomalies created by the introduction of asymmetric devolution raised questions in the public's mind, while reform of the Lords was undoubtedly regarded as unfinished business. But so far as securing legitimacy is concerned, New Labour's reform programme must be regarded as a considerable success.

Trust

When it comes to the second test—whether Labour's programme of constitutional reform helped to restore public trust and confidence in the political process—a dark cloud immediately comes to mind: the MPs expenses scandal that broke out in the summer of 2009. That event unleashed an unprecedented degree of public anger at MPs. If Labour had had any success in restoring public trust up until that event, presumably its good work was undone by that event?

Table 1 shows how levels of trust in the political system have ebbed and flowed during the last twenty years according to one key, and far from untypical, indicator.[21] It shows what has happened when people have been asked on various occasions how much they trust 'British governments of any party to place the needs of the nation above the interests of their own political party'.

There are three key points to note. First, it appears that levels of trust were indeed eroded in the wake of the 'sleaze' allegations that surrounded the 1992–97 Conservative administration. The proportion who trusted govern-

Table 1: Trends in political trust, 1987–2009 (percentages)

Trust government	1987 (1)	1987* (2)	1991	1994	1996	1997 (1)	1997* (2)	1998	2000	2001	2002	2003	2005	2006	2007	2009
Just about always/most of the time	37	47	33	24	22	25	33	28	16	28	26	18	26	19	29	16
Some of the time	46	43	50	53	53	48	52	52	58	50	47	49	47	46	45	42
Almost never	11	9	14	21	23	23	12	17	24	20	24	31	26	34	23	40

Source: British Social Attitudes, except * British Election Study.

ments at least 'most of the time' fell from around a third to a quarter between 1991 and 1994, and levels of trust did not subsequently recover. Labour's claim before coming to power in 1997 that the bonds of trust between politicians and the public were in need of repair was not without foundation.

Second, New Labour had relatively little success in restoring levels of trust, even before the MPs expenses scandal broke. Indeed, on occasions during its first ten years in power the proportion trusting governments at least 'most of the time' fell well below the level of a quarter or so that the party inherited. A number of the readings in the table that suggested some recovery might be afoot were in fact taken immediately after an election had been held. Levels of trust are always higher after elections, only to fall again subsequently.[22]

Third, the MPs expenses scandal did indeed do further damage. In 2009, in the immediate wake of the scandal, no less than two in five said that they 'almost never' trusted governments, more than ever before and almost twice the proportion that pertained immediately before the 1997 general election. Doubtless some of this lack of trust will have subsided once the immediate headlines of the MPs expenses scandal have faded from memory, but, nonetheless, it seems safe to conclude that Britain was even more sceptical, if not necessarily cynical, about politicians when Labour left office in 2010 than it had been thirteen years earlier.

Why did Labour's reform programme do so little to restore trust in politics? The key tools that it deployed were transparency and regulation. In particular, freedom of information legislation was designed to shed light on the dark corners of government, ensuring that those who might be tempted to engage in shady or undesirable practices were dissuaded by the fear of public exposure. [23] Meanwhile, tighter regulation of political parties was intended to reduce the risk that unknown wealthy donors might secure excessive influence.

However, there are potential downsides to this approach.[24] If politicians and political parties have to be heavily regulated, then presumably they are not to be trusted. In any event, tighter regulation can increase the risk that politicians commit a technical breach of the rules, and thereby be made to appear untrustworthy, even though their breach might have had little to do with the kind of behaviour that the regulation is designed to avoid. Arguably this was the fate that befell both former cabinet minister, Peter Hain, and the former Scottish Labour leader, Wendy Alexander—both of whom were forced to resign in the wake of errors made in financing internal party election campaigns. In making it more likely that alleged 'wrongdoing' is exposed, its apparent prevalence can be highlighted, [25] undermining people's trust even further. Indeed, it was ironically the passage of the freedom of information legislation that set in train the sequence of events that eventually led to the MPs expenses scandal.

So the second test of the effectiveness of New Labour's programme of constitutional reform appears more challenging. It seems to have done little to restore people's trust and confidence in politics and the political system. It could even be argued that, despite the best of intentions, some of the measures Labour adopted in practice proved to be positively counterproductive.

Participation

Perhaps the greatest risk that Labour took in creating new, devolved institutions in Scotland and Wales was not that those institutions would become the focus of public opposition, but rather that they would simply be ignored altogether. Although the new bodies might symbolise the distinctive national identities to which many people in those two parts of the United Kingdom now adhere, this does not guarantee that voters will consider it worthwhile to turn out and vote in elections to the new institutions. The electorate might well feel that the Scottish Parliament and, certainly with its more limited powers, the National Assembly for Wales, were not sufficiently important to merit their participation. That, after all, is a fate that befalls many 'sub-state' elections elsewhere in the world.[26]

In the event, turnout was indeed lower in the two sets of devolved elections than in general elections, and especially so in Wales. Just 46.4 per cent voted in the first devolved Welsh election—well down on the 73.5 per cent who had done so in the 1997 general election. In the subsequent two contests, just 38.2 and 43.5 per cent did so. Such turnouts were in fact no better than the norm for local elections in the principality.[27] In Scotland, turnout was rather higher, but still less than in general elections: in 1999, 58.2 per cent voted, whereas two years previously 71.3 per cent had turned out in the general election. In the 2003 Scottish election turnout fell to just below a half (49.4 per cent) before recovering slightly to 52.4 per cent in 2007. Devolved elections have not proved to be particularly successful at drawing voters into the electoral process.

Meanwhile, one of the arguments put forward in favour of mayoral elections was that they would secure higher levels of interest and participation than local elections usually manage to achieve.[28] In the event, this has largely not occurred. Just 33.6 per cent voted in the first London mayoral election in 2000, and only slightly more (36.9 per cent) did so in the second contest in 2004. This was little different from the 33 and 38 per cent, respectively, that participated in the London borough elections of 2002 and 2006. Only the third contest, held in 2008 when 45.3 per cent voted, attracted rather greater interest. The first mayoral elections in the twelve authorities outside London that adopted the system secured an average participation rate of just 29 per cent—rather less than the norm in local elections.[29]

One of the arguments sometimes put forward in favour of proportional representation is that it encourages more people to vote—a claim for which comparative cross-national research provides a degree of support.[30] Yet not only did the use of proportional representation fail to ensure a high turnout in the devolved elections in Scotland and Wales, its introduction in European elections failed to rescue those contests from the abysmally low turnouts that had become the norm in Great Britain. In the first European election to be held under proportional representation, in 1999, just 23.1 per cent participated—a drop of 13 points compared with the last contest to be held under first-past-the-post in 1994. True, turnout did rise sharply to a record high of 38.2 per cent in 2004, but on this occasion the participation rate was boosted by the fact that the election was held using an all postal ballot in several regions of England.[31] In 2009, turnout slipped back to 35.9 per cent, more or less in line with the norm for European elections since their introduction in 1979. It seems that the switch to proportional representation in determining Britain's representation at Strasbourg made little difference either way.

Yet if the introduction of proportional representation had little obvious beneficial impact on levels of electoral participation, it can hardly be said that voters flocked to the polls in contests held under the traditional first-past-the-post system either. Indeed, turnout in elections to the House of Commons plummeted to unprecedented lows.[32] At 71.4 per cent, turnout in Great Britain had already been lower in 1997 than in any previous postwar election. In 2001, however, only 59.1 per cent voted—a lower proportion than on any occasion since 1918 when participation was affected by the war that had only just ended. In 2005, the figure was little better at 61.3 per cent, and the 65.3 per cent turnout recorded in 2010 was still well below the 70 per cent mark that had hitherto been regarded as the 'floor' level of turnout in British elections.

Much of this decline in turnout may in fact have been circumstantial rather than the result of a decline in voters' motivation to engage in the electoral process as a result of declining political trust. It seems that those with relatively little interest in politics felt that there was little point in voting in elections where the outcome appeared to be a foregone conclusion, and when there appeared to be little difference between the parties.[33] However, a major reason why many voters saw little difference between the parties was because of New Labour's perceived shift to the centre-right. In this respect at least, the party seems to have undermined its efforts to strengthen the bonds between public and politicians. Moreover, even if originally occasioned by circumstance, there were signs that such a sequence of low turnouts was having a longer-term impact. Young voters appeared less likely to develop the habit of voting that they would then retain for the rest of their lives.[34] Meanwhile, there were indications towards the end of Labour's time in office that the recent sequence of low turnouts had begun to undermine the feeling that people had a duty to vote.[35]

So far as electoral participation was concerned, the bonds between politicians and the public looked even weaker by the time Labour lost power in 2010. Electoral participation reached a record low, while turnout in the new institutions created by Labour's constitutional reforms showed little sign of helping to fill the gap. The high hopes of 1997 had come to seem a world away.

Conclusion

The 1997–2010 Labour government largely avoided serious difficulties in introducing its radical programme of constitutional reform. A few proposed measures such as regional devolution in England failed to win public support when put to a popular vote in a referendum, but most of the reforms gained public assent and soon became part of the legitimate fabric of the British constitution. To that extent, the new institutions created by those reforms added useful additional links in the chain between politicians and the public.

Yet Labour's experience also revealed some of the potential pitfalls of constitutional reform. It revealed that greater transparency and tighter regulation of the political system do not necessarily enhance public trust and confidence. Indeed, they may even serve to undermine it. Meanwhile, even new political institutions whose legitimacy may not be widely questioned can still struggle to attract sufficient interest and attention in persuading voters to go to the polls. Consequently, by the time that Labour left office, the gulf between the public and politicians seemed to be even wider than it had been in 1997.

Yet despite or perhaps because of this experience, the search for constitutional reforms that might succeed in strengthening the bond between politicians and the public goes on. Labour's successor in power—the Conservative–Liberal Democrat coalition—is committed to a programme of constitutional reform at least as radical as that introduced by Labour, ranging from a referendum on the Commons electoral system to the introduction of directly elected police commissioners.[36] In introducing these reforms the coalition hopes, according to Nick Clegg, to persuade people 'to put your faith in politics once again'.[37] He should be aware, given Labour's experience, that he has not set himself an easy task.

Notes

1 P. Mandelson and R. Liddle, *The Blair Revolution: Can New Labour Deliver?*, London, Faber & Faber, 1996.
2 Report of the Labour/Liberal Democrat Joint Consultative Committee on Constitutional Reform, March 1997.
3 Labour party, *New Labour Because Britain Deserves Better*, London, Labour party, 1997.
4 See also, J. Straw, D. Henderson and D. Foster, *New Politics, New Britain: Restoring Trust in the Way We are Governed*, London, Labour party, 1996; R. Hazell, 'Constitutional eform and the New Labour government', CIPFA/Times Lecture, 14 July 1997, http://eprints.ucl.ac.uk/113588/; P. Dunleavy, H. Margetts, T. Smith and S. Weir, 'Constitutional reform, New Labour in power and public trust in government, *Parliamentary Affairs*, vol. 54, 2001, pp. 405–24.
5 R. Ormston and J. Curtice, 'Resentment or contentment? Attitudes towards the Union ten years on', in A. Park, J. Curtice, E. Clery and C. Bryson, eds, *British Social Attitudes: the 27th Report—Exploring Labour's Legacy*, London, Sage, 2010, pp. 158–77.

6 J. Curtice and B. Seyd, 'The citizens' response: devolution and the Union', in J. Curtice and B. Seyd, eds, *Has Devolution Worked? The Verdict from the Policy-makers and the Public*, Manchester, Manchester University Press, 2009, pp. 116–37; gfkNOP Social Research, *Research to Support the Work of the All-Wales Convention*, London: gfkNOP Social Research, http://allwalesconvention.org/?skip=1&lang =en

7 T. Dalyell, *Devolution: The End of Britain?*, London, Jonathan Cape, 1977.

8 Ormston and Curtice, 'Resentment or contentment?'.

9 Curtice and Seyd, 'The citizens' response'; gfkNOp Social Research, *Research*.

10 Ormston and Curtice, 'Resentment or contentment?'.

11 J. Curtice and M. Sandford, 'Does England want devolution too?', in A. Park, J. Curtice, K. Thomson, C. Bromley and M. Phillips, eds, *British Social Attitudes: the 21st Report*, London, Sage, 2004, pp. 201–19; M. Sandford, ed., *The Northern Veto*, Manchester, Manchester University Press, 2009.

12 Ormston and Curtice, 'Resentment or contentment?'.

13 I. McLean, G. Lodge and K. Schmuecker, *Fair Shares? Barnett and the Politics of Public Expenditure*, London, IPPR, 2008.

14 J. Curtice, *Where Stands the Union Now? Lessons from the 2007 Scottish Parliament Elections*, London, IPPR, 2008.

15 Ormston and Curtice, 'Resentment or contentment?'.

16 J. Curtice, B. Seyd and K. Thomson, 'Do mayoral elections work? Evidence from London', *Political Studies*, vol. 56, 2008, pp. 653–78.

17 Independent Commission on Proportional Representation, *Changed Voting, Changed Politics: Lessons from Britain's Experience of PR since 1997*, London, Constitution Unit, 2003; J. Curtice, B. Seyd, A. Park and K. Thomson, *Wise after the Event? Attitudes to Voting Reform after the 1999 Scottish and Welsh Elections*, London, Constitution Unit, 2000; J. Curtice and B. Seyd, 'Attitudes to voting rules and electoral system preferences: Evidence from the 1999 and 2003 Scottish Parliament elections', *Electoral Studies* (forthcoming).

18 J. Curtice, S. Fisher and L. Lessard-Phillips, 'Proportional representation and the disappearing voter', in A. Park, J. Curtice, K. Thomson, M. Phillips and M. Johnson, eds, *British Social Attitudes: the 23rd Report—Perspectives on a Changing Society*, London, Sage, 2007, pp. 119–41.

19 Dunleavy et al., 'Constitutional reform'.

20 See State of the Nation surveys 2006 and 2010, both available at: http://www.jrrt.org.uk/.

21 For further evidence and discussion, see C. Bromley, J. Curtice and B. Seyd, 'Political engagement, trust and constitutional reform', in A. Park, J. Curtice, K. Thomson, L. Jarvis and C. Bromley, eds, *British Social Attitudes: the 18th Report—Public Policy, Social ties*, London, Sage, 2001, pp. 199–225; J. Curtice and A. Park, 'A tale of two crises', in Park et al., *British Social Attitudes: 27th Report*, pp. 131–54.

22 The second of the two readings, in 1987 and 1997, together with those of 2001 and 2005, were taken after the elections in those years. The first of the two readings in 1987 and 1997 were obtained shortly before that year's election. We might also note that the levels of trust in 2001 and 2005 were below those pertaining in 1987 and 1997.

23 C. Hood and D. Heald, *Transparency: The Key to Better Government?*, Oxford, Oxford University Press for the British Academy, 2006.

24 Public Administration Select Committee, *Ethics and Standards: The Regulation of Conduct in Public Life*, Fourth Report of Session 2006–7, HC121, London, Stationery Office: 2007.

25 Indeed, evidence from the British Social Attitudes survey suggested that the public were just as likely in 2009 to think that Labour and the Conservatives do 'favours for people or companies who give the party large sums of money' as they had been seven years previously (see Curtice and Park, 'A tale of two crises').

26 K.-H. Reiff and H. Schmitt, 'Nine second-order national elections: a conceptual framework for the analysis of European election results', *European Journal of Political Research*, vol. 8, 1980, pp. 3–44; R. Dinkel, 'Der Zusammenhang zwischen Bundes- und Landtags-wahlergebnissen', *Politische Vierteljahresschrift*, vol. 18, 1977, pp. 348–60; C. Jeffery and D. Hough, 'Devolution and electoral politics: where does the UK fit in?', in D. Hough and C. Jeffery, eds, *Devolution and Electoral Politics*, Manchester, Manchester University Press, 2006, pp. 248–56.

27 C. Rallings and M. Thrasher, *British Electoral Facts, 1832–2006*, Aldershot, Ashgate, 2007.

28 G. Stoker, *The Reform of the Institutions of Local Representative Democracy: Is There a Role for the Mayor-Council Model?*, London, Commission for Local Democracy.

29 Rallings and Thrasher, *British Electoral Facts*.

30 D. Amy, *Real Choices/New Voices: The Case for PR Elections in the United States*, New York, Columbia University Press, 1993; A. Blais and K. Aarts, 'Electoral systems and turnout', *Acta Politica*, vol. 41, 2006, pp. 180–96.

31 J. Curtice, S. Fisher and M. Steed, 'Appendix: an analysis of the results', in D. Butler and M. Westlake, *British Politics and European Elections 2004*, Basingstoke, Palgrave Macmillan, 2005, pp. 190–208.

32 Turnout also fell to a record low of less than 30 per cent between 1997 and 2001 in local government elections, though thereafter it returned to the more regular level of a little over a third or so (see Rallings and Thrasher, *British Electoral Facts*).

33 C. Bromley and J. Curtice, 'Where have all the voters gone?', in A. Park, J. Curtice, K. Thomson, L. Jarvis and C. Bromley, eds, *British Social Attitudes: the 19th Report*, London, Sage, 2002, pp. 148–67; Curtice et al., 'Proportional representation'.

34 J. Curtice, 'Losing the voting habit', in R. Gough, ed., *2056: What Future for Maggie's Children?*, London, Policy Exchange, 2006; H. Clarke, D. Sanders, M. Stewart and P. Whiteley, *Political Choice in Britain*, Oxford, Oxford University Press, 2004.

35 S. Butt and J. Curtice, 'Duty in decline: who still feels a duty to vote?', in A. Park, J. Curtice, K. Thomson, N. Phillips, E. Clery and S. Butt, eds, *British Social Attitudes: the 26th Report*, London, Sage, 2010, pp. 1–18; Curtice and Park, 'A tale of two crises'.

36 Indeed, it is a programme that is particularly notable for its greater emphasis on instruments of direct democracy that are of interest to those with low levels of trust and confidence in government (see J. Curtice, 'Switching off the lights in the corridors of power', *Parliamentary Brief*, vol. 13, no. 5, 2011, pp. 9–10; V. Bogdanor, *The New British Constitution*, Oxford, Hart, 2009; R. Dalton, W. Bürklin and A. Drummond, 'Public opinion and direct democracy', *Journal of Democracy*, vol. 12, 2001, pp. 141–53.

37 N. Clegg, 'Deputy PM's first speech on constitutional reform', 19 May 2010, http://www.dpm.cabinetoffice.gov.uk/news/deputy-pms-first-speech-constitutional-reform

New Labour and the Distribution of Power: Constitutional Reform, Human Rights and Civil Liberties

FRANCESCA KLUG

BEFORE the 2010 general election, the then aspiring leader of the Labour party, Ed Miliband, asked the following rhetorical question: 'How did we go from a government which started with windfall taxes and the minimum wage to one which defended bankers bonuses?'[1] The intention behind the question was clear. It was to stake out the journey New Labour had travelled in government from a party associated with protecting the low paid to one which defended the interests of the very rich. The terrain Ed Miliband chose to illustrate this point was the one most closely associated with the Labour party since its inception: social justice, inequality and the redistribution of wealth.

Yet this was not the only searching question that needed asking about New Labour's journey. The then prospective leader might just as well have asked the following question: How did we go from the party of the Freedom of Information Act, the Human Rights Act, Devolution, the abolition of hereditary Peers, the Enquiry into the murder of Stephen Lawrence, the Race Relations Amendment Act, the Equality and Human Rights Commission, civil partnerships, the Equality Act and so forth to a party with a reputation for being 'casual'—or worse—about civil liberties; not trusted to tell the truth about statistics, party funding or, for that matter, weapons of mass destruction in Iraq; and an advocate of anything from 42 to 90 days detention without charge?

The raft of constitutional and legal reforms, particularly in the early days of Blair's tenure, that Miliband could have drawn upon to illustrate this line of enquiry arguably *did* add up to 'the biggest shake up of our democracy since 1832 when the Great Reform Act' was passed. This was the boast Deputy Prime Minister, Nick Clegg made about the Coalition's proposed 'power revolution' in the rosy dawn of the new administration's life—a brag he may yet come to regret on sober reflection.[2]

The New Labour journey

A dispassionate evaluation of Labour's record in office from 1997 must begin with an acknowledgement of the advances in democratic accountability and enhanced rights and freedoms that were made, particularly in the government's first term. The state was far more centralised before the

Published by Blackwell Publishing Ltd, 9600 Garsington Road, Oxford OX4 2DQ, UK and 350 Main Street, Malden, MA 02148, USA

devolution measures to Scotland, Wales and Northern Ireland that defined Blair's reforms.[3] Before the 1998 Human Rights Act,[4] the courts had no mandate to hold the executive to account beyond the relatively constrained powers of judicial review that they developed for themselves.[5] The equalities measures were substantial. Even David Cameron acknowledged on becoming prime minister that 'compared with a decade ago, this country is more open at home and more compassionate abroad'.[6]

So why, in so many commentators' estimations across the political spectrum, did this not *feel* like an era where power was dispersed from the centre rather than concentrated in it? Why is it that the claim that 'we distributed power' is rarely presented as New Labour's most enduring legacy? How, as former political secretary to Tony Blair, John McTernan has pondered, did 'a party which brought in the Human Rights Act come to be seen as an enemy of liberty'?[7] Why have claims like Labour 'has abused and eroded fundamental human freedoms and historic civil liberties',[8] or 'under Labour our civil liberties have been undermined, eroded, lost',[9] chimed with the views of young people and those who turned away from Labour to the Liberal Democrats and Greens, in particular, reflected in a stream of political blogs and polling evidence?[10]

The largely successful labelling of New Labour as 'arrogant' and 'all-controlling' has impacted on the fortunes of all the main political parties.[11] Tony Blair convincingly described in his book *A Journey* how, over time, the 'big tent' support New Labour had amassed became weakened by a coalition of what he called the 'Daily Mail/Guardian alliance'.[12] It was this coalescing of erstwhile opposing forces, united above all by an apparent regard for the freedoms that New Labour appeared to disdain, that significantly contributed to the 'mood music' which bled Labour's support and provided the nest egg for the Clegg–Cameron nuptials. A new cross-party fault line had opened up in British politics, revolving around the powers of the state rather than the state of the economy.

It is not difficult to see how the trajectory of New Labour paved the way for such an alliance. Common ground developed between 'economic liberals', who combine their adherence to a 'small state' with a patriotic attachment towards what they regard as 'traditional British liberties', and 'social liberals' who, while supporting an enabling state, are concerned to limit its power where it encroaches on human rights.

Although the contradictions between these approaches are starting to strain the marriage, their common thread provided the prelude to the Liberal Democrats' and Tories' coupling. It opened the door for the new Coalition government to present their shared agenda as one of freedom for the citizen even when this is really camouflage for freedom for the market. Cameron's catch-all depiction of the New Labour creed as 'statism',[13] enabled him and his partners to discredit the social democratic elements of New Labour's programme as all of a piece with its disregard for civil liberties—both evidence that 'Labour just don't trust people'.[14]

Attempts by the last government to improve the quality of life of most United Kingdom citizens by curbing 'postcode lotteries' and providing accountable standards of public services could be dismissed by the opposition as Labour's culture of 'targets, directives and central control'.[15] Explicitly or implicitly, public health measures and NHS reform were derided as 'Labour's mania for controlling and directing things from the centre'[16] building new schools and enhancing benefits as 'high-spending, all-controlling, heavy-handed' government.[17] The largely traditional Tory case for rolling back the state was refreshed under the guise of presenting Labour as 'secretive, power-hoarding . . . [and] arrogant'.[18]

The success of both Coalition partners in portraying the state under the previous administration as 'authoritarian'[19] and 'controlling'[20] occurred despite the fact that one of the major purposes of the New Labour project was to represent a break with its centralised and collectivist past. It is well documented that in government, New Labour presided over a deregulated financial sector and an enhancement of market freedoms that was unprecedented in Labour history.

Conversely, whilst the Conservative leader set out to 'rebrand' his party from its previous reputation as 'nasty', the Thatcher administration that he continues to laud as a byword for individual freedom ushered in a range of measures which reduced the freedom of the individual[21]—in some cases specifically targeted at minority groups or trade unions.[22] But it was the growing association of New Labour with 'encroaching state power'[23] that allowed Cameron to fudge this heritage and brand his 'Big Society' as being about 'liberation' involving 'the biggest, most dramatic redistribution of power from elites in Whitehall to the man and woman in the street'.[24]

By the end of its term of office, it was not uncommon for the last government to be labelled as 'arrogant, inflexible [and] authoritarian', even by some of its supporters.[25] How did the party of constitutional reform and equality legislation develop this widely held reputation? The nature of the New Labour project, when tested against specific catastrophic events that could not have been predicted before the party came to power,[26] is the usual explanations for this journey.[27]

The New Labour project

Conscious of a longstanding reputation for championing the 'collective, exercised through the state' at the expense of 'the fundamental rights of the individual', the architects of New Labour, according to Peter Mandelson, saw the case for distinguishing themselves from 'Old Labour' by demonstrating that 'individuals have inalienable rights' which 'should be clearly and unambiguously expressed'. This was the early justification for 'why Labour now advocates as a first step the incorporation of the European Convention on Human Rights into British law, as the basis for Britain's own bill of rights'.[28]

In his inaugural conference speech as Leader, Tony Blair declared 'We are the party of the individual because we are the party of community'[29]— suggesting that New Labour was bent on integrating liberty and fraternity, even if it was to be lighter on Labour's traditional concern with (social and economic) equality. In the same speech he promised 'the biggest programme of change to democracy ever proposed by a political party' and that 'every citizen [will] be protected by fundamental rights that cannot be taken away by the state or their fellow citizens, enshrined in a bill of rights'. But in a classic illustration of New Labour 'triangulation', in the next breath he suggested that rights would be *dependent* on responsible behaviour as a demonstration that under his leadership, the party would be firmly on the side of victims of anti-social behaviour, many of whom were Labour's traditional 'core' supporters.

Blair undoubtedly struck a chord in implying that until this time Labour had been 'too casual' about the victims of crime. Castigating 'the left' for having 'undervalued the notion of responsibility and duty', Blair coined what was arguably New Labour's most successful sound bite: 'tough on crime and tough on the causes of crime'.[30] But there was also a hint of things to come. Being tough on crime was not just to mean taking steps to deter and prevent it, which human rights law itself requires,[31] but being demonstrably tough on criminals, regardless of the link to public protection. Seeking to out-flank the then Home Secretary from 'the right', Blair mocked Michael Howard as 'the man in charge of prison catering'. He continued: 'Last year he told the Tory conference he was building six tough new prisons. Butlins wouldn't win the contract he said. He was right. The Savoy got it.'[32]

'No rights without responsibilities' became the mantra of New Labour and its then fashionable 'third way politics'.[33] Tony Blair went so far as to claim that 'the theme of rights and responsibilities' lay 'at the heart of *everything* New Labour stands for'.[34] For Blair this was an asymmetric equation. Duties are pre-eminent and 'the rights we enjoy reflect the duties we owe'.[35]

As a statement of *philosophy* this assertion was open to debate and sits ill with the human rights framework introduced by the 1998 Human Rights Act (HRA) as a fulfilment of Blair's commitment to introduce a bill of rights.[36] Most of the rights in the European Convention on Human Rights, which are included in the HRA, are subject to a range of legitimate limits but this is not because responsibilities determine rights. It is because it can be 'necessary in a democratic society' to protect the wider community or 'the rights and freedoms of others'.[37]

As a statement of *policy*, the Labour leader's assertion that the rights of individuals reflect the duties they owe was significant. It heralded what Ed Miliband has since described as 'government' becoming 'a vested interest when it comes to civil liberties'.[38] Once they had passed the HRA, the New Labour government acted as if it had fulfilled its commitment on rights and freedoms. Time and again ministers sounded surprised when the courts applied the very standards they had introduced to hold the state to account. Promoting its alternative framework of rights and responsibilities, New

Table 1: Labour measures impacting on rights and freedoms

Year	Measure	Coalition plans/actions
1998	ASBOs introduced, including for children aged 10+.[a]	To 'simplify and improve' the ASBO regime.[b]
2000	Empowered over 500 public bodies, including local authorities, to self-authorise covert surveillance of individuals in public places or access communications data.	Require judicial approval for local authorities to use these powers.[c]
	Created an offence of photographing something of potential use to terrorists, which has been used to stop journalists and others taking photographs of landmark buildings and the police.	Change the relevant guidance.[d]
2001	Introduced indefinite retention of DNA of all those charged with offences, extended in 2003 to anyone *arrested* of most offences, regardless of conviction.[e]	Remove DNA from the database of those arrested or charged, but not convicted, of minor offences.[f]
	Fingerprints taken of children in schools without parents' consent or regulation.	Introduce a system of dual consent by parents and children.[g]
2002	Removed asylum support from certain categories of asylum seekers.	
2003	Introduced power to impose curfews for young people under 16 in designated areas.[h]	Coalition are considering retaining this power.[i]
	Relaxed the law to permit extradition to the EU and several other countries (including the US) without providing *prima facie* evidence.	Review the operation of the law.[j]
	Allowed greater admissibility of evidence of 'bad character' to juries in criminal trials.	
2004	Created a database on all children and young people, accessible to a wide range of public bodies.	Closure of the ContactPoint database in August 2010.
2005	Criminalised unauthorised demonstrations within a kilometre of Parliament Square.	Replace this with restrictions on protest in Parliament Square Garden.[k]
2006	Created a National Identity Register for the introduction of identity cards.	Abolished the ID card scheme and the Register in the Identity Documents Act 2010. However, biometric permits for non-EEA nationals remain.
2009	Introduced gang injunctions ('gangbos'), similar to ASBOs. Later extended to children aged 14+ through the Crime and Securities Act 2010.	Powers brought into force for adults in January 2011 (and 'gangbos' for children will be piloted later in 2011).

Government empowered to suspend inquests into unexplained deaths in favour of (potentially secret) inquiries. Where the deceased suffered a violent or unnatural death, the cause of death is unknown or the deceased died while in custody or otherwise in state detention (s.1, Coroners and Justice Act 2009).

These powers have not yet been implemented.[m]

Presided over a threefold increase in the number of CCTV cameras controlled by local authorities (by 2009).[n]

Produce a Code of Practice on CCTV (Clause 29 of the Protection of Freedoms Bill).

Notes:

[a] The House of Lords ruled that although ASBO proceedings were civil in nature, when deciding whether antisocial behaviour took place the criminal standard of proof should apply. However, the normal restrictions on hearsay evidence that exist in criminal case do not apply to ASBO proceedings and hearsay evidence is permissible (*McCann v. Manchester Crown Court* [2002] 4 All ER 593).

[b] 'More Effective Responses to Anti-Social Behaviour', Home Office, February 2011. This consultation document proposes to repeal ASBOs and replace them with Crime Prevention Injunctions (a civil order similar to ASBOs where hearsay evidence would still be permitted) and Criminal Behaviour Orders, which can be attached to criminal convictions.

[c] Chapter 2, Part 2 of the Protection of Freedoms Bill; 'Review of Counter-terrorism and Security Powers', HM Government, January 2011. The Review also proposes that covert surveillance in public should be limited to cases where the offence under investigation carries a maximum custodial sentence of six months or more.

[d] Ibid.

[e] See Note 57.

[f] Included in the Protection of Freedoms Bill, which also proposes the retention of DNA for three years for those charged but not convicted of a serious or sexual offences.

[g] Ibid.

[h] Under the Anti-Social Behaviour Act 2003 the police have the power to move on or send home any young person under 16 not accompanied by an adult who is in a 'dispersal zone' between 9pm and 6am. The police do not have to believe that that the young person is involved in or likely to be involved in anti-social behaviour.

[i] The coalition government has suggested retaining these powers, as a 'Direction Power', as part of their changes to the anti-social behaviour regime. Curfews are also one of the tools proposed to help enforce the replacement for ASBOs. See Note b above.

[j] 'We will review the operation of the Extradition Act—and the US/UK extradition treaty—to make sure it is even-handed', the Coalition Programme for Government. See Note 8.

[k] The Police Reform and Social Responsibility Bill repeals ss132–138 of the Serious Organised Crime and Police Act 2005, which restricts the right to protest in the vicinity of Parliament but replaces them with similar restrictions on protest in Parliament Square Garden.

[l] However, the coalition government argued during the inquest into the 7/7 bombings that the coroner had the power to exclude the victims' families from some parts of the hearing on grounds of security. The coroner did not accede to this request.

[n] 'Big Brother is Watching', Big Brother Watch, December 2009.

Table 2: Labour counterterrorism measures

Year	Measure	Coalition plans/actions
2000	Bypassed the need for the police to have 'reasonable suspicion' to stop and search in a 'designated area'.	Searches suspended under s44 of the Terrorism Act 2000 in July 2010 to comply with a European Court of Human Rights (ECtHR) ruling that they were a breach of the right to respect for private life.[a] The Protection of Freedoms Bill will allow searches necessary to prevent 'reasonably suspected' terrorist activity. Searches will also be narrowed in time and place.[b]
	Increased precharge detention for terrorist offences from 7 days (2000) to 14 days (2003) then 28 days (2006) with failed attempts to increase it to 90 days under Blair's premiership (2005) and 42 days under Brown's (2008).	Precharge detention reduced to 14 days.[c]
	Widened power to proscribe terrorist organisations,[d] of which membership or support is an offence.[e]	
2001	'Certifying' of foreign nationals the Home Secretary suspected of involvement in terrorism, to detain them indefinitely without charge.[f]	
2005	Introduced 'control orders', putting suspects under virtual house arrest on the basis of closed hearings.[g]	Control orders to be renamed TPIMS with some less restrictions.[h]

Notes:
[a] *Gillan and Quinton v. UK*, ECtHR, 12 January 2010.
[b] See also 'Review of Counter-terrorism and Security Powers', Lord MacDonald QC, January 2011.
[c] The previous 28-day order was allowed to elapse (see Clause 57 of the Protection of Freedoms Bill). However, emergency legislation was also drafted extending the period to 28 days for a 3-month period, in case it is required in urgent situations.
[d] The power to proscribe an organisation, initially created in 1973 in the context of terrorism in Northern Ireland, was subsumed by the Terrorism Act 2000 (and then the Terrorism Act 2006) and now applies to international organisations and the grounds for proscription are much wider.
[e] 'Review of Counter-terrorism and Security Powers'. The Review concluded that this would be disproportionate and possibly ineffective.
[f] Declared a breach of the Human Rights Act, Articles 5 (right to liberty) and 14 (prohibition of discrimination), by the House of Lords in December 2004 in *A and others v. Secretary of State for the Home Department* [2004] UKHL 56.
[g] In Control Order hearings neither the suspect nor their lawyer are provided with the full evidence against them. Government appointed 'special advocates' receive this secret evidence instead. In 2009 the House of Lords ruled that the right to a fair hearing under Article 6 requires that the 'controlled person' be given sufficient information to know the case against them (*Secretary of State for the Home Department v. AF and others* [2009] UKHL 28).
[h] 'Review of Counter-terrorism and Security Powers'.

Labour proceeded on the basis that it is the government of the day which is responsible for determining the duties of the individuals and the limits of their liberties, rather than a set of fundamental values which bind state and citizen alike. Attempts by anyone, from the judiciary to protesters, to challenge these limitations were met with frustration and derision.[39]

Human rights and civil liberties

Once in power, New Labour introduced a wide range of measures that reflected its stated approach to fundamental rights and freedoms, as Tables 1 and 2 illustrate.[40] Some of these policies are due to be overturned, regulated or diluted if the Coalition government honours its commitments, although in some cases—notably 'Anti-Social Behaviour Orders' (ASBOs) and 'control orders'—the replacement is largely a 'rebranding' exercise. There are other changes, such as cutting back the recording of police stop-and-searches, introduced in response to the disproportionate stops of black and Asian people, that are a retrenchment on policies introduced by the last government to enhance fairness.

Following the terrorist atrocity in New York in 2001, and subsequently in London four years later, a further range of measures (some covert) were introduced that impacted almost entirely on Britain's Muslim community or foreign nationals, surpassing those designed to counter IRA terrorism in the 1970s and 1980s. In addition to these formal measures, the government eventually acknowledged in that following 9/11 and the initiation of George Bush's so-called 'war on terror', United Kingdom airspace and territory had been used for so-called 'extraordinary rendition'[41] and that British forces had handed over individuals to the United States who were later 'rendered'.[42] In 2009, Attorney General Patricia Scotland asked the Metropolitan Police to begin investigating allegations by former Guantanamo Bay detainee Binyam Mohamed that MI5 had been complicit in his ill-treatment. Mohamed and other former detainees subsequently received compensation from the Coalition government in an out-of-court settlement. In July 2010, the new Prime Minister, David Cameron, announced the establishment of an inquiry into concerns about 'the improper treatment of detainees held by other countries, involving British authorities, in the aftermath of 9/11', which is to be chaired by Sir Peter Gibson, the Intelligence Services Commissioner.[43]

This series of allegations, and the ratcheting-up of policing, surveillance and anti-terrorism measures, was one of the key drivers of a new 'unholy alliance' across the political spectrum. During Labour's period in office it is estimated that a staggering 4,300 new criminal offences were created[44] and over fifty new criminal justice, public order and related bills were introduced,[45] whilst the prison population increased 35 per cent between 1997 and 2008. Traditional Conservatives, many of whom were on the right of the party and were deeply uncomfortable with the European roots of the HRA, were affronted by what one described as a 'surreptitious and relentless erosion of fundamental British freedoms'.[46] Liberals (with a small and large 'L'), for whom support for human rights and civil liberties (often used interchangeably) is a priority, were 'outraged' by how the New Labour government 'dealt with terrorism . . . by how they pressed on and on for further detention without trial . . . by the unquestioning willingness to see the prison population go up and up and up'.[47]

A growing number of current or former Labour supporters, some of whom were initially silent about many of these measures or supported them as necessary to fight crime or terrorism, became increasingly disillusioned by their accumulative effects and started to speak out. There was a cacophony of criticism about 'Labour's authoritarian streak',[48] 'the ultra-authoritarian New Labour years'[49] and 'ever-encroaching authoritarianism and pandering to the right on criminal justice'.[50] Once the election was lost, the then Labour leadership candidate, Ed Miliband, 'accept[ed] that in government we were too draconian on aspects of our civil liberties'.[51]

Some of the harshest measures, like the proposal to detain terrorist suspects for three months before they were even charged with an offence, were of course in the context of the severe pressure the government faced in the aftermath of 9/11 and then 7/7. It is a matter of speculation whether other parties in power would have acted differently.[52] If these atrocities had not occurred, and in the light of peace in Northern Ireland (for which Tony Blair and his government can rightly take much credit), the New Labour years might have had a different flavour.

Many of the government's more controversial crime and punishment measures, while of variable effect, were undeniably a popular response to legitimate public concern about violence and anti-social behaviour in many inner city areas which can blight the lives of some of the most disadvantaged communities in the United Kingdom. The neglect of these issues by much of the left in the past allowed the New Labour government to dismiss those who opposed many of its measures as an elite, out of touch with 'the real world'. Where New Labour increasingly disappointed much of its 'core' constituency on tax and income redistribution policies, it could appeal to a section of its traditional supporters with tough anti-crime initiatives and a burgeoning prison population—often outflanking the Conservative party with the harshness of its approach.

This was not just a matter of courting popularity on a tabloid-driven agenda. There is evidence that some of the measures, at least, were effective. Although the precise causes are the subject of academic dispute, crime in England and Wales, including violent crime, dropped over 40 per cent between 1997 and 2010 according to the British Crime Survey.[53] There is little doubt that CCTV can enhance people's sense of security, particularly for women and elderly people, and, there is growing evidence that, along with advances in DNA, it has helped to solve some crimes and even reduce miscarriages of justice.[54]

All that would have been necessary to comply with human rights principles and restore faith in the fairness and accountability of *some* of the measures New Labour introduced was enhanced regulation (flagged for inclusion in the current government's pending Freedom Bill in relation to CCTV) or a curtailment of the scope of a measure (as with the retention of DNA[55]). Commentators who opposed liberty-reducing policies, who were not motivated by party-political advantage, might have softened their critiques had these necessary safeguards been adopted.[56]

Tone and values

It was not just a question of legislation and policy. It was also the tone, style and approach of a number of senior Labour figures—on issues ranging from immigration and identity to crime and terrorism—which alienated those who look to the Labour party to provide an ethical root to politics. Tony Blair's declaration, two weeks after the 7/7 attacks, that 'the rules of the game are changing', [57] or former Home Secretary John Reid's call for 'reform (of) our human rights' because 'the world has changed',[58] signalled the contingent nature of fundamental rights and freedoms as they saw it, and was reminiscent of the refrain heard by countries under pressure throughout the world.[59] There was rarely a trace in ministers' statements of the view nurtured in the Enlightenment, and brought to maturity after the Second World War,[60] that there are certain fundamental rights and freedoms—whether stemming from the 1215 Magna Carta or the 1950 European Convention on Human Rights— that no democratic state should tamper with without demonstrable justification that this is absolutely 'necessary' to protect others or the common good.[61] As with the previous Conservative government, judicial scrutiny of government decisions—a feature of virtually all modern democracies—was greeted with increasing outrage.[62]

When Gordon Brown first became prime minister in June 2007 a different tone was adopted, which initially led some human rights campaigners to hope that this signalled a change of policy. In his speech on British liberty, early in his tenure, Brown said: '[F]rom the time of Magna Carta, to the civil wars and revolutions of the 17th century, there has been a British tradition of liberty—what one writer has called our "gift to the world".' But in the very same speech he foreshadowed his subsequent (failed) attempt to extend detention without trial from 28 to 42 days.[63]

Ed Miliband, in his first statement on being elected leader, returned to this theme when he reminded the Labour party that 'we must always remember that British liberties were hard fought and hard won over hundreds of years' and 'we should always take the greatest care in protecting them'.[64] There was probably no more obvious example of what the new leader termed, in the same speech, the Labour government's 'casual' approach to 'British liberties' than identity cards. A succession of Labour Home Secretaries championed them for a range of reasons from 'tackling illegal working, immigration abuse

. . . health tourism and benefit fraudsters'[65] to promoting 'the most fundamental civil liberty in our society, which is the right to live free from crime
and fear'.[66] Both the Tories and Liberal Democrats fought the last election on a
platform of opposition to identity cards, safe in the knowledge that they had
attracted no broad support. The very first piece of legislation introduced by
the Coalition government in May 2010 was the Identity Documents Bill to
repeal the 2006 Identity Cards Act.

Is Ed Miliband right to suggest that this 'casualness' he complained of is a
recent phenomenon, a product of New Labour which somehow 'forgot' that it
was 'supposed to be the party of civil liberties'?[67] If he *is* right, then it would
be a relatively straightforward task, as the Labour leader has suggested, to
'reclaim' the 'British tradition of liberty' which the Tories and Liberals have
'take[n] ownership of'?[68] The problem with this formula is that it skips over a
longer and deeper rift between 'the left' and an earlier tradition of what might
be called 'radical' or 'progressive' liberalism,[69] reflected in an inconsistent
approach by Labour to the value of individual liberties (often conflated with
individualism) and a negligent attitude to the power of the state. This
approach long predates the last Labour government.

Labour's historic approach to liberty

It is impossible to do justice to this history in this short chapter,[70] but the
rupture between these traditions of radical thought in this country can be
dated back to Marx's disdain for 'the so called rights of man',[71] discarding the
liberal egalitarian legacy of the Levellers, Tom Paine[72] and the Chartists with a
stroke of his pen.

From the seventeenth century onwards, radicals (or what we might now
call 'progressives') routinely discussed the nature of political power in a
democracy and what measures were necessary to keep the state's oppressive
and centralising tendencies in check. This philosophical tradition, with its
focus on democratic accountability, liberty and pluralism, alongside social
justice, was largely airbrushed out of the Labour movement's DNA as a
political framework, except as heroic stories of individual struggles.

While the British Labour party may have 'owed more to Methodism than to
Marx', the influence of the intellectual tradition which never really saw the
problem with the state—provided it was in the right, or rather left, hands—
was pervasive. The purpose of the Labour party was not so much to *change*
the state, but to *control* it. It was the current Labour leader's father, Ralph
Miliband, who provided one of the most influential early challenges to the
left's lack of interest in the state as a potentially oppressive force in liberal
societies.[73]

The championing of a strong and active state by the bulk of the Labour
movement throughout its history should not obscure a long tradition of
participation in specific campaigns for human rights, civil liberties or justice,
often in alliance with other political forces. In the 1970s and 1980s, for

example, Labour party members, and other sections of the left, were often at the forefront of protests against successive Prevention of Terrorism Acts, miscarriages of justice and trade union restrictions—regardless of which party was in power. Whilst the civil liberties record of previous Labour administrations was variable, the Labour government of the mid-1960s, with Roy Jenkins as Home Secretary, famously presided over a period of unprecedented liberalisation and reform.[74] It is this tradition that, presumably, Ed Miliband is asking his party to 'reclaim'[75] with his description of Labour as 'a party that has liberty at its core'.[76] Yet in contrast to liberals or libertarians, the left's critique of state power can sometimes sound selective and inconsistent, based on opposition to particular laws rather than a coherent analysis of the state and a recognisable set of principles to enhance its accountability.[77]

After New Labour came to power—and particularly following 9/11—the emphasis changed from a strong state as necessary for economic security, to a strong state as essential for physical security. Successive Home Secretaries tended to sound like the direct descendents of the seventeenth-century authoritarian, Thomas Hobbes, with their repeated assertion that 'the first duty of the state is to protect the citizen'.[78] Whilst all governments understandably assert this, what was conspicuous by its absence was the current Home Secretary's repeated rider to this obligation, that this 'duty must never be used as a reason to ride roughshod over our civil liberties'.[79] It was as if Labour ministers were unaware that the question of what the state is for had been the subject of 'hot debate' for over 200 years. They seemed unfamiliar with the Enlightenment thinkers who maintained that the first duty of the state was to protect the rights and freedoms of men and women, *including*, but *not solely*, their security.[80] If the great project of progressive politics is to work through the synthesis and tensions of liberty, equality and fraternity (to which could be added security[81]), it is the first of these which has been most readily dismissed by the left and least valued by the Labour party, both Old and New.[82]

Conclusion

Labour entered office committed to a radical programme of democratic policies, influenced by the constitutional change pressure group Charter 88 and the informal alliance between Labour, Liberal Democrat and Green supporters that defeated the last Conservative government. Once the then Prime Minister began to treat the first flush of democratic reforms like embarrassing youthful indiscretions, the link between these measures, and the distribution of power from the state to citizens, became obscure and ultimately lost.

By the time they left office, their Conservative opponents were able to label the last government as 'statist', painting New Labour as far more distinctively left-of-centre than it actually was. The more salient fact, as the psephologist John Curtice has argued, was that the ideological gap between the main political parties had narrowed considerably.[83] But as former Labour minister James Purnell has refreshingly acknowledged, New Labour was 'too hands off with the market and too hands on with the state'.[84] Where the characterisation of the last administration as controlling and centrist particularly rang true was in its apparent lack of trust in people to 'get it right'.[85] As the writer and activist Neal Lawson has remarked, New Labour 'trusted the state and trusted the market, but it didn't trust the people'.[86]

It is an irony that while the central mission of New Labour was to distinguish itself from both the New Left and Old Labour, it was no more successful than its predecessors in relinquishing a longstanding association between the left and authoritarianism. Although many who are immersed in the Labour tradition can be oblivious to this, it is an association that did not begin with New Labour. As the Coalition government's commitment to rights and freedoms is increasingly tested by protests, demonstrations and probable strikes over unprecedented cuts to benefits and public services, and by its determination to replace the HRA with a less universal 'British Bill of Rights . . . written down here in this country',[87] what will be the opposition's response?' Will this new epoch signal a reappraisal of what the Labour party is for? A chance to 'draw breath' and 'go back to first principles in many areas', as Shadow Justice Secretary, Sadiq Khan, has proposed?[88]

A party that stands for 'the many not the few'[89] can conflate *democracy* with *populism*. Sometimes it is the few who need protection from the many—particularly if they are unpopular or small minorities. New Labour struck a chord with a concern the left had long neglected when it focused on anti-social behaviour and crime. But the whole point of fundamental rights is to provide safeguards for those who cannot rely on the ballot box or the opinion poll to protect them. In any case, as the polling expert Peter Kellner maintains, there are now two distinct Labour-supporting electorates.[90] One of these was increasingly unimpressed by 'playing tough in order not to look soft,' as Khan has put it.[91] Whilst 'what my constituents tell me' did not determine New Labour's policy on tax avoidance or bankers' bonuses—or for that matter on joining George Bush in invading Iraq—'popularity' was invariably the clincher with regard to rights issues. When Nick Clegg described the detention of the children of asylum seekers as 'shameful' before the last election,[92] it was a word that reverberated with many erstwhile Labour supporters who had once been drawn to what they saw as the party's ethical heritage, repelled by the harsh, high handed approach of the Thatcher era.

To this extent, references to New Labour being too 'casual' about 'civil liberties' do not dig deep enough. It is the soul of the Labour party, and the moral compass of the left, which is at stake in Labour's approach to the dignity of the individual and the accountability of the state.[93] Polling by Demos in August 2010 found that Labour voters had lost faith in the state as a force for good.[94] The late academic and author Tony Judt spoke for many disillusioned Labour supporters in concluding that 'there is something deeply incoherent about a radical politics grounded in aspirations to equality and social justice that is deaf to broader ethical challenges and humanitarian ideals'.[95]

Notes

1 'Ed Miliband pledges to put the co-operative ideal at the heart of public services', *Politics For People blog*, 31 August 2010.
2 N. Clegg, Speech, London, 19 May 2010.
3 Including the introduction of locally elected Mayors from 2000 in London and elsewhere.
4 For a discussion of the background to Labour adopting the HRA, see F. Klug, 'A bill of rights—what for?', in C. Bryant, ed., *Towards a new Constitutional Settlement*, London, Smith Institute, 2007, pp. 130–44; and F. Klug, 'The Human Rights Act: origins and intentions', in J. Milner et al., eds, *Confronting the Human Rights Act: Contemporary Themes and Perspectives*, London, Routledge, forthcoming.
5 This is with regard to domestic legislation. The courts were empowered to review compliance with EU Directives by the European Communities Act 1972.
6 D. Cameron, first statement as Prime Minister, Downing Street, 11 May 2011.
7 'Which way will he lead?', *Daily Telegraph*, 27 September 2010.
8 'Coalition Programme for Government', May 2010. Available at: http://www.cabinetoffice.gov.uk/sites/default/files/resources/coalition_programme_for_government.pdf
9 N. Clegg, speech on civil liberties, Institute for Government, 7 January 2011.
10 See, for example, 'Why voters left Labour', Open Left and Demos, 2010; 'Labour may be losing support from traditional supporters', Ipsos MORI, June 2008; M. Ryder, 'Civil liberties crucial to Labour revamp: Labour must change its position on human rights if the party is to retrieve its core supporters—and its soul', guardian.co.uk, 17 May 2010.
11 D. Cameron, 'Rebuilding trust in politics' speech, 8 February 2010.
12 T. Blair, *A Journey*, London, Hutchinson, 2010, p. 275.
13 D. Cameron, speech, Conservative party conference, 6 October 2010.
14 D. Cameron, speech, Conservative spring conference, 19 March 2007. Nick Clegg was still arguing that 'freedom for individuals is one of the core values of the Coalition Government' in a speech on multiculturalism in Luton, 3 March 2011.
15 D. Cameron, speech, Conservative party conference, 1 October 2006.
16 D. Cameron, speech, Note 15 above.
17 D. Cameron, speech, Note 14 above.
18 D. Cameron, speech , Note 11 above.
19 'Coalition Programme for Government', Note 8 above.
20 D. Cameron, speech, Note 11 above.
21 For example: Public Order Act 1986; 1988 ' broadcasting voice ban' directed at Sin Fein and the IRA; the Prevention of Terrorism Acts 1984, 1989; Emergency Provisions Act 1991; Criminal Justice and Public Order Act, 1994; the introduction of 'Exclusion Orders'; the watering down of 'the right to silence'.
22 For example: s28 Local Government Act 1988, which banned the dissemination of information on gay and lesbian family life by local authorities; also restrictions on the rights of travellers and a raft of trade union laws.
23 'Coalition Programme for Government', Note 8 above.

24 D. Cameron, 'Our Big Society agenda' speech, Liverpool, 19 July 2010. At the time of writing there are already signs that 'the Big Society' project is fraying under the weight of public spending cuts. See 'Big Society Setback', *Guardian*, 4 February 2011.

25 'Which way will he lead?', *Daily Telegraph*, Note 7 above; see also M. Harris, *Left Foot Forward*, 10 January 2011.

26 In particular the terrorist atrocities in New York and London, which have come to be known as '9/11' and '7/7', respectively, and all that flowed from them, including the invasion of Iraq and war in Afghanistan.

27 See, for example, R. Smith, 'Labour, civil liberties and human rights', *Justice Journal*, vol. 7, no. 2, 2010, http://www.justice.org.uk/resources.php/29/justice-journal-volume-7-number-2

28 P. Mandelson and R. Liddle, *The Blair Revolution: Can New Labour Deliver? An Insider's Account of New Labour's Plans for Britain*, London, Faber & Faber, 1996, p. 193.

29 T. Blair, Labour party conference speech, Blackpool, 1994.

30 T. Blair, speech, Note 29 above.

31 The European Court of Human Rights has repeatedly asserted that the state has an obligation to put in place 'effective criminal law provisions to deter the commission of offences against the person backed up by law-enforcement machinery for the prevention, suppression and sanctioning of breaches of such provisions' (*Osman v. UK* [1999]). See F. Klug, 'Human rights and victims', in Legal Action Group (eds), *Reconciling Rights? Analysing the Tension between Victims and Defendants*, London, Legal Action Group, 2004.

32 T. Blair, speech, Note 29 above.

33 Professor Tony Giddens suggested that 'no rights without responsibilities' was a 'prime motto' for 'the new politics' (A. Giddens, *The Third Way: The Renewal of Social Democracy*, London, Polity Press, 1998, p. 65).

34 T. Blair, speech, Cape Town, 14 October 1996. Emphasis added.

35 T. Blair, *The Third Way: The New Politics for the New Century*, London, Fabien Society, 1998, p. 4.

36 T. Blair, speech, Note 29 above.

37 European Convention on Human Rights, Articles 8–11.

38 'The New Generation', Ed Miliband's first speech as Labour leader at Labour party conference, Manchester, 28 September 2010.

39 See, for example, D. Blunkett, Zurich/Spectator Parliamentarian of the Year awards ceremony, London, 8 November 2001; and J. Rozenberg, 'Is David Blunkett the biggest threat to our legal system?', *Daily Telegraph*, 13 November 2001. See also J. Reed, speech to Labour party conference, 28 September 2006.

40 Boxes 1 and 2 contain measures introduced by Labour which impact on rights and freedoms and on counterterrorism. Where the coalition government has responded to these measures they are included, otherwise we are unaware of any significant changes planned to alter these measures.

41 D. Miliband, statement to House of Commons, 21 February 2008, confirming that the British island of Diego Garcia had been used by the United States for rendition flights. 'Extraordinary rendition' refers to the transfer of detainees from one state to another, outside normal legal processes, for the purpose of interrogation.

42 J. Hutton, statement to House of Commons, 26 February 2009, confirming that British troops in Iraq handed over individuals to the United States who were then 'rendered' to a prison in Afghanistan.

43 Announcing the inquiry in the House of Commons, David Cameron said: 'It will look at whether Britain was implicated in the improper treatment of detainees held by other countries that may have occurred in the aftermath of 9/11' (6 July 2010).

44 C. Huhne, website, 22 January 2010. Research based on parliamentary questions.

45 Between 1997 and 2004, the Home Office passed 49 Acts of Parliament dealing with aspects of crime, disorder, policing, criminal justice and punishment (I. Loader, 'Fall of the "platonic guardians"', *British Journal of Criminology*, vol. 46, 2006, p. 561).

46 D. Davies, statement on resigning from the House of Commons to force a by-election to campaign against 42-day detention, 12 June 2008.

47 Shirley Williams Interview by Iain Dale for *Total Politics*, September 2010.

48 J. Harris, *Guardian*, 25 September 2010.

49 M. Hasan, *Guardian*, 18 December 2010.

50 S. Tall, 'John Kampfner backs the Lib Dems', *Liberal Democrat Voice*, 10 March 2010.

51 Interview with Liberal Conspiracy, July 2010.

52 In an interview with Henry Porter in the *Observer* (13 February 2011), Nick Clegg honestly warned: '[Y]ou shouldn't trust any government, actually including this one. You should not trust government—full stop. The natural inclination of government is to hoard power and information; to accrue power to itself in the name of the public good.'

53 A review by the former Prime Minister's Strategy Unit concluded that 80 per cent of the crime reduction was attributable to economic factors (quoted in R. Reiner, 'Success or statistics? New Labour and crime control', *Criminal Justice Matters*, vol. 67, 2007, pp. 4–5, 37). According to British Crime Survey (BCS) figures, violent crime in England and Wales fell from 3,593,000 crimes in 1997 to 2,104,000 in June 2010 (41 per cent), but the BCS figures do not include murder or rape. For the crime types and population it covers, the BCS provides a better reflection of the extent of household and personal crime than police recorded statistics because it includes crimes that are not reported to the police.

54 The number of suspects who were identified by the Metropolitan Police using CCTV cameras went up from 1,970 in 2009 to 2,512 in 2010 ('"Six crimes a day" solved by CCTV, Met says', BBC News website, 26 December 2010). In 2008, only 1,000 crimes were solved using CCTV images ('CCTV in the spotlight: one crime solved for every 1,000 cameras', *Independent*, 25 August 2009).

55 In 2001, retention of DNA for all those charged with an offence became indefinite, regardless of whether they were later acquitted. In 2003, this was extended to include all those arrested for a 'recordable offence', which is all offences that could lead to at least one year's imprisonment and other minor offences. The blanket retention of fingerprints and DNA samples of those suspected but not convicted of offences was found by the ECtHR to breach the right to respect for private life in *Marper v. UK* ECtHR Grand Chamber, 4 December 2008.

56 See, for example, K. Ewing, *Bonfire of the Liberties*, Oxford, Oxford University Press, 2010, p. 55. 'There is no law on CCTV cameras, authorising their installation, determining the circumstances by which they might be used, and subjecting those who use this technology to any form of supervision.'

57 T. Blair, Statement on anti-terror measures, Press Conference, 5 August 2005.

58 *Daily Telegraph*, 19 January 2001.

59 The statements were particularly reminiscent of a similar tone emanating from George Bush's White House at the same time.

60 With the drafting of the 1948 Universal Declaration of Human Rights and the 1950 European Convention on Human Rights.

61 In line with the Human Rights Act, which establishes a framework for legitimate limitations on individual rights where it is 'necessary' to protect others and the wider community 'in a democratic society'.

62 See Note 41 above. This resistance to judicial scrutiny is despite the fact that parliamentary sovereignty has been preserved by the Human Rights Act, which does not permit the Courts to strike down legislation, in contrast to most bills of rights (or their equivalents) elsewhere.

63 G. Brown, speech, University of Westminster, 25 October 2007.

64 E. Miliband, speech, Note 41 above.

65 D. Blunkett, 'National ID card scheme to be introduced', Home Office Press Release, 11 November 2003.

66 C. Clarke, 'ID cards defend the ultimate civil liberty', *Times*, 20 December 2004.

67 G. Brown, address to Reading Constituency Labour party during the leadership campaign, http://duncanbruce.blogspot.com/2010/12/year-in-review.html

68 See E. Miliband, speech, Note 41 above.

69 The antecedents of today's 'social liberals'.

70 See, for example, D. Marquand, *The New Reckoning: Capitalism, States and Citizens*, London, Polity Press, 1997, Chapter 4; M. Glasman, 'Labour as a radical tradition', *Soundings Journal*, Winter 2010.

71 K. Marx, *On the Jewish Question*, 1848.

72 Tom Paine effectively produced a blue print for a welfare state 150 years before William Beveridge (T. Paine, *Rights of Man, Part Two*, Harmondsworth, Penguin, 1984 [1792].

73 R. Miliband, *The State in Capitalist Society: The Analysis of the Western System of Power*, London, Littlehampton, 1969.

74 As Home Secretary from 1965–1967, Roy Jenkins sought to build what he described as 'a civilised society', with measures such as the effective abolition of capital punishment and theatre censorship, the decriminalisation of homosexuality, relaxing of divorce law, suspension of the birch as a form of punishment and the legalisation of abortion. Although many of these were backbench measures, they were passed with support of Harold Wilson's Labour government. In 1984 Jenkins became one of the 'gang of four' who founded the Social Democratic party, now merged with the Liberal party to form the Liberal Democrats.

75 E. Miliband, speech, Note 41 above.

76 E. Miliband, speech to Labour's National Policy Forum, November 2010.

77 See F. Klug, *Values for a Godless Age: The Story of the UK's New Bill of Rights*, Harmondsworth, Penguin, 2000, pp. 84–8.

78 For example, Gordon Brown said after an attempted car firebombing at Glasgow airport: 'The first duty of the government is the security and safety of all the British people' ('Britain under attack as bombers strike at airport', *Sunday Times*, 1 July 2007). David Blunkett said at the Labour party conference in 2001: 'Our first duty is to protect our people' ('Blunkett unveils anti-terror curbs', *Independent*, 3 October 2001).

79 T. May, statement to House of Commons on counterterrorism and security powers, Hansard, 13 July 2010, col. 797.

80 For the framers of the 1789 French Declaration of the Rights of Man and Citizen, 'the aim of all political association is the preservation of the . . . rights of man'.

81 Influenced by the Socialists and Social Democrats who (along with liberals and communitarians) largely drafted it, the 1948 Universal Declaration of Human Rights (UDHR) was an early attempt to develop a framework to address when individual freedoms should be limited to (a) protect the common good and (b) enhance the equality of those who need the greatest protection. The ECHR is a direct descendent of the UDHR and is incorporated into our law through the 1998 Human Rights Act.

82 But see N. Lawson, *Dare More Democracy*, London, Compass, 2005, p. 26. He maintains that: '[T]he goal of the left is not dull uniformity but true liberty—the ability of people to shape and reshape their world as they see fit.'

83 See 'Blair steers return to Thatcher attitudes: voters in shift to the right', *Herald*, 9 December 2003.

84 Quoted in M. Glasman, 'Heart-broken Britain', *Fabian Review*, Winter 2010/11.

85 From which David Cameron was able to strike a chord with his 'big society' idea (D. Cameron, 'The Big Society', Hugo Young lecture, 10 November 2009).

86 N. Lawson, Compass Rally, Labour party conference, Manchester, September 2010.

87 Prime Minister's Questions, House of Commons, 1 December 2010.

88 S. Khan, speech, Hansard Society, 7 March 2011, responding to Justice Secretary Ken Clarke's stated plans to reduce the prison population and focus on rehabilitation.

89 Clause IV, Labour constitution, as amended in 1995.

90 Peter Kellner is President of the YouGov opinion polling organisation. He was speaking at the Q&A session of a Fabian Society book launch for *Europe's Left in the Crisis*, 15 March 2011.

91 See also M. Riddell, 'Ed Miliband is right—Labour got it wrong on crime and its causes', *Daily Telegraph*, 7 March 2011.

92 'Brown urged to free the children locked up in asylum centres', *Daily Mail*, 15 December 2009. Some 1,000 asylum seeker children were detained in Labour's last year in office.

93 Former Labour Prime Minister, Harold Wilson, memorably said: '[T]he Labour Party is a moral crusade or it is nothing' (Labour party conference, 1961).

94 See Note 10 above.

95 T. Judt, *Ill Fares the Land*, London, Allen Lane, 2010, p. 234.

Localism under New Labour

GUY LODGE and RICK MUIR

Introduction

GOVERNMENTS are judged not just by the objectives they pursue, but by the way they pursue them. Every administration is characterised by a form of 'statecraft'—a dominant mode of operating. The Labour government of 1997–2010 came to be known for a centralist style of political management. Although there were significant acts of political devolution (most importantly to the different nations within the United Kingdom and to London) and although 'new localism' was at times emphasised rhetorically, New Labour had every intention of keeping hold of the political power it had secured. Central–local relations were not radically recast—if anything, the grip of central government was tightened, making England one of the most centralised liberal democracies in the world. Not only did this centralist statecraft prevent Labour from revitalising local democracy within England, ultimately it also proved counterproductive in terms of transforming public services.

This chapter explains why Labour's centralists won out over those who wanted to see much more devolution of power downwards to the regions, cities and localities of England.[1] It argues that Labour's centralist approach is explained by five interconnected factors:

- An instrumentalist approach to the exercise of state power: the party lacked any guiding theory of the state and instead simply used the existing state machinery to pursue its broader agenda.
- Labour's strategic priority during this period was to improve England's public services and it believed that the best way to do this was to set targets and introduce reforms from the centre, side-lining local government in which it had little confidence.
- Parts of the party were worried that decentralisation would exacerbate geographical and social inequalities by allowing service standards to vary in different parts of the country.
- There was never any great demand for more localism from the public, which remained concerned about so-called 'postcode lotteries'.
- Labour ministers were worried that in our highly centralised political culture even if they did devolve powers to local bodies they would still be blamed when things went wrong. This made them very reluctant to 'let go'.

Published by Blackwell Publishing Ltd, 9600 Garsington Road, Oxford OX4 2DQ, UK and 350 Main Street, Malden, MA 02148, USA

The characteristics of Labour's statecraft

Within the Labour party there has always been a tension between those who see the decentralisation and redistribution of political power as central to the party's purpose, and those who see a powerful central state as a precondition for the attainment of social justice. This tension continued during the New Labour period, with the government drawing at different points on both of these traditions.

Looking back to Labour's early years, this tension was at the centre of debates between the guild socialism of G. D. H. Cole and the democratic collectivism of Sidney and Beatrice Webb. Cole envisaged socialism as a decentralised association of democratic workplaces and cooperatives, whereas the Webbs believed that social equality was predicated on a redistribution of resources through a powerful central state. The tension re-emerged during the debates about the creation of the NHS, with some, like Herbert Morrison, advocating a network of municipally controlled hospitals, while Nye Bevan believed that equity and universal access demanded a fully *National* Health Service administered from London.[2] Bevan famously said that he wanted the sound of a bedpan dropping on the floor at Tredegar general hospital to reverberate in the corridors of Whitehall.

It was Bevan who triumphed over the more localist Morrison and it was the former's thinking which best reflected the intellectual zeitgeist of the post-1945 settlement: the creation of a *national* welfare state was considered essential to achieving social rights for citizens. The writings of T. H. Marshall on the subject of social citizenship were also to have a major and lasting influence on the way that the democratic left thought about the distribution of power—and on public expectations about the nature of the services to which they were entitled. For Marshall, citizenship rights were 'national' rights and thus he argued that welfare *should* be delivered on the same terms to all citizens across the whole of the national territory. If it is not, and devolution undermines common standards, then it 'threatens the Welfare State', marking the end of 'the belief that a benign government at Westminster can secure the distribution of benefits and burdens on the basis not of geography but of need'.[3] In other words, this conception of social citizenship considered decentralisation to be anathema to the achievement of equality.

Dichotomous attitudes to power also affected the party's approach to constitutional reform. Throughout its history, Labour has generally supported the view that the constitution worked best with minimal checks and balances: an elective dictatorship was fine so long as both sides had 'their turn' from time to time. But Labour's majoritarianism came under fire in the 1980s and 1990s precisely because of its sustained exclusion from power—and the fact that the elective dictatorship had enabled Thatcherism to flourish unchecked. The long years of opposition witnessed a renaissance of the pluralist voices in the party who championed a programme of constitutional reform to limit executive power.

When in power, New Labour set about transforming Britain's constitution, though in an *ad hoc* manner. The ancient British constitution, based on parliamentary sovereignty and majoritarianism, was changed into a system characterised by a stronger separation of powers and a more robust set of checks and balances. Vernon Bogdanor argues that power has been 'cut to pieces'.[4] There is much in this view as it can be seen that power was indeed constrained in a number of important ways. The Human Rights Act strengthened the role of the judiciary in the constitution and reinforced the more assertive role of judges. Devolution limited the reach of Westminster in the affairs of Scotland, Wales and Northern Ireland on devolved matters. The removal of the hereditary peers, combined with the absence of single-party control, made the Lords more willing to challenge and defeat the government. The Labour years also saw the expansion of independent regulators (such as an independent central bank) and arms-length constitutional bodies (such as the Electoral Commission and the Information Commissioner), which have added further constraints on the executive. However, such changes did little to overhaul the power relations that prevailed *within* England, between central government and localities. As if to compensate for the power it ceded to the devolved bodies, Whitehall's stranglehold over local government and public services within England intensified during Labour's period in office. Here power was hoarded, not dispersed.

Labour approach to local democracy

In opposition, Labour had been critical of the centralism of the Thatcher and Major governments and promised to strengthen local democracy. Among the localist measures in Labour's 1997 manifesto was the commitment to abolish controversial rate capping and compulsory competitive tendering, as well as proposals to give councils 'well-being' powers. None of this, however, amounted to a major transformation of central–local relations. Aside from the genuinely radical plans for the creation of a London Mayor and Assembly, and Scottish and Welsh devolution, Labour's localist agenda was short on details and highly cautious in nature. Indeed, though Labour's approach to central–local relations evolved during their time in office, the most salient features of their attitude towards localism were apparent from the outset.

Senior Labour ministers (and Whitehall officials) felt that local government lacked the competence to be trusted with real power.[5] Many believed that the record of several so-called 'loony left' Labour councils in the 1980s had badly damaged the party's brand, and others maintained that local government was antiquated and amateurish. For this reason, the first Blair government used the Local Government Act 2000 to overhaul internal governance arrangements by forcing councils to replace the traditional committee system with either a leader and cabinet model, a directly elected-mayor (the policy Blair strongly favoured himself) or the opaque 'mayor and council manger' model. In particular, New Labour did not trust councils to deliver public services to a high standard, and this gave rise to a highly intense and over-prescriptive regime of targets and performance management. Under the Best Value regime, councils were assessed against hundreds of inflexible national indicators. This was later supplemented by the Comprehensive Performance Assessment (CPA) process, which introduced league tables for councils. Such measures initially stimulated improvements in the performance of councils, but over time they became criticised for their cost, distortions and stultifying impact on local initiative.

This lack of faith in councils later underpinned the concept of 'earned autonomy' which ensured that only high performers were to be trusted with more freedom. Yet despite some fairly compelling evidence demonstrating significant improvements in the performance of local government over time (not least that generated through the government's own inspection regimes), many in Whitehall continued to lack confidence in those running England's town halls.

Also absent from the start was any intention to deliver the localist Holy Grail: stronger fiscal powers for local government. The lesson Blair had learned from Thatcher's disastrous experience with the poll tax was that the box labelled 'local government funding reform' should not be opened under any circumstance. Blair instead chose to review into the political long grass. Neither the Balance of Funding Review 2004 nor the review led by Sir Michael Lyons (published in 2007) produced significant changes to council tax, and the modest proposals in the latter's final report (council tax revaluations, and changes to banding) was instantly rejected by the ministers who had commissioned the review in the first place.

The early promise to scrap universal capping was jettisoned in 2003 on the back of double-digit council tax increases (a product of the 'gearing effect' arising from the stark imbalances between local and central funding), while the decision to transfer education funding to a specific grant tightened the screws further. Less adverse for local government was the move to give councils prudential borrowing powers for capital projects (though many were reluctant to use the new powers) and rather late in the day (2007) a commitment to a supplementary business rate. At the end of Labour's time in power English local government remained a 'one-club golfer', solely dependent on a highly visible property tax, which accounted for just 25 per cent of its spending with the rest provided by central government grant (representing one of the lowest ratios in the OECD). If funding reform is the truest test of localist credentials, then the Blair and Brown governments can be seen to be unequivocal centalisers.

Labour consistently struggled to define what it meant by localism, which also inhibited progress. It was originally divided between a minority, including figures such as Nick Raynsford who championed bolstering local government powers, and an even smaller minority led by John Prescott who dreamt of introducing regional government within England. Both camps were significantly outnumbered by the localist sceptics in the Cabinet and Parliamentary Labour party (PLP) who successfully thwarted efforts to devolve real powers. Prescott's plans for regional government were heavily watered-down—a contributory factor to the resounding 'no' vote in the North East referendum of 2004. Later internal divisions arose between city-regionalists, including David Miliband during his time at the Department for Communities and Local Government, and 'administrative regionalists' in the form of Ed Balls and John Healey. There were also 'new localists'—perhaps the dominant group among the decentralisers—arguing that local government should not be directly responsible for public services, but should instead perform a 'place-shaping' role. Labour policy makers thus struggled to agree on the appropriate tier of subnational government it wanted to strengthen. The situation was made more difficult by England's disparate and non-coterminous administrative boundaries which further impeded reform.

There were some important exceptions to Labour's overwhelmingly dirigiste statecraft within England. The creation of an elected mayor for London was a major localist achievement: indeed, once established and having shown itself much better at governing the capital than any Whitehall department (in particular, overseeing huge improvements in the capital's public transport system), the London mayoralty has gradually accumulated more powers. Importantly, after an initial phase of target-driven public service reform, the second- and third-term Blair governments also started to introduce market-based experiments in public services. This represented a push to make some public service providers more autonomous from central or local political control, and to give managers greater flexibility and users greater choice.

The so-called 'new localism' entailed the creation of a number of new local institutions to deliver public services, which further eroded local government's role as a service provider. Academies were explicitly designed to be 'free' schools from local education authority (LEA) control, while the establishment of Arms-Length Management Organisations (ALMOs) put more distance between local authorities and social housing. As service delivery was increasingly fragmented, Labour promoted the concept of 'place-shaping' for local government, which required councils to work with other local service providers to deliver a range of shared objectives for their area. Labour unleashed a drift towards technocratic fixes—through devices such as Local Area Agreements and Multi-area Agreements—as they sought to try and manage the diverse governance ecosystem they had created.

This is not to suggest that there was no effort to reinvigorate local democracy: but the focus tended to be on strengthening models of participatory, rather than representative, democracy (that is, strengthening local councils). The government believed that greater citizen engagement was integral to designing and then holding to account services. There were some important initiatives, such as the spread of participatory budgeting, new duties on councils to respond to local petitions, experiments with citizens' juries, and the direct engagement of communities in regeneration schemes such as the quietly popular New Deal for Communities. David

Blunkett wrote about the need to renew the civic realm. Hazel Blears wanted to see more power handed directly to local communities, particularly in disadvantaged areas. David Miliband argued for the 'double devolution' of power from local councils to communities, as well as from the centre to local councils. Tellingly, however, there was little progress made on the second part of the equation. Local government's precarious role in the constitution was further undermined, while the steady expansion of local partnership bodies has helped to generate a profound accountability muddle that confused the public and helped depress local political participation.

Explanations

So, why did Labour's statecraft develop in the way that it did? Why did the early promise of constitutional devolution not feed into a wider agenda of spreading and devolving power? We argue that Labour's centralist approach to governance was a consequence of five main factors: the party's lack of any theory of the state, the priority it gave to improving public services, its belief that social justice was incompatible with a decentralised polity, the lack of any real public demand for greater localism, and the problem of devolving power in a highly centralised political culture in which the public tend to hold ministers in Whitehall responsible for most public policy questions.

Labour lacked a theory of the state

The Labour party has never really had a developed or coherent theory of the state. The Labour tradition has always had an instrumentalist approach to the political system and has focused almost exclusively on its search for social justice. The statecraft used to deliver those objectives has always been seen as simply a means to pursuing that end. The Blair/Brown governments were little different from their 'old' Labour predecessors in this respect, helping to explain the many inconsistencies in their statecraft. The constitutional reforms brought in during Blair's first term were the most radical to have taken place in 300 years. And yet these were never brought together as elements in a wider strategy for dispersing and checking state power. Many reforms were a hangover from John Smith's leadership—most obviously, Scottish and Welsh devolution. Other measures were either a response to specific problems (such as attempts to improve local government leadership), or to the dynamics created by the government's own reform programme (for instance, the creation of the Supreme Court).

The over-riding imperative of public service improvement

The same inconsistencies and lack of guiding principle can be seen in the area of public service reform. Here we see a reform agenda that can be characterised as a curious mix of Keith Joseph and Aneuran Bevan. In many services there was *both* an emphasis on top-down direction, and initiatives to extend user choice through the introduction of quasi-markets. So the NHS was set up to respond both to top-down pressure in the form of waiting times targets and bottom-up demands with patients being able to choose the hospitals where they should be treated.

The Redcliffe-Maud Report (the Royal Commission into local government) published in the late 1960s asked whether the ambition of local government reform was to foster autonomous local democratic sites of power or to improve the local delivery of national services. All governments since Redcliffe-Maud, but especially the New Labour ones, have chosen to prioritise the second of these goals. Labour's approach to central–local relations was powerfully shaped by its commitments to public service reform—a programme that was inherently centralist in nature.

Public service improvement was best achieved, it was thought, by the introduction of either a set of targets, and additional funding from the centre, or by the use of choice and competition (although not to the extent envisaged by the current Coalition government). Neither of these approaches is likely to be compatible with the promotion of a flourishing civic locale. Targets dictate the work of local actors and crowd out any space for local democratic decision making, while markets fragment the delivery of local services into a series of multiple contractual relationships between (often national) commissioners and autonomous providers, with little scope for inputs from local communities.

Added to this was a belief, deeply entrenched in Whitehall, but also within the party leadership, that English municipal government was generally poor at service delivery. So, local councils themselves were subjected to a plethora of best-value and key performance indicators. While these measures unquestionably did improve some services delivered by local government, they also reflected a view of councils as essentially the local delivery arm of the central state. And if local government itself were perceived to be of poor quality, a government that prioritised public service improvement was not about to hand the country's schools, hospitals or police over to local town halls.

Failure to address the equity–diversity conundrum

In power, New Labour was haunted by the ghost of that iconic 'Old Labour' figure, Nye Bevan. Most ministers took the view that the goals of equality and decentralisation are irreconcilable. Decentralisation implies pluralism, difference and inequality; equality implies uniformity and imposition. As we have seen, the concern that decentralisation will undermine social justice is a longstanding one on the left. Public services were based on the principle that benefits and burdens would depend on need, not geography. Devolution, it is argued, negates that philosophy.[6] Such concerns undoubtedly played on the minds of ministers.

Looking forward, Labour will need to move beyond the Bevanite imprint upon its thinking—not least because postwar history suggests that many of the assumptions underpinning it are flawed. To start with, we can observe empirically that centralism in itself has signally failed to achieve equity in terms of public service provision. The Black Report published in 1970s shattered the illusion that a centralised health service would automatically deliver uniformity by exposing significant variations in health outcomes across the country. Since then, the extent of the information on geographical inequalities in public service availability, quality and consequently outcomes has grown enormously, as evidenced, for example, by various Healthcare Commission, Audit Commission and Ofsted reports. Most of this data, much of it produced during Labour's time in office, across the range of public services, indicates wide variations in delivery. Postcode lotteries, in other words, exist when centralised systems become dysfunctional. Differences may well emerge where there is greater devolution, but they often reflect local political choices, sanctioned through the ballot box. Reflecting on this evidence Geoff Mulgan, a former Director of Policy at Number Ten, has warned that: '[W]e can now say with certainty that a generation of centralisation has not improved the relative standing of Britain's public services.'[7]

International evidence reveals that some of the most egalitarian countries in the world have strong local governance and highly decentralised polities. Nor is it the case that decentralisation inevitably leads to wide variety in service quality or in a 'race to the bottom' regarding standards. It can often promote policy convergence through the power of example: devolution, for instance, has seen a number of important policies, like the smoking ban and Children's Commissioner, successfully rolled-out across the United Kingdom. There is also evidence to suggest that decentralisation can boost welfare standards and even promote a 'race to the top'.[8] When France regionalised in the 1980s, it drew attention to the major disparities that existed under the *centralised* system which acted as an engine for driving up standards.

Part of the problem with this debate in England is the weight attached to public services to do all heavy lifting when it comes to achieving social justice. In other countries, distributive justice in public services is strongly supported by greater egalitarianism in the economy and wider society, and by using the tax and benefit system to ensure more equity between people and areas. Moreover, many countries put in place constitutional safeguards to ensure forms of territorial equity by stipulating minimum standards in service provision, and by using fiscal equalisation grants to ensure that these are met. Such measures are crucial for resolving the devolution–equity conundrum.

Ironically, given his reputation as a torchbearer for social democratic traditionalism, it was Gordon Brown who came closest to resolving this longstanding problem. His nascent 'entitlements' agenda envisaged replacing Labour's top-down targets with a bottom-up system of entitlements guaranteeing citizens a certain level of service from their hospitals, schools and police. *Potentially* it offered a way of devolving power while also ensuring fair provision. Brown, however, got to this agenda far too late in the day for it to have any impact.[9] Labour should, however, revisit and refine this idea if it is to regain power equipped with a strategy for achieving greater political pluralism *and* a greater commitment to equality.

Popular scepticism?

One of the greatest obstacles to the introduction of greater localism appears to be the British public itself. T. H. Marshall's ideas have not only shaped Labour's postwar thinking, but have also contributed to the strong sense among the British that services must be the same everywhere. Such expectations, however unrealistic, represent a powerful, centripetal force in British politics. Irritation with 'postcode lotteries' tends to trump public support for the flexibility to respond to local needs and preferences. Devolution has prompted concerns about health and education 'apartheid' given the decision of the Scottish Parliament to abolish tuition fees and introduce long-term care for the elderly, with neither of these policies having been introduced in England. Table 1 shows that in England, Scotland and Wales there are clear majorities in support of standard provision of the main public services, with the strongest support in England: 66 per cent say that standards for services such as health, schools, roads and police should be the same in every part of Britain. Public fears about 'difference' in terms of services will have to be carefully managed, and suggest the importance of enshrining a basic minimum of national standards.

Low political salience was also important. Even the more devout localists in the Labour governments realised that this was never going to be a political priority. Localism might fascinate policy experts, but it has singularly failed to capture the public's imagination. Voters in the North East were considered most supportive of regional government, which led to them being asked to give their verdict ahead of other possible regions: they overwhelmingly rejected the proposals by 78 per cent 'against' to 22 per cent 'for'. The lack of public demand ensured only a half-hearted effort. Blair was personally committed to directly elected mayors, but was not prepared to invest the effort to take on the forces in Labour's local government power base who opposed the policy.

Localism in a centralised political culture

Perhaps the most significant factor underpinning Labour's reluctance to decentralise to the local level was the fear that having let go it would still be held to account for the actions of local actors. England's highly centralised and adversarial political and media cultures tend to direct accountability back to ministers in Westminster. Consequently, Labour ministers were regularly held to account for problems arising at the local level. Of course, given the highly centralised nature of English governance, particularly in relation to funding, responsibility

Table 1: Attitudes towards policy variation in Great Britain, 2003 (percentages)

	Should be the same in every part of Britain	Should be allowed to vary
England		
Standards for services such as health, schools, roads and police	66	33
Scotland		
Standards for services such as health, schools, roads and police	59	40
Level of unemployment benefit	56	42
University tuition fees	56	40
Wales		
Standards for services such as health, schools, roads and police	55	44
Level of unemployment benefit	57	41
University tuition fees	58	40
Cost of NHS prescriptions	63	37

Sources: British and Scottish Social Attitudes 2003, Wales Life and Times 2003. Data provided by John Curtice.

often does reside with national politicians. Ministers worried, not unreasonably, about whether this centripetal political culture would cope with the responsibility being exercised at the sub-national level. The situation is made worse by the absence of strong accountability mechanisms at the local level—evidenced by the low profile and visibility of many local council leaders—which ensures that the buck is often passed back to the centre.

These two themes—a belief in the omnipotence of national politicians and the relative weakness of local accountability structures—are connected and have produced a vicious cycle of centralism: because ministers are held responsible for the performance of services at a local level they naturally seek to control those services, hence the proliferation of targets and the appetite to micro-manage from the centre. Such interventions further erode the role of local government and serve to reinforce the accountability of ministers. The way out of this centralist bind is to put in place highly visible and accountable forms of local leadership, such as directly elected mayors, to reassure ministers that it is safe to let go. The London Mayoral example shows that central government is more inclined to devolve power where lines of accountability are clear. Localists in local government will therefore need to drop their opposition to measures like directly elected mayors if these are a *quid pro quo* for a meaningful devolution of power.

Conclusions

As with its predecessor government, under New Labour the party's minority, pro-pluralist wing was overruled by its dominant majoritarian and instrumentalist faction. For most Labour figures the distribution of power has always been a second-order question compared to the focus on the power of the state to achieve social justice. Under Tony Blair this instrumentalist and dirigiste statecraft was buttressed by the overwhelming priority the government gave to improving public services, and its view that such an important task could not be left to tiers of local government that were perceived as simply not up to the job. It was to Whitehall and to markets that Blair turned to drive his programme through. This was further reinforced by Gordon Brown's traditional social democratic view that decentralisation would whittle away at common social entitlements, and also by a political culture that made it hard for ministers to devolve responsibility downwards when they felt they would still be blamed when things went wrong. Crucially, however, just as there was no sustained push for decentralisation from the government itself—nor was there any real pull from below.

In opposition, Labour has an opportunity to rethink its position on central–local relations. This is because we know that countries with much more equitable social structures than our own also have more decentralised political systems. The empirical evidence simply does not sustain the view that devolution automatically increases social inequalities.[10] Moreover, a system structured around a regime of central targets produces too much rigidity and demoralises professionals. High-quality public services require greater local flexibility and space for innovation. So long as there are clear lines of accountability at the local level, more freedom at the frontline should not come at the expense of quality. Finally, a flourishing local, civic realm should itself be a desirable objective for any social democratic party.

In retrospect, Labour's great mistake on central–local relations was to see democratic renewal as being in tension with public service improvement. In looking to the future, Labour should integrate the goal of public service improvement with a commitment to political pluralism and the wider dispersal of power. This dual focus would entail a judicious mix of elected mayors in our cities and city-regions, greater fiscal autonomy for local councils, stronger tools for holding services to account locally, and a small set of minimal universal social entitlements. Such measures are essential for a radical programme to democratise the governance of England.

Notes

1 This chapter considers Labour's policy in respect of England only.
2 See K. Morgan, *Labour in Power*, Oxford, Oxford University Press, 1985.
3 V. Bogdanor, *Devolution in the United Kingdom*, Oxford, Oxford University Press, 2001, pp. 153–4.

4 V. Bogdanor, *The New British Constitution*, London, Hart, 2009.
5 See D. Wilson and C. Game, *Local Government in the United Kingdom*, Basingstoke, Palgrave Macmillan, 2006.
6 V. Bogdanor, 'The elements of a codified British constitution', *Financial Times*, 8 December 2003.
7 G. Mulgan and F. Bury, 'Introduction: local government and the case for double devolution', in G. Mulgan and F. Bury, eds, *Double Devolution: The Renewal of Local Government*, London, Smith Institute, 2006, p. 9.
8 C. Jeffery 'Wales, the Referendum and the Multi-level State', St David's Day Lecture, Wales Governance Centre, 2011, p. 5, http://www.aog.ed.ac.uk/__data/assets/pdf_file/0007/63286/St_Davids_Day_Lecture.pdf.
9 A. Seldon and G. Lodge, *Brown at 10*, London, Biteback, 2010, pp. 285–99.
10 G. Lodge, 'Central–local relations: why it's so hard to let go', in R Brooks, ed., *Public Services at the Crossroads*, London, IPPR, 2007, pp. 80–1.

Labour's Record on the Economy

KITTY USSHER

THE LABOUR government's record on the economy goes to the heart of what the New Labour project was all about.[1] The experience of the International Monetary Fund (IMF) crisis of the 1970s, exacerbated by the party's inability to reassure the public that it could lead the way out of recession at the 1992 general election, was ringing in the ears of Tony Blair, Gordon Brown and Peter Mandelson in the run-up to the 1997 general election. Their first priority was to restore the party's economic credibility. In this chapter it will be argued that they largely succeeded. Clearly from the vantage point of the period after the 2010 election, however, this is highly contested territory. The first act of the Coalition government in June 2010 was to introduce an emergency budget, the political purpose of which was to ram home to the public the supposed incompetence of the Labour government. Both parties know that Labour cannot win an election if it is perceived as weak on the economy. Hence the Tories must attack, and Labour must vigorously defend its record. That is why it is so important properly to examine Labour's period in government.

This chapter has three main objectives. First, it examines the macro-economic record of the 1997–2010 government through objective measures of success. Second, it considers Labour's performance against the tests it set for itself. I argue that Labour succeeded at the former, but failed at the latter. Finally, the chapter considers what economic policy lessons should be drawn from the experience of Labour's period in office and, in particular, lessons from the economic crisis of 2008–9 and its aftermath.

Objective measures of success

Until the financial crisis hit, Labour's record on economic growth had been fairly remarkable. Not only had there been no downturn, where other countries had fared worse, but in terms of gross domestic product (GDP) per head, the United Kingdom economy grew faster than any other country in the G7 between 1997 and 2009, up by 20 per cent compared to 15 per cent in France, 12 per cent in Germany and 4 per cent in Japan.

While undergraduate textbooks were still showing that there was a trade-off between unemployment and inflation, the experience of the United Kingdom was indicating something very different. The consumer price index grew by an average of 1.8 per cent in the years 1997–2009—around half the average of the previous ten years and a validation of the early decision to give independence to the Bank of England. Meanwhile, unem-

Published by Blackwell Publishing Ltd, 9600 Garsington Road, Oxford OX4 2DQ, UK and 350 Main Street, Malden, MA 02148, USA

ployment was also low: averaging around 5.5 per cent of the workforce from 1997–2009, compared to just below 10 per cent during the years of the previous Conservative government.

To a large extent, it appeared as if the chronic weaknesses in the British economy during the 1980s and early 1990s had been resolved. In particular, the stubborn productivity gap between the United Kingdom, France and Germany was dented, as Figure 1 shows, although productivity growth in the United States was roughly the same as in Britain. Overall, productivity in the United Kingdom increased by 24 percentage points between 1997 and 2007— the fastest of all the G7 countries. This impressive rate of growth has led to productivity (GDP per worker) above that of Japan, and similar to that of Canada and Germany. The figures are given in Table 1.

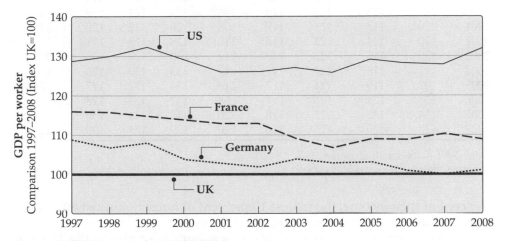

Figure 1: GDP per worker, 1997–2008.
Note: UK = 100.
Source: Office For National Statistics.

On the issue of fairness, the answer rather depends on the question. On a pure measure of income inequality, such as the Gini coefficient, the United Kingdom became more unequal under Labour simply because the number of 'super-rich' rose. However, a rather different picture is obtained if you look at the experience of the vast majority of the population. Taking out the bottom and top 10 per cent, the effect of higher employment and tax credits was to significantly improve the living standards of those on lower than average earnings.

The Institute of Fiscal Studies (IFS) has estimated the effect in 2010–11 of all tax and benefit reforms introduced by Labour since 1997 across the income distribution. It shows that reforms during Labour's first and second terms were highly progressive. Over all three terms, Labour's reforms led to the poorest 10 per cent of households gaining, on average, a figure equal to 12.8

Table 1: GDP per worker (constant purchasing power parity—PPP)

Year	Canada	France	Germany	Italy	Japan	UK	USA	G7	G7 excluding UK
1991	100	100	100	100	100	100	100	100	100
1992	102	102	104	101	100	102	103	102	102
1993	104	102	104	106	100	106	104	104	103
1994	107	104	108	110	101	110	106	106	106
1995	108	106	110	114	102	112	107	108	107
1996	108	107	111	115	105	114	110	110	109
1997	111	108	114	116	105	116	112	112	111
1998	112	110	114	117	104	119	115	113	113
1999	116	112	117	117	104	121	119	116	116
2000	119	113	120	119	108	124	121	119	118
2001	120	113	121	119	108	126	122	120	119
2002	120	114	122	118	110	128	125	121	121
2003	120	115	123	117	112	130	127	123	122
2004	121	118	125	117	115	133	130	126	125
2005	123	119	124	117	116	134	132	127	126
2006	124	121	125	117	118	137	133	128	128
2007	124	122	125	118	120	140	134	130	129
2008	123	120	125	116	120	139	135	130	129

Note: 1991 = 100 for all countries.
Source: Office for National Statistics.

per cent of their income; the richest 10 per cent of households lost an amount equal to roughly 8.7 per cent of their net income.[2]

The experience under the previous government—in particular the Thatcher era—was quite the opposite. During the 1980s, the gulf between the top and bottom 20 per cent widened by 60 per cent—much the most dramatic widening of income differences on record. Since then, the gap between the top and the bottom has remained stubbornly similar, but data from the Office for National Statistics (ONS) show that without the redistributive measures introduced by Labour, the United Kingdom would be a far more unequal society today.

Looking at the response to the crisis, the Labour government's record also appears commendable. Systemic failure in financial services was avoided (even if the banks came very close to collapse on several occasions) and the British government's policy to help recapitalise the most distressed institutions by taking ownership stakes was replicated around the world. Indeed, at the G20 summit held in Britain in April 2009 it looked as if Britain was 'leading the world' in the economic response to the financial crisis. Although instigating a so-called 'bailout' of the banks was unpopular—not least because it made the public feel that they needed to pay for the mistakes of the richest in society—it is still possible that the stakes in these institutions will yield a profit to the taxpayer when they are eventually sold.

Although the contraction in GDP that occurred in 2008–09 was particularly acute in Britain, the impact on households was not as harsh as had initially been predicted at the start of the recession. It is not yet clear whether this is because the economy had become more flexible and therefore more resilient, or because of the government's initial interventionist response to the crisis including: a £2 billion[3] package to help those who were having difficulty paying their mortgage, additional help for jobseekers and support for businesses who were given greater flexibility over the rate at which they spread payments owed to HM Revenue and Customs. Overall, the increase in repossessions came in 40 per cent lower than anticipated by the Council for Mortgage Lenders at the beginning of the crisis, and by 2010 the rise in unemployment was around a million lower than originally forecast. Similarly, while the rate of small business insolvency rose, its peak was still far lower than in the 1990s. Levels of debt, which have been by far the most contentious issue as Labour's record has been debated, are comparable with those experienced by similar industrialised nations. In the run-up to the crisis, while spending did increase, the structural deficit was around 2.6 per cent of national income—well within historical levels, as Figure 2 indicates. And as we discuss below, even if this structural deficit had been zero, or a surplus, it would have made little difference to the overall levels of debt we now experience because they were driven by the effect of the recession.

While the first act of the Coalition government has been to seek to portray Labour as over-spending in the run-up to the crisis, it ought to be remembered that the Conservative party as late as 2009 had pledged to keep to Labour's own spending plans.

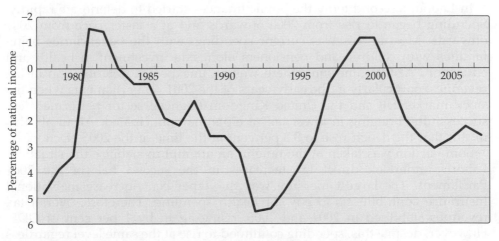

Figure 2: Structural budget deficit (public sector net borrowing).

KITTY USSHER

Labour's own golden rules on debt and the deficit

If the Labour government's performance under objective measures of success was strong, the same cannot be said for the party's performance under its own rules, mainly due to the effects of the recession on levels of debt in the United Kingdom economy. In the run-up to the 1997 election, Gordon Brown set out the golden fiscal rules that would determine his approach to the management of the public finances. These were: first, that current spending would balance over the cycle—in other words, any borrowing over the cycle would only be for the purposes of long-term investment; and second, the stock of debt would remain under 40 per cent of GDP. Looking at the history of what actually happened indicates that these rules did alter behaviour at the margin, and that had there not been a financial crisis, it does not seem implausible that the rules would have been met.

In Labour's first term, the government eliminated a deficit of 3.4 per cent of GDP and ran a surplus of 1.9 per cent. In doing so, it reduced net debt from 42.5 per cent of GDP to 30.7 per cent. On the spending side, restraint came in the first two years from Labour sticking to the spending plans it inherited from the Tories, causing both current spending and investment to fall. At the same time, government revenues rose due to above average economic growth; hikes in fuel and tobacco duties inherited from the Tories were accelerated under Labour; controversial decisions like the abolition of dividend tax credits on pension funds brought in £5 billion a year after the 1998 Budget; raising income tax thresholds as quickly as incomes meant a greater proportion of people's incomes being taxed at higher rates ('fiscal drag'); and the auctioning off of 3G mobile phone licences raised £22.5 billion to pay off net debt. Overall, this meant that Britain actually ran a budget surplus of 1.9 per cent of GDP in 2000–01.

In Labour's second term, the public finances started to deteriorate rapidly. Spending began to rise from 2000 onwards and at a faster pace from 2001 onwards. Most of this was current spending, with the beneficiaries being families with children and pensioners alongside investment in health and education. At the same time, there was an unexpected deterioration in tax revenues, particularly in the early years of the 2001–05 Parliaments when the stock market fell and the United Kingdom financial sector performed less successfully, bringing in lower tax receipts than anticipated. All in all, this meant that the deficit rose to 3.3 per cent at the time of the 2005 election.

Some action was taken at the time in an attempt to stabilise the situation. Labour undertook direct tax increases in the second half of the 2001 Parliament. The largest measure was the 1 per cent increase in National Insurance contributions to pay for health spending. Therefore, overall tax revenues stabilised in 2004 and 2005, rising again by 1 per cent of GDP. However, despite this, spending continued to rise at the same level regardless of the fall in tax revenues, and the Chancellor refused to raise taxes before the 2005 election.

By the time of the 2005 election, the deficit was back to 3.3 per cent of GDP—roughly the same level inherited from the Tories—and net debt had started rising in 2001 from 29.7 per cent of GDP to 34 per cent in 2005. To avoid breaking the golden rule of balancing the current budget over the course of the economic cycle, after the election Labour announced net tax increases in the 2005 Pre-Budget Report (PBR), the 2006 Budget and the 2006 PBR. These were sufficient to raise an extra £6.9 billion a year. In total they amounted to an increase of £200 per family. These, along with a slowdown in the growth of public spending, contributed to the improvement in the fiscal position seen between the time of the 2005 election and the recession. During this time, tax receipts rose again by 1.3 per cent of GDP, and spending only rose by 0.5 per cent of GDP. This closed the deficit by 0.9 per cent, making it 2.4 per cent of GDP on the eve of the crisis. In addition, in these three years before the recession, increases in investment were making up a larger proportion of GDP than rising current spending. Investment increased by 0.3 per cent of GDP, while current spending only increased by 0.2 per cent.

At the time of the crisis in 2008, investment made up 83 per cent of United Kingdom borrowing. The annual level of investment was higher than at any point in the Labour government's period in office. It was also one of the highest investment levels as a proportion of borrowing throughout the party's time in government. Net debt was still rising, from 34 per cent of GDP in 2005 to 36.5 per cent on the eve of the crisis. This was still considerably lower than the 42.5 per cent inherited from the Tories.

So while the risks were increasing before the crisis hit, the golden rules were more or less met, with a caveat that there was some debate as to when the cycle actually started or finished. For example, in 2004, the IFS commented that:

If our forecasts are correct, then between April 1999 and March 2006, the average current budget surplus as a share of national income will be zero. As a result, our central estimate implies that the golden rule will just be met over the current economic cycle on the retrospective method of calculation currently favoured by the Chancellor.[4]

The following year, they wrote:

On these figures [the IFS Green budget 2005 public finance forecasts], the government would narrowly break its golden rule over the current economic cycle, if the cycle ends in 2005–06 as the Treasury expects. But if there is less spare capacity in the economy than the Treasury thinks, and the cycle is already in its final year, the rule should be met narrowly.[5]

And even the year after they still concluded via their own forecasts that there was a 50 per cent chance of the golden rule being met. If the opposite were to occur, then it would have only been broken very narrowly, with a cumulative deficit of £0.7 billion.[6]

So although there was a budget deficit in the run up to the 2008–09 crash, it remained just about consistent with the first golden rule for the simple reason that much of the spending was on investment—notably transport, public service infrastructure and buildings—rather than revenue spending.

Once the recession hit, however, both rules became impossible to stick to. Not only did the government bring forward spending that had been earmarked for future years (particularly in construction projects to maintain the level of aggregate demand in the economy), but there was also a targeted fiscal stimulus aimed at supporting the most vulnerable groups. But dwarfing all of this was the effect of the automatic stabilisers that kicked in as the economy weakened. Revenue from taxation began to fall, beginning in the financial services sector which caused the Treasury to breach the second golden rule that the stock of debt should be under 40 per cent of GDP. As confidence began to weaken, revenues from the wider corporate sector beyond financial services also began to weaken. As the effects then began to be felt in the unemployment figures, expenditure on benefits rose at the same time as revenue from income tax fell. The budget deficit rose sharply and any attempt to get it to balance over the cycle was soon jettisoned.

It is important to understand, however, that it was not the breaching of the debt and deficit rules that caused the financial crisis. Labour did not spend profligately in a way that hurt the economy. Rather the levels of debt rose as a consequence of the crisis. If there had been no crisis, then it seemed likely that the government would have remained within its self-imposed rules, even if the margin for error was getting tighter. Crucially, if the Labour government had not incurred any kind of deficit in the period after the 2005 election, then it would not have prevented the recession and the golden rules would still have been broken. The severity of the financial crisis was such that it would have required decades of running surpluses and a net debt stock of around zero, rather than 40 per cent of GDP, to be able to absorb the shock and meet the golden rules. That the rules could not cope with an external shock of this magnitude was nonetheless a weakness. Conversely, the fact that the rules were quite tight meant that in the event of a crisis there was still enough room for manoeuvre without leading to a sovereign debt crisis, even if the rules were broken in the process.

Lessons to be learned

So if the Conservatives are wrong to try to pin the blame on Labour for the economic ills that befell the country in 2008–09, what lessons should be drawn from this period? The cause of the crisis did not lie in Britain, but the United Kingdom economy was particularly vulnerable to its effects. The problem was one of the mispricing of risk in the financial markets, primarily in the United States.[7] It had become far too easy to borrow money to buy a property in America. A deliberate loosening of the regulatory environment, coupled with low interest rates, and a celebration of the role of subprime markets to enable greater access to homeownership proved an explosive cocktail, causing the value of outstanding subprime mortgages to rise by nearly 300 per cent to US$1.3 trillion in early 2007, up from £332 billion in 2003.[8]

The main contributory factors were:

- A clear political decision by the Bush and Clinton administrations to ratchet up the affordable housing goals set by the government for Fannie Mae and Freddie Mac. This encouraged the agencies not only to purchase securities backed by subprime loans, but to originate such loans as well.
- The Commodities Futures Modernisation Act 2000 reduced supervision of financial commodities such as 'interest rates, currency prices and stock indices' and enabled the rapid rise of credit default swaps in an unregulated fashion, which later led to the collapse of AIG as well as problems elsewhere.
- A relaxation in 2004 by the Securities and Exchange Commission (SEC) of the 'net capital rule' for five investment banks: Bear Stearns, Lehmans, Goldman Sachs, Merrill Lynch and Morgan Stanley. Previously this had limited firms' debt:capital ratios (that is, leverage) to 12:1. Once removed, firms were free to invest in a far greater volume of riskier assets, causing debt ratios to rise sharply—in the case of Bear Stearns to 33:1. By October 2008, the chairman of the SEC, Christopher Cox, was forced to concede what many would say was self-evident—namely that 'voluntary regulation does not work'.[9]
- A general failure of the regulators to see the rise in systemic risk in the system. Instead, the lead of Alan Greenspan was followed, who as late as April 2005 was making speeches praising the role of computer-based risk models that used past credit scores rather than predictions of future incomes to decide whether loans should be made.

As profits rose, checks and balances seemed to become even more unfashionable. Online applications for mortgage loans became common, with some companies making a virtue of a product that required no documentation at all. Their online offerings included products such as 'no doc' mortgages, which required no supporting documentation, and 'ninja' mortgages (no income, no job, no assets) to people in receipt of benefits. Overall it appeared that the constraining factor in granting a loan was not the individual's ability to repay, but the company's ability to securitise it.

Of course, subprime and excessive lending were not exclusively an American phenomenon. In the United Kingdom the growth of the buy-to-let market in 2000–07 and the easy availability of mortgages that offered more than the value of the property was evidence that things were getting out of hand. However, this merely increased our vulnerability to the effects of the crisis rather than caused the crisis itself: the transmission mechanism that led to the recession in the United Kingdom began in the United States rather than the domestic housing market. In any case, the proportion of toxic assets held by financial institutions that were American in origin vastly outweighed those that originated in the United Kingdom, even after accounting for population size. The International Monetary Fund (IMF) estimates that the value of America-originated toxic assets is around US$3.1 trillion, compared to US$900 billion in assets originating from Europe and Asia combined.[10]

Once the 'bad' loans had been made and some bankers had bought them, problems were inevitable. But the severity of the impact of the crisis in the United Kingdom was due to the low savings ratio in its economy. Up until 2007, the British consumer was feeling confident. Low inflation and low interest rates had caused house prices to rise, bestowing a feeling of affluence across much of the economy. As a result, consumer spending rose, and with it so did levels of debt. Indeed, by 2006 the savings ratio had fallen below 3 per cent—the lowest it had been at any time since the 1950s (Figure 3).

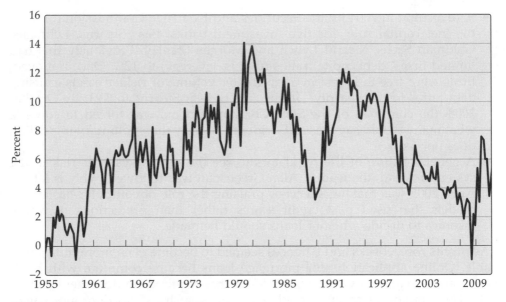

Figure 3: Households savings ratio.

Up until 2007 the official government response was that, like in the 1950s, voters were feeling upbeat about their prospects, a reflection of the success of economic policy rather than something to be concerned about. In mid-2008, oil and food prices rose simultaneously pushing heating, petrol and shopping bills up rapidly. This occurred at the same time that the banks started reining in credit, such that for a few months a mortgage was virtually impossible to come by, and employees began to feel less secure at work. As we saw in the previous chapter, this led to a collapse in consumer confidence, causing a reining-in of discretionary spending and a paying-down of debt, which eventually contributed to a full-scale economic slowdown. Had there been less consumer debt, this effect would have been less pronounced and the recession not as severe. The conclusion that follows is certainly that the British government should have taken earlier action to discourage and prevent British households from being so indebted; however, their failure to do so was not of itself a cause of the recession.

It was not just consumers who lacked a financial safety cushion to shield them against adverse financial effects. Many financial institutions did as well. Labour has received criticism for its failure to put in place an adequate regulatory regime for Britain's banks, yet the failure of the regulators to make the banks more resilient was a problem for the FSA rather than the government. In order to have a licence to trade from the FSA, banks need to demonstrate they have sufficient capital to withstand unforeseen events. These limits are set by the FSA with a backstop provided by the Basel committee. Its failings in the run-up to the crisis were twofold: first, it provided a limited challenge to the institutions that had weak internal risk management; and second, it failed to ensure that banks had sufficient capital and liquidity to survive a sharp downturn in the housing market, leading to the requirement to raise capital in the heat of the crisis. These failings were recognised by the FSA at an early stage. In 2008 it ran a number of stress tests on each of its regulated entities and advised on the level of capital required to be raised accordingly in order to bring stability to the system. At the end of 2007, British banks had a core tier one capital ratio of 6 per cent; by mid-2009 this had risen to 7.7 per cent.

Being forced to engage in frenzied capital-raising in the heat of an economic and financial crisis is not, however, a situation in which a bank likes to find itself. Investors are already nervous about the sector, increasing the risks of a failed rights issue, which could precipitate even more instability not only in the share price of the company concerned, but in the financial system as a whole. And, of course, the price of the capital rises in troubled times. Moreover, some took the view that having to keep more capital in reserve was the last thing a firm needed when its balance sheet was already under huge pressure. The countercyclicality of the FSA's capital raising requirements was far from popular.

The alternative of continuing with inadequate capital, however, would have been far worse. The banks that remained needed to demonstrate they had sufficient buffers against the next shock that might occur in order to restore confidence in the system and make it less likely that that shock would ever happen.

What could have prevented it? These two aggravating factors—low savings in the United Kingdom as well as insufficient capital held among British banks—share many similarities. Even if British consumers had higher savings, and the banks had stronger reserves, the recession probably would not have been avoided, but the impact of the recession and the instability in the markets would probably have been less severe.

A further lesson to be learned arises from the whole issue of asset price bubbles. House prices in the United Kingdom rose rapidly in the years leading up to the crisis. Yet with inflation and interest rates low, and the

Bank of England independent, there were no policy tools available to deal with this phenomenon. There are two possible answers to these issues. The first is regulatory—namely to implement specific loan-to-value ratios for lending into the housing market, which have the capability of being tightened in a countercyclical fashion as house prices rise in order to curb the bubble. In Hong Kong, for example, the government has implemented a system of loan-to-value caps in residential mortgage lending in order to curb short-term property speculation and reduce the risk of asset bubbles forming. The caps are linked to property value, so the maximum permitted loan-to-value ratio is lower on high value properties. For example, on residential properties over US$1.5 million, the loan-to-value cap is 50 per cent.

The second is fiscal—namely to have the ability to raise property taxes when house prices rise, and potentially lower them when confidence is low. Governments have already conceded the principle of using stamp duty as a proactive policy lever. In 1997 a new higher rate of stamp duty of 2 per cent for properties over £500,000 was introduced and then raised to 4 per cent by 2000 as the market boomed. Conversely, the minimum threshold for stamp duty was raised from £125,000 to £175,000 in 2008 in an attempt to restore some confidence to the market during the worst of the credit crunch. Around 2,000 poorer areas in the United Kingdom have for some years had a higher threshold in an attempt to boost activity. And a brief attempt was also made in 2010 to introduce a 'first-time buyer' stamp duty exemption. The British government should use this tool more aggressively, giving an explicit commitment to use stamp duty as a countercyclical tool for dampening a house price boom. Again, Hong Kong provides an example of how such a policy might operate in practice. In November 2010, Hong Kong introduced a special stamp duty of 15 per cent on housing transactions conducted within six months of the owner buying the property, 10 per cent on transactions taking place between 6–12 months and 5 per cent on those taking place between 1–2 years.

The advantage of using a fiscal tool rather than a regulatory one is that it gives an opportunity to strengthen the public finances in advance of an economic slowdown; politically, however, it may be less attractive. Either way, it was a missed opportunity for the Labour government to make the United Kingdom less vulnerable to the effect of the crash when it eventually came.

An important distraction: the so-called need to 'rebalance'

This chapter has argued that the main causes of the financial crisis were the lax regulatory environment in the American mortgage markets, which caused a large number of bad loans to be made, the nature of the financial markets which allowed this risk to be spread around the world and management failure in some global financial institutions. The British economy was particularly vulnerable to the loss of consumer confidence that resulted from the banking crisis because of our historic low levels of savings. The situation was not helped by regulatory failings, which meant that the emerging signs of crisis were missed. The lessons to be learned, and some policy conclusions that flow directly from these observations, have already been outlined. Now is the time to address the regrettable and difficult fact that the public debate on the banks has been following an entirely different chain of logic. We hear repeatedly from politicians on left and right the argument that the recession was caused by our 'over-dependence' on financial services and peculiar vulnerability to financial crises. It is frequently said that it is desirable to rebalance the economy so that a smaller proportion of our national wealth is created from the financial services sector—perhaps in favour of manufacturing—to make our economy more robust in the future.

This, however, is a poor argument, for a number of reasons. For a start, the financial services sector is not the largest sector in the United Kingdom economy. At its peak it was around 10 per cent of GDP—less than manufacturing (around 14 per cent). It is therefore illogical to argue that there is an over-dependence on the former that requires a rebalancing in favour of the latter. Second, those advanced economies that had a proportionally smaller financial services sector did not have a shallower recession, so it does not follow that having a relatively large financial services sector makes a country more vulnerable. Table 2 shows that there is no obvious connection between the size of a country's financial services sector as a percentage of GDP and the contraction of its economy in the recent crisis. Germany and Japan generate proportionally less of their GDP from financial services than the United Kingdom, but their economies contracted more than Britain's. The percentage of GDP attributable to the American financial services sector is nearly as high as in the United Kingdom, but the recession in the United States was mild in comparison with Britain.

Data published by TheCityUK shows that the financial services sector employs around a million people in the United Kingdom, of whom around a third work in 'City-type' jobs in the square mile and Canary Wharf. In addition, there is important indirect employment—for example, an increasing

Table 2: Change in real GDP during 2008–09 recession and financial services share of GDP in seven countries (percentages)

Country/region	Change in real GDP in 2008–09 recession	Financial services share of GDP
Canada	3.1	Unknown
France	3.2	4.6
Germany	6.3	3.8
Italy	6.5	Unknown
Japan	8.0	6.7
United Kingdom	5.9	8.3
United States	3.5	7.5

© 2011 The Author. The Political Quarterly © 2011 The Political Quarterly Publishing Co. Ltd demand for professional services from accountants and lawyers, who tend to cluster around professional services. The total tax contribution of the financial services sector in the financial year to 31 March 2010 has been estimated at £53.4 billion in a report commissioned by the City of London from PricewaterhouseCoopers. This equates to 11.2 per cent of total government receipts from all taxes. Each person employed in the financial services sector pays an average of £25,000 in tax. For every pound granted in bonuses, 50 pence goes to the government and a further 20 pence in VAT if the remainder is spent. There are several hundred banks in London, only a handful of which are high street names. Yet the rest are paying tax to the British government. The United Kingdom runs a surplus in financial services in its balance of trade; the Pink Book, which publishes details on Britain's balance of payments, showed a trade surplus that peaked at £46 billion at its peak in 2008, falling back to around £40 billion the subsequent year, although TheCityUK considers that this might actually be an underestimate.

Although necessarily based on subjective measures, London still ranks top of the global competitiveness index for financial services, as can be seen in Figure 4. In an increasingly competitive world, does it make economic sense to try to constrain a sector that is yielding significant revenues, employing large numbers of people, helping to counterbalance the persistent current account deficit in manufacturing and in which we appear to be a global leader? The evidence points to the opposite: as long as we can ensure that the activity of the financial services sector is regulated in ways that minimise the impact and frequency of economic shocks affecting the wider economy, perhaps it is better to promote it, rather than to try to weaken it.

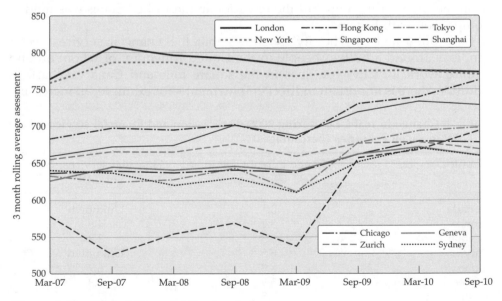

Figure 4: The Global Financial Centres Index.

Conclusions

I have argued in this chapter that using objective measures, Labour's economic performance has been generally successful. Examining the key economic indicators since Labour was elected in 1997 until the economic crisis in 2008 the United Kingdom has enjoyed quarter on quarter growth and low inflation which has remained expertly close to the Bank of England's mandate of 2 per cent. At the same time the labour market has absorbed a growth in population of more than 5 per cent, yet unemployment has remained at historically low levels unlike many of Britain's Continental European neighbours. Even on the Achilles heel of productivity, Britain has narrowed the gap between France and Germany, and kept up with the post-1995 American 'productivity miracle.'

I have also argued that while success measured by Labour's own golden rules may tell a different story to objective measures, this is mainly due to the effect of the recession on levels of debt. If you look at the level of debt on the eve of the crisis, which stood at 36.5 per cent of GDP, you can see that it was still consistent with the second golden rule, and considerably lower than the 42.5 per cent inherited from the Tories. In terms of the much discussed structural deficit, year on year the IFS public finance forecasts, while slightly less optimistic than the Treasury's, still show how Labour was well placed to meet the self-imposed fiscal rules over the course of the economic cycle before the crisis hit. They predicted that if Labour were to break the golden rules, then they would only do so narrowly. It is therefore not the case that spending was profligate in the run-up to the banking crisis.

Tory criticisms of the previous government's economic policy are rooted in a wish to blame Labour for a global financial crisis that saw almost all the major developed countries experience one of the worst economic downturns in history. In fact, the cause of the crisis was external to Britain and whilst there are some policies that could have mitigated the effect of the recession to a degree, there is little if anything that could have been done to prevent it. Labour's economic policies announced to deal with the crisis received wide international praise, and the bank 'bailout' was replicated globally. The government's supply-side response to the crisis, coupled with the increased flexibility of the economy, led to repossessions, unemployment and small business insolvencies that were all lower than originally anticipated.

The real lessons to be learned relate to Britain's vulnerability to the effects of the global financial crisis. I have identified the low savings ratio as one significant weakness, which fell below 3 per cent in the build up to the crises. In the future we must be wary of such high levels of debt in the United Kingdom economy, rather than simply viewing it as a sign of economic prosperity. Second, the issue of asset price bubbles: regulatory and fiscal measures have been identified that could provide the answer on how to deal with them in the future. Finally, the well documented issue of financial regulation. Banks need to become more resilient to mitigate the effects of the next crisis, with higher capital requirements and a better understanding of risk.

Almost by definition, it is not known where the next crisis will come from. However, there is nothing in the previous government's record that should prevent Labour from being the party that prepares the United Kingdom economy to withstand the crisis when it does next appear.

Notes

1 The author would like to thank Andy Stuckey for his help researching and editing this chapter
2 J. Browne and D. Phillips, *Tax and Benefit Reforms Under Labour*, London, Institute for Fiscal Studies, 2008.
3 http://www.parliament.uk/briefingpapers/commons/lib/research/briefings/snbt-04968.pdf
4 The IFS Green budget, January 2004.
5 The IFS Green budget, January 2005.
6 The IFS Green budget, January 2006.
7 This section draws on the pamphlet *City Limits* by Kitty Ussher, published by Demos, March 2011.
8 United States Centre for Responsible Lending.
9 *New York Times*, 2 October 2008.
10 International Monetary Fund, 21 April 2009.

Labour and the Economy, 1997–2010: More than a Faustian Pact

DAN CORRY

THERE appears to be an emerging consensus about the Labour government's economic policy between 1997 and 2010 in the light of election defeat, but it has real dangers.[1] It is dangerous in part because it presents an overwhelmingly negative interpretation of United Kingdom economic performance under New Labour, detracting from many positive achievements. But this consensus also adds weight to the view, asserted continually by the right, that Labour cannot be trusted to manage the economy. Ironically, the left has ended up ventilating a critique of British economic management over the last thirteen years that started on the free market right of British politics. The underpinning argument of the consensus is that New Labour did too little to try to reform the model of capitalism that it inherited from Thatcherism: that is why it all ended in tears. The narrative is to be found in Will Hutton's writings[2] and in various contributions from academic commentators on the left. The claim is that Labour made a 'Faustian pact' with the City and with capitalism more generally. There was an implicit pact in which markets would be allowed to function without regulatory interference, particularly the financial sector and the banks, provided they generated sufficient tax revenue to fund investment in Britain's public services.

Of course, there is certainly some truth in the claim that given thirteen years in office, a healthy majority and generally stable global economic conditions, Labour could have done more on the economy—just as it could have in other areas such as education, health and child poverty. But this should not obscure the fact that an enormous amount was achieved. It is certainly not the contention of this chapter that Labour made all the right calls, nor was its government sufficiently brave enough on certain public policy issues. Above all, there was a failure, shared by most on the left and the right both here and abroad, to comprehend the scale of the transformation underway in the financial sector, and the potential risks attached to many of the new products and transactions that were devised.

It is very dangerous, however, merely to assume that New Labour's chosen policy agenda was the result purely of a lack of political will and a 'Faustian pact' with the financial markets. This suggests that Labour could somehow run the economy very differently if only it had the inclination to be radical and bold. This is dangerous, and will lead to a return to lazy centre-left thinking that dominated the 1980s.

The argument of this chapter is that we need to remember just how hard it is to run a policy against the underlying structural trends in the economy and

Published by Blackwell Publishing Ltd, 9600 Garsington Road, Oxford OX4 2DQ, UK and 350 Main Street, Malden, MA 02148, USA

society, given fast-moving global financial markets and the constraints of operating in the world economy. These have always been challenges for the left and they have not gone away. There were mistakes of both a technical and political nature but overall in the New Labour years, a valiant attempt was made to change how capitalism worked—and in many areas, such as improving working conditions and eliminating low wage routes to competitiveness, the situation in the United Kingdom was transformed for the good.

Debates pre-1997

In the period leading up to New Labour's victory in 1997, there had certainly been many important debates on the centre-left regarding economic policy. There was in fact a remarkable turn-around from the 'siege economy', public-ownership-orientated view that predominated in the early/mid-1980s, to the market-orientated, pro-European, supply-side socialism of the early 1990s, which led inexorably to the Blair and Brown eras.[3] There were still lively debates as Labour's view shifted. Of relevance was the debate about how much to bias policy towards the revival of manufacturing not least through keeping the exchange rate low, and how far to rely on regulation and the enabling state, rather than ownership and planning, creating a 'developmental state'.[4] Attitudes to markets still varied within Labour thinking too. Some analysts see in the shift towards New Labour a move to policies being about accommodation with the electorate and with powerful players in the city and business—the theory of 'structural dependence'—not least because of the need to ensure continued investment by the private sector.[5] Moves to scrap Clause 4 fit neatly into this theory.

However, much of the change can be seen as a pragmatic response to being out of power for eighteen years rather than a major step backwards or an embrace of the neoliberal model that existed in the Thatcher/Major years—focused on ends not means and toning down some of the flowery anti-market rhetoric while toning up the pro-business vocabulary. The Mitterrand experiment of the early 1980s had convinced most of the British left that interventionism and fiscal Keynesianism in one country could not work, while other thinking led to a shift away from the idea that high inflation (supposedly in return for lower unemployment) was a trade-off worth making—if it existed at all.

As full-on Keynesianism—epitomised by the 364 economists who wrote to the *Times* in response to the money supply monetarism of the 1981 Budget—ebbed away over the decade, thinking started to focus more and more on how to get long termism into the economy. One manifestation of this was the focus on supply-side socialism. But it is also what led to an increasing emphasis on stability, especially in the macro policy where boom and bust were seen to be one of the major impediments to investment and innovation. This focus led to policy moves to grant the Bank of England independence and to get behind fiscal rules rather than fiscal activism. It was a long-termist version of capitalism that was being searched for, and in the run up to the 1997 election there was reasonable consensus within the leadership on the overall direction of economic policy.

However, important areas of debate about economic policy continued in Labour circles—one of the most interesting being that raised by Hutton's conception of stakeholder economics. There is an argument made by many on the left, but also by some in the centre, that Blairism was far too much of an acceptance of the neoliberal market economy. David Marquand, for example, argues that:

[T]he intellectual ferment of the early 1990s, with its debates over alternative models of capitalism, had had virtually no impact on [New Labour]. . . . For New Labour, as for the Thatcherites, capitalism was capitalism. There was no point in trying to redesign the architecture of British capitalism . . . the only question was how to adapt it.[6]

One counterargument made at this time was that there should be more of a pitch to the German model of capitalism, supposedly characterised by long-termism, investment and equal rights for workers, in contrast to the Anglo-Saxon model which New Labour was believed to have embraced. This alternative tended to be labelled 'stakeholder capitalism' in Labour debates.[7] Famously Blair, after running with this idea for a short while, panicked when it was interpreted as returning to a corporatist vision, with trade unions being more involved in policy and within firms, increasing costs for business.[8] Arguably the 1992 manifesto of Kinnock and Smith had more of the Hutton approach with, for example, a National Investment Bank and regional banks, than the 1997 manifesto.

Nonetheless, New Labour did attempt to create a new capitalist model. This was a mixture of stakeholderism—in the sense of trying to increase long-termism, boost investment and so on—and of Clintononics, which was characterised more by a focus on skills and education,[9] as well as competition and innovation. Some of this 'new Keynesianism' was pursued in the pages of the Institute for Public Policy Research (IPPR) journal *New Economy*, and summarised by Corry and Hutton, who commented, perhaps too optimistically, that:

A new critique of capitalism is emerging that while accepting wholeheartedly the role of price incentives and entrepreneurship is offering a new basis for public initiative that would reliably promote more equity, investment and employment. . . . There are choices over the configuration of British capitalism and they can and should be made.[10]

Different terms were also used, like the infamous 'post neo-classical endogenous growth theory' that pointed towards believing that purposeful action could lead to improvements in growth rates. The IPPR's Commission on Public Policy and British Business published its findings in 1997; the fact that they were drawn up with leading left-sympathising business players showed where the agenda was heading.[11]

This was not setting out to try to create a totally different economy or even a totally different market economy. Nor was it a robust, full-on challenge to what Gamble categorises as the neoliberal and 'Washington consensus'—privatisation, deregulation, free trade, fiscal discipline, shareholder value, financialisation, residual welfare, and so on.[12] But the aim was undoubtedly to change the context in which capitalism—its firms and economic agents—operated.

Altering capitalism: policy, 1997–2010

There are 'big bang' ways of changing how a system works. Arguably it is easier to go from a statist to a liberal model since all one has to do is cut back and abolish what exists, as both Thatcher showed and the Tory-led Coalition is demonstrating. Building institutions for a reformed model of capitalism is considerably harder. It is not one or two big changes that matter, but a whole nexus of them that in aggregate alter the incentives on markets and other players, fill in gaps in missing markets, and stop the race to the bottom as a profit-making strategy. So if a dramatic shift towards the German model was not undertaken, there were numerous more modest moves towards the same goal.

The changes can be seen as falling into several different categories. First were important alterations to the external environment faced by firms. Some of the measures here were deliberate attempts to alter the set of incentives facing firms. Most clearly in this external market space was the radical strengthening of competition policy. Stemming from the historic left tradition which was anti-trust and anti-big business, this attempted to stop firms raising profits through anti-competitive practices and mergers that stifled competition to the detriment of consumers. Of course this is contested terrain on the left—some believe that going too far in this area stops firms taking long-term decisions, and stops collaboration for innovation.[13]

Others measures, like a great deal of the reregulation of the labour market, had social aims at their core but were clearly understood as altering the profit-maximising strategies of firms.[14] The achievement, after many decades, of introducing a national minimum wage is perhaps the best known, blocking off profit-making strategies by paying very low wages, but other significant steps included a blend of collective rights-making union recognition easier, giving union members a right to be accompanied in hearings, ending the 'check-off' system for union subscriptions—and individual rights like bringing in paid holidays, rights for part-timers (even if not from day one as the labour movement wanted), rights to time off, a right to request the right to work flexibly, and the halving of the period people had to work before being able to claim unfair dismissal.

In the public sector, although outsourcing did not cease, clear enforcement of Transfer of Undertakings (Protection of Employment) (TUPE) and the new two-tier code to protect terms and conditions of new employees to outsourced services, meant that the use of the private sector to deliver public services was not just done on the basis of a 'race to the bottom'. The impact of these changes was greatly understated due to the business-friendly rhetoric from the leadership that emphasised that, despite all this, Britain still had one of the most flexible labour markets in the world. Although this was true—unsurprising given the nature of the deregulated labour market that Labour inherited—these were a profound set of changes to the way that capitalism worked in the United Kingdom.

An additional attempt here was to encourage partnership working. This fell well short of what some wanted (that is, social partners, German-style), but did try to 'nudge' towards different forms of behaviour on both sides of industry: mechanisms ranging from the new union modernisation fund and partnerships funds, to bringing in rights to information and consultation arrangements for firms over a certain sizes. Unions were also brought into dialogue with government far more. There was no return to NEDO or more corporatist models—not possible in the United Kingdom anyway due to the weakness of the union and employer organisations—but a much greater attempt to get the two sides of industry working together than had happened under Labour's predecessors. Indeed, the biggest problem that I experienced at Department for Trade and Industry (DTI) was that the unions in general no longer had the capability or capacity to discuss intelligently industrial issues, outside a few key sectors like automotive.

There was also an attempt to start influencing market pricing to capture externalities, especially environmental externalities. This included the first real green taxes in the Climate Change Levy, landfill levies, aggregate taxes and environmentally motivated changes to the structure of car taxation.

The second category of attempts to modify British capitalism was altering how firms utilised and accessed labour and capital. The focus on skills was crucial. This was a tricky area and one central idea—the University for Industry—while a great slogan, never really amounted to much. Before 1997 the old policy of compulsory levies to fund training—in effect to force all firms to contribute to training rather than having collective under-supply of training due to 'poaching'—had been ditched. The alternative was in fact a very radical one: an attempt to allow people to have their own funds to pay for the training they wanted and so to really empower workers and citizens. The early days of the Individual Learning Account showed a great deal of 'additionality' and it was very popular; at its height, 2.5 million members registered as eligible to undertake subsidised learning and some 9,000 organisations registered as learning providers. Unfortunately, the scheme was bedevilled by poor design which allowed a small percentage of providers who were playing the system to discredit it—and it was closed to new entrants in 2001.

A second bold attempt to tackle the issue was the 'Train to Gain' scheme born out of the Leitch review of 2006. This offered employees full funding for a first level 2 qualification (broadly equivalent to five good GCSEs) with the hope that this would allow people to have a transferable certificated level of skill to help them progress within or across firms and sectors. Although this made a significant difference to many people's lives and helped many firms up-skill, overall it turned out not to be as great a success as predicted partly because it tended merely to give a certificate for skills people already had rather than give them new skills and partly due to the difficulty in getting take up in smaller firms where there are the most acute skill problems.

In addition to trying to force firms to use more skilled labour—both to improve productivity overall and the prospects of those on lower incomes and skills—there was heavy investment in the physical and more intangible infrastructure on which firms depend. These mainly collective goods are core to economic success. Thus, impetus was placed on improving public services and 'public' infrastructure ranging from schools and universities, where science in particular, was transformed in the Labour years, to areas like Broadband and information technology, rail and roads. Regulation of the privatised utilities was also changed, although until more recent times this was less about industrial policy and the need for investment than depersonalising regulation and making outcomes fairer.[15]

The phrase 'industrial policy' was not a term frequently used as it smacked too much of a return to the old 'picking winners' approach. It also suffered from a very hostile Treasury, at the official and 'political' levels, towards interventionism of any kind, which was seen as offering soft subsidies to firms who were better at lobbying than being innovative and efficient, and was also strongly against sectoral policy as opposed to horizontal policy agendas. Moves of this kind had to be disguised to get through—like the support to the car industry given via Regional Selective Assistance and to the aerospace sector though Launch Aid.

Labour Secretaries of State for Industry did, however, talk about 'active' policy even in the first term of pure Blairism and, within certain parameters, were seeking to promote manufacturing and innovation, as well as newer industries. In terms of manufacturing, even the Treasury was aware that ministers wanted action, and many attempts were made to boost the sector in a way that had been absent from the previous regime: papers were written, groups met, a Manufacturing Advisory Service was set up in 2002. However, this was effectively drowned out by the opposite of the often-feared collapse in the pound when Labour came to office—namely a steady appreciation of the pound in the late 1990s. This led to a significant squeeze on manufacturing and a large number of jobs were lost in the first half of the Labour government, which helps explain the comparative underperformance of the West Midlands and some other regions.

Tax credits for research and development (R&D) were a major and important change; investment allowances were also used, and the general drift of Labour policy was towards this type of 'guided' approach to 'good' investment rather than the classic free-market focus on reducing corporation tax generally—a policy that would clearly help banks as much as manufacturing firms.

In addition, the end of pension tax credit in the 1997 Budget was motivated partly to remedy a perceived distortion in the tax system that led to institutions with funds receiving tax credits which pressured companies into paying higher dividends (on which they got relief) rather than re-investing in the firm, and thus encouraging short-termism.

Regional policy moved heavily away from the 'get on your bike' approach of the Thatcher years or the garden festival/enterprise zone approach of Hesiltinian activism in the Major period, with the regional development agencies (RDAs) representing a major attempt to locate centres of industrial policy closer to the firms and localities that needed help. This policy, associated closely with John Prescott, was at first rather unfairly resisted by Blairites and some Brownites who feared it as the kernel of a more dirigiste approach to economic policy that harked back to older Labour thinking, but in time was embraced as a key way to try and even out growth across the country. Had the referendum for an elected tier to oversee regional governance been successful in the northeast in 2004, we may have seen this develop more. In its place was a renewed attempt at boosting and supporting city regions, with Greater Manchester the most successful of these in emulating the governance and power of what is in effect a city-region in London, but Liverpool (European City of Culture in 2008), Leeds, Newcastle and Sunderland, amongst others, began to make good progress and contributed to a northern urban renaissance after many years of decline under the Conservatives.

Finance for industry has been a tricky issue throughout British history. This was not solved under Labour, but from the time of Peter Mandelson's Knowledge Economy White Paper in 1998, major steps forward were taken to build up venture capital, start-up support and encourage university spin-offs.

Third—and perhaps most profound of all when one thinks about altering the way that capitalism works—were attempts to alter how firms operated, and how they interacted with their shareholders and other stakeholders. There were various steps taken to give shareholders a bigger role in determining the remuneration of executives—arguably one of the key levers to influence firm behaviour. Over time, pension trustees were given new duties to make them a bit more open and accountable. A potentially big intervention that never quite delivered was a major review of company law set up by the first Department for Trade and Industry (DTI) Secretary of State, Margaret Beckett. Its steering group contained interesting thinkers on the nature of shareholder value capitalism, ranging from Professor John Kay and John Plender of the *Financial Times* to John Parkinson, Professor of Law at Bristol, whose 1994 book *Corporate Power and Responsibility* argued that company law needed to take account of the range of stakeholders, other than shareholders, who have an interest in the activities of modern corporations. The review looked at the duties of directors, at links to corporate governance and at shareholders influence over pay. Unfortunately, ministers' attention wavered, the Treasury view was to be cautious, and the whole exercise was largely taken over by lawyers and officials more keen to re-write company law so that it was neater and more efficient than to progress the original aim of the radicals who wanted to turn it into something that really changed the way in which firms worked.

Added to this were a number of bold reforms that aimed to make welfare policy more of a trampoline than a safety net. Tax credits made work more rewarding, as did the minimum wage. Analysis by experts like the Institute for Fiscal Studies (IFS) shows that the net effects of all this were progressive, and Treasury figures show that over the period from 1997 the number of families facing marginal deduction rates (MDRs) in excess of 70 per cent more than halved, although as a consequence of the introduction and increased generosity of tax credits those facing MDRs between 60 and 70 per cent increased.[16] In addition, a version of a more active, European-style labour market policy was introduced via the New Deal for Young People.

Where New Labour did not go far enough

This is an important set of measures. Of course even in their own terms some will criticise them as lacking enough ambition and not really going to the heart of the issues around company governance, workers power, privatisation, shareholder value capitalism and the power of financial capital.[17] Although this is an important perspective and one that is always useful to the centre-left in government as a counter to excessive compromise, it ultimately fails to hit home since it does not consider the plausible options available to Labour in the period, and its limited room for manoeuvre, not least given the strength of the prevailing orthodoxy.

Perhaps more to the point, and more painful, are the critiques which say that while at face value these measures could have been transformational, in too many cases successive Labour ministers pulled back from the more difficult and radical versions of them, or did not see them fully through, and so weakened the impact overall.

The company law review severely underperformed. The Treasury even got the then Chancellor to withdraw the proposed Operating and Financial Review (OFR) in a speech to the Confederation of British Industry (CBI) in November 2005 primarily for short-term tactical reasons. This would have required companies to produce an annual statement on environmental and social issues rather than such statements being voluntary.

More compulsion on training was never really pushed. Equally, while there was intervention to make more finance available for innovation, this was not far reaching enough; and Labour was slow on empowering the great cities.

In the realm of finance, the bubble was very unhelpful and obscured many of the real underlying issues from policy makers. For a period, finance was readily available to many business ventures and business start ups; profitability in the Labour years was good; and it was not as apparent as it should have been that too many of these did not provide the deep beginnings of companies in new, growth sectors, but were ephemeral firms that were as much about manipulating financial capital as about producing goods and services.

In the labour market, although it was right to bring in the minimum wage at a low, risk-averse level, especially for younger people, there was great reluctance to raise it that quickly—not least as business was extremely hostile. More importantly, the combination of British labour and product markets was not producing enough jobs with decent prospects at lower skill levels, and was supporting too many firms who could make profits despite low productivity and investment. The bubble allowed this to be masked by the 'good' times.

Why did this happen?

There is, of course, a good argument to suggest that Labour bought too much into the neoliberal model, and in some areas that may have been true. The financial markets are discussed below. In competition policy, the strengthening undoubtedly contributed to firms having to innovate to succeed—rather than indulge in anti-competitive practices—and gave hard-pressed families fairer prices for many products. However, a consequence of the honourable desire to depoliticise competition policy, and in general to back innovation and higher productivity, meant that there was almost a sense of pride in being indifferent to the nationality of ownership. The net result was that, for instance, almost all our utilities ended up being foreign-owned since the competition regime would not allow British firms to merge but would allow foreigners to buy them. Takeover policy is another area where, with the laudable aim of not defending weak and inefficient firms, we did not take the opportunity to put as much 'grit in the wheels' as we could have.

Political economy factors also mattered. There was an acute sense of trying to keep business on board and more-or-less behind a Labour government. This led to reluctance from Downing Street and beyond to bring in too many measures that business genuinely opposed. In this sense, the CBI and organised businesses bluff was probably called less often than it should have been. This stemmed from a memory of the dark years where business was so hostile to Labour, influencing the public view of the party's economic competence.

Another reason for what can look like excessive caution was a belief—probably well founded—that the nature of globalisation really does make capital mobile and creates certain limitations on how much one can impose regulation, forms of working and so on that add to business costs at least in the short run.

There were several infamous quotes from senior figures about a general lack of concern about the distribution of income. But the real worries that many ministers and advisers did have about the distribution of wages, incomes and wealth were offset by a fear that we were hemmed in on the

40 pence tax rate by globalisation, the antipathy of business to such a move and the fear of being seen as hostile to aspiration. While the constraints always seemed exaggerated, it was only after the crash in 2008 that a 45 pence and then a 50 pence top rate of tax seemed viable. Then, we felt able to start to attack some of the most generous tax breaks at the top, like pension tax relief, addressed at last in Budget 2009, as the search to raise funding in a fair way outweighed all the previously binding factors.

The much maligned redistribution by stealth was in fact fairly intelligent in policy terms. Radicalism for left governments has too often been judged by the size of the top marginal rates, whereas what matters more are overall moves to redistribute and what incentive effects they have. A lot of effort into giving back via tax credits therefore made sense, at the same time as keeping marginal tax rates competitive and raising revenue in other ways. More generally though, there was a hope that the achievement of near full employment would be one of the key 'equalising' forces in society not only because people in work do better than those out of it, but because it was also widely held that if employers were short of labour they would have to help their workers up-skill and end discrimination against them. That this did not work as hoped may owe something to migration as well as the success of policies to boost labour market participation, but these are issues that the left needs to ponder carefully for future reference.

Government did try to work with manufacturing—there were, for instance, innumerable publications, strategies and summits on the topic, which had been absent from the previous Tory years. In this sense, Gamble's accusation that '[t]he British government actively encouraged the growth of financial sector and the service sector to replace the gap left by the decline of manufacturing'[18] is only half right with respect to the Labour years. Yet in some ways the Labour government was not quite sure what to do, faced with a long underlying trend of a shift away from manufacturing, certainly in employment terms if not so greatly in output terms.

The knowledge economy angle was used to try to help think about high-end manufacturing, and those areas connected with high tech and the science base, which was funded very well indeed and blossomed in the New Labour years. However, a desire not to pick winners (even winning sectors), a suspicion of subsidy of firms or sectors, and a rather simple version of free trade and against 'infant industry' arguments often led to a lack of ambition, while an obsession for a period with trying to recreate Silicon Valley in the United Kingdom probably led to the wrong focus. Possibly a better link with the European Union would have helped here as more attempts to embrace the successful aspects of the German and French approaches to growth, rather than just the American model, might have been fruitfully followed.

Another factor limiting options was the poor condition of the social partners in the United Kingdom, which made certain approaches unfeasible. The trade union movement was not only declining, it was becoming less able to engage in serious strategy discussions.

Financial services: the biggest New Labour failure?

The biggest failure, clearly in retrospect, concerned financial services and the tipping of the economy into that area of activity—either via the growing size and power of investment banks, equity funds, mergers carried out to manipulate short-term financial advantage or the excessive degree of credit and leverage individuals and firms took on. The failure was less about having a successful financial sector—that turns out to be a relative advantage and many of our highly skilled jobs and exports derive their strength from this—but rather in letting it become too dominant a sector within our economy and society.

And of course in the end what brought the period of growth to an end were the banks. So Labour must take some responsibility for a failure to regulate this sector as strongly as it ought to have done. The Labour governments' culpability lies in the facts that we were neither aware of the pace and scale of change in the financial sector, nor did we comprehend its potential risks.

There are reasons for this, and one must remember that the Conservative party during these years argued for less regulation rather than criticised the rather light-touch approach that was the fashion at the time.

In the first place, a serious analysis of financial capital had arguably been missing from Labour thinking. Thompson and MacDougall argue that 'capital markets do matter and they are not benign in their effects', but New Labour was reluctant to challenge this.[19] Writing in 2003, they blame this to some extent on the capturing of policy thinkers by the 'New Times analysis' of ex-*Marxism Today* acolytes, with their stress on 'dynamic markets, decentralised corporations, discriminating consumers and multiskilled, knowledgeable workers' and away from the 'varieties of capitalism literature'. There is some truth in the accusation that excitement with these new developments blinded some key figures to the underlying economic truths that had not really altered. Certainly much of the light touch and deregulatory talk of the times—especially around financial markets—looks very naïve from today's perspective.

In terms of the direct activity of City traders there had also been a lack of analysis, except for a general cry against 'casino capitalism'. Those who did more detailed work on derivatives[20] were rare, and concerns pre-1997 were more about the possibility of a run on the pound and the currency speculation that has always haunted the left. As Robert Shiller has argued, it was very easy to get the 'social contagion of boom thinking' as things seemed to be working.[21] The way that a nexus of factors, including cheap Chinese goods, came together to cause the crisis was not going to become clear until after the crash.

In addition, almost nobody understood exactly what was going on in the markets, or the degree to which moral hazard really was affecting risk taking. Like so many, the government largely bought into an idea of the financial sector as being the ultimate in efficient, calculating market rationality. In practice, we now know there was a cycle of irrational exuberance with people dealing in exotic financial instruments that they did not fully understand, and assuming reckless levels of risk. Even with a more sceptical eye, the identification of systemic risk would have been very difficult.[22]

Instead, the City and United Kingdom financial services looked to be a success story. There did not seem to be a very good reason to get in its way, especially, as at the start of the Labour government, there was still talk about possible threats from Frankfurt and Paris—not least if the United Kingdom kept out of the euro.

Given that neither the experts at the Bank of England, focused on macro-economics, nor the FSA, which took too narrow a view of its regulatory role, were raising much of an alarm, it is perhaps unsurprising that Labour also missed what was happening.

The City is a major relative advantage for the United Kingdom on a global stage with extensive benefits in terms of spin-offs in areas like legal and accounting services to add to its direct job- and wealth-creation impact, and any future government will want to nurture it. However, it is also one with an unusual degree of international mobility, which makes governments acutely conscious of the possibility of movement from the United Kingdom of people, capital or headquarters.

Just as important was a lack of a proper growth strategy owned by the whole government—not just HM Treasury—which would have allowed one to measure how the rest of the economy was doing, and so helped judge moves on banking alongside the overall health of the economy. In fact, a strong, growing economy, with unemployment down to low levels and money to spend on public services and other good deeds, blinded people to the fact that wages for many were stagnating from around 2003.[23] Some regions were far too reliant on public-sector activity, and property and mortgage debt were growing far too much.

This also meant that the government was too vulnerable in the place that matters most for economic policy—namely the Treasury—to the endless lobbying of the financial markets themselves and less exposed to the views of other areas of industry. This lobbying is not as blatant as Acemoglu suggests it is in the United States, but it undoubtedly had an impact in Britain.[24]

The bubble eventually burst with significant consequences for the rest of the economy. Through vigorous action, Labour mitigated the worst of those consequences.[25] Some of the economy's strong performance, in retrospect, was froth from the United Kingdom and global asset price bubble, but it would be wrong to dismiss economic performance before the crash. There was real productivity growth and real jobs were created for many people.

Was New Labour wrong on macro policy?

Some argue that the policies that ended up encouraging consumption and house price inflation were the cause of the financial crises.[26] But things went wrong because everyone was fooled by the bubble and it was hard to know what else to do, especially when faced with the prospect that other countries would outgrow us if we just stood still. True, better policies on the taxation of housing, including land taxes and capital gains on homes, might have helped, but were never seen as viable policies. Most economists, including those at the Bank of England, kept predicting a 'soft landing' and turned out to be utterly wrong.

The other major critique revolves around spending too much and letting debt rise too high. This is quite hard to sustain—at least without the benefit of hindsight—as the facts show.

In 1979 public-sector net debt as a proportion of GDP stood at 44 per cent after the difficult decade of the 1970s. This proportion gradually fell as the economy recovered and growth accelerated in the later 1980s, and reached a low of 26 per cent in 1991 as the United Kingdom economy returned once again to recession.

From 1991 until 1997 the proportion increased to 42 per cent as real growth in GDP stalled and attempts were made to stimulate the economy. The Labour government then got the figure down to 29 per cent in 2002, during which time the British economy enjoyed a strong and stable boom period. Interestingly, the government resisted calls to spend the proceeds of the surprisingly lucrative sale of spectrum, which raised £22 billion in 2000,[27] and used it to reduce the national debt instead. From 2002, however, despite growth continuing, public-sector net debt as a proportion of GDP did not fall further—instead increasing from 29 per cent in 2002 to 36 per cent in 2007. This was still low—even internationally.

It is only in retrospect and with the benefit of a lot of hindsight that it appears relatively high. Both the fiscal expansion and automatic stabilisers led to the debt rising to levels that the credit rating agencies did not like. As Crafts and Fearon have put it, one of the lessons of the Great Depression of the 1930s is that 'at times when fiscal policy is a valuable weapon, it is highly advantageous to enter the crisis with a history of fiscal prudence'.[28]

Doing Keynesianism?

When the crisis began, the Labour government followed the text book Keynesian approach.[29] This meant introducing policies that pushed up the deficit and also debt levels. Most of this was due to the action of the automatic stabilisers and the decision to let them fully play out. Some was due to discretionary policy and some the result of the important decision to stick to, rather than cut back on, the spending plans for the next three years set out in the precrash 2007 Comprehensive Spending Review. One of the problems this created was that markets were hovering over us, asking, even as we tried to deal with the crisis, how we were going to get the deficit and debt down again. Markets, especially credit rating agencies, are not, of course, at all sympathetic to Keynesian policies: they distrust debt, see little case for an orderly transition back to sustainable public finances, and demand their pound of flesh now, whatever it costs in domestic policy terms.

Labour also suffered because the markets do not, as a rule, entirely trust centre-left governments. That means they have to act even more vigorously than right-wing governments to keep bond yields down—much as we once had to have interest rates higher in order to convince the markets we were not looking to devalue or inflate. For the same reason that an independent central bank or even the European single currency have been seen as beneficial for the left,[30] Labour would have been helped by an independent fiscal body, along the lines argued for by Simon Wren-Lewis[31] for many years and brought in in a particular form via the current Office of Budget Responsibility.

Going forward, it is clear that banks will need to hold much more capital and be able to fail without causing systemic risk. The United Kingdom will also need to go beyond interest rate policy as the only tool outside fiscal policy, with more powerful macro-prudential regulation and a reassessment of the targets that the Bank of England is trying to hit.[32]

The beginnings of new centre-left radicalism? The crisis and beyond

In government things go wrong. From a certain perspective, what happened after 1997 can look like an ill-conceived pact with the financial sector. However, this chapter has argued that this does not capture what policy makers were seeking to achieve.

Some think economic policy in this period involved acquiescing to the neo-liberal model—and had been for some years. As Colin Hay put it: 'Labour [by 1990] had ceased effectively to be a social democratic party committed as it had then become to a pervasive neo-liberal economic orthodoxy.'[33]

This ignores the substantial changes that were made, however. The British economic model was modified: it was neither a German social model, but nor was it a Thatcherite market economic model either. The financial crisis and the exposure it created through dependence on financial services was the great lacuna in this process. It did reflect an over reliance and comfort with markets, a weakness in the face of international capital and finance, but one that was an international weakness too well beyond the United Kingdom.

Overall rightly or wrongly, what was done was what was deemed possible at the time. As Martin McIvor has noted: 'New Labour's compromises and calibrations were the result of hard headed calculations by people convinced that the realities . . . left them no other line of advance.'[34] The policies carried out in this period were a coherent and radical project in relation to British capitalism, unrecognised because rarely framed in that way. But policies shift as events unfold. We have learned lessons—and indeed adapted accordingly—in part as a result of the crisis. People who had been hostile to interventionism changed their spots: Peter Mandelson, some year after his first spell as Business Minister, became convinced of the need for intervention in what in Whitehall became know as the 'NINJ agenda' (New Industry, New Jobs).[35] The Labour Manifesto of 2010 was radical on takeovers—not least in the wake of the Kraft/Cadbury affair—proposing a steep rise to two-thirds of shareholders in the threshold needed for success, for bidders to set out how they would finance their bid, more transparency on fees, and more requirements on shareholders to declare how they voted.[36]

Business, too, has changed to an extent, with more small and medium-sized enterprises (SMEs), entrepreneurs, women and black, minority and ethnic (BME) persons involved, and policy needs to reflect these realities. However, we should not forget that the large mobile, multinationals still carry most weight, pay the most tax and provide the business elite and the main business voice for the country.

As John Kay has put it, the left needs to focus on the dynamic capacity of markets to innovate and experiment, rather than to attack public intervention in the name of an unquestioning belief in the allocative efficiency of competitive markets.[37] We need to take more risks in our policy making, but we also need more balance so that we can cope with shocks which, in an internationalised world, are bound to happen, perhaps with greater frequency.

Ideas about how to effect change at the international level are needed, too: international action on global finance cannot be allowed to fail as the memory of the financial meltdown slips away and lobbyists for banks and low tax emerge once again. Proposals such as a financial transaction tax, and other ways of taxing banks and flows need to be explored. More generally, the British left needs to strengthen its links with the European Union.[38]

This project can broadly be characterised as what Gamble calls the 'social market' version of neoliberalism, which believes that 'for the free market to reach its full potential the state has to be active in creating and sustaining the institutions that make that possible'.[39] As social democrats operating in a world where options are significantly constrained—from mobile capital to tax-resistant voters—Labour will always have to make tough choices. Those constraints will not go away. Indeed, the pace of growth in China, Brazil and India means they will tighten. And despite popular anger at bankers, it does not appear that the electorate have emerged from the 'crisis' radicalised in their attitudes towards government and the economy.

The Labour record over thirteen years was a sound one for social democrats in the modern world. Trashing our record, or arguing that we could have transformed the world if only we had been bolder and not entered into an unholy alliance with the City, is neither going to deliver a better economic policy nor is it going to persuade voters to support us again.

Hill has described Labour's search for a new economic approach after 1979 as 'chaotic, diffuse and slow'.[40] That was probably inevitable. What matters now is to build on the experiences of 1997–2010 by reflecting openly and critically about what worked in policy terms, and what did not. The view that New Labour was crippled by its lack of radicalism is seductive but flawed, and negates the fact that any centre-left political economy has to deal with the real world of changing circumstances and material constraints. Labour ignores this at its peril.

Notes

1 Many thanks for helpful comments and discussion from the editors, from former colleague and No 10 and BIS adviser Geoffrey Norris, and from Joe Corry-Roake.

2 For example, W. Hutton, 'It's the Conservatives who are now promising real reform in the City', *Guardian*, June 2009, ttp://www.guardian.co.uk/commentis free/2009/jun/14/conservatives-george-osborne-business-banking

3 See R. Hill, *The Labour Party and Economic Strategy, 1979–1997: The Long Road Back*, Basingstoke, Palgrave Macmillan, 2001.

4 Hill, *The Labour Party*, p. 70.

5 Hill, *The Labour Party*, p. 11.

6 D. Marquand, *Britain since 1918: The Strange Career of British Democracy*, London, Phoenix, 2008, p. 376; see also A. Gamble, *The Spectre at the Feast: Capitalism's Crisis and the Politics of Recession*, Basingstoke, Palgrave Macmillian, 2009, p. 106.

7 G. Kelly, D. Kelly and A. Gamble, eds, *Stakeholder Capitalism*, Basingstoke, Macmillan, 1997.

8 Hill, *The Labour Party*, pp. 118– 121.

9 R. Reich, *The Work of Nations: Preparing Ourselves for 21st Century Capitalism*, New York, Alfred A. Knopf, 1992.

10 D. Corry and W. Hutton, 'New Labour, New Economy', *New Economy*, vol. 3, no. 3, 1996, pp. 143–9.

11 Commission on Public Policy and British Business, *Promoting Prosperity: A Business Agenda for Britain*, London, Vintage, 1997.

12 Gamble, *The Spectre at the Feast*, pp. 85–7.

13 D. Corry, 'Labour's industrial policy', *New Economy*, vol. 8, no. 3, 2001, pp. 127–33.

14 D. Corry, 'Should we continue with the de-regulated labour market?', *Renewal*, vol. 5, no. 1, 1997, pp. 35–49.

15 D. Corry, *The Regulatory State: Labour and the Utilities, 1997–2002*, London, Institute for Public Policy Research, 2003.

16 HM Treasury, *Budget 2010: Securing the Recovery*, HC 451, London, HM Treasury, March 2010, Table 5.2.

17 D. Coates and C. Hay, 'The internal and external face of new Labour's political economy', *Government and Opposition*, vol. 36, n. 4, 2001, pp. 447–71.

18 Gamble, *The Spectre at the Feast*, p. 16.

19 P. Thompson and A. MacDougall, 'The politics of New Labour's economy', *Renewal*, vol. 11, no. 4, 2003, introduction.

20 For example, A. Hudson, 'Derivatives problems', *New Economy*, vol. 1, no. 4, 1994, pp. 249–53.

21 R. Shiller, *The Subprime Solution*, Princeton, NJ, Princeton University Press, 2008.

22 A. Milne, 'Macro prudential policy: what can it achieve?', *Oxford Review of Economic Policy*, vol. 25, no. 4, 2009, pp. 608–29.

23 J. Plunkett, *Growth without Gain? The Faltering Living Standards of People on Low-to-middle Incomes*, London, Resolution Foundation, 2011, p. 29.

24 D. Acemoglu, *Thoughts on Inequality and the Financial Crisis*, Cambridge, MA, Massachusetts Institute of Technology, 2011, http://econ-www.mit.edu/files/6348

25 D. Corry, 'Power at the centre: is the National Economic Council a model for a new way of organising things?', *The Political Quarterly*, 2011, forthcoming.

26 C. Crouch, 'What will follow the demise of privatised Keynesianism', *The Political Quarterly*, vol. 79, no. 4, 2008, pp. 476–87.

27 D. Corry, 'Communications bill': inside story, *Prospect*, April 2003, pp. 48–53.

28 N. Crafts and P. Fearon, 'Lesson from the 1930s Great Depression', *Oxford Review of Economic Policy*, vol. 26, no. 3, 2010, p. 310.

29 A. Seldon and G. Lodge, *Brown at 10*, London, Biteback, 2010; Corry, 'Power at the centre'.

30 D. Corry, *Restating the Case for EMU: Reflections from the Left*, London, Institute for Public Policy Research, 1995.

31 S. Wren-Lewis, 'Avoiding fiscal fudge: More openness on fiscal policy would boost Labour's credibility', *New Economy*, vol. 3, no. 3, 1996, pp. 128–32.

32 D. Corry and G. Holtham, *Growth with Stability: Progressive Macroeconomic Policy*, London, Institute for Public Policy Research, 1995.

33 C. Hay, *The Political Economy of New Labour: Labouring under False Pretences*, Manchester, Manchester University Press, 1999.

34 M. McIvor, 'The lessons of powers', *Renewal*, vol. 18, nos , 2010, p. 7.

35 Department for Business, Innovation and Skills (BIS), *New Industry, New Jobs White Paper*, London, BIS, 2009, http://www.bis.gov.uk/files/file51023.pdf

36 Labour party, *Manifesto 2010: A Future Fair for All*, http://www2.labour.org.uk/manifesto-splash

37 J. Kay, 'Market failure', in P. Diamond and R. Liddle, eds, *Beyond New Labour: The Future of Social Democracy in Britain*, London, Politico's, 2009, pp. 83–4.

38 L. Thurrow, *Building Wealth: The New Rules*, London, HarperCollins, 1999, p. 109.

39 Gamble, *The Spectre at the Feast*, p. 71.

40 Hill, *The Labour Party*.

New Labour and the Politics of Ownership

STUART WHITE

Introduction

ANY political economy has to take a view about the nature of wealth and ownership rights. What view—or series of views—did New Labour take? What questions must Labour and the wider left confront in developing its view afresh? To explore these questions, this chapter begins with a brief account of views on the ownership question within the British centre-left prior to the New Labour period, and looks at the debate surrounding the idea of 'stakeholder capitalism' in the early, formative years of New Labour. The chapter then explains how Labour adopted the rhetoric of stakeholding, while radically transforming its content and goes on to discuss the rise of 'asset-based welfare' as a distinctive New Labour policy consistent with its revised, highly individualistic notion of stakeholding. It further discusses how, following developments in the housing market, New Labour was put firmly on the defensive in relation to the taxation of wealth and wealth transfers. The chapter considers how the banking crash of 2008 has prompted the start of a reappraisal of the politics of ownership within Labour, with a partial return to some of the ideas around stakeholding from the 1990s. It concludes with some thoughts on the key questions that a future Labour, or wider centre-left, politics of ownership must address.

Ownership: the centre-left tradition

The early Labour party asserted a distinct identity by adopting a constitution that committed the party to the 'common ownership of the means of production, distribution and exchange'. In due course, the objective of common ownership became identified with the nationalisation of specific firms and industries. However, by the end of the 1945–51 Labour government, influential currents within the party had started to question the idea that progress consisted of further nationalisation. This 'Revisionist' current developed during the 1950s, with some of its supporters arguing that Labour should drop clause four of the party constitution which had become associated with the goal of nationalising industry. Anthony Crosland's book *The Future of Socialism* is usually seen as the exemplary text here.[1]

There is a tendency to portray the Revisionists as rejecting common or public ownership in favour of a social democratic politics focused reductively on the 'Keynesian welfare state': management of aggregate demand to sustain

Published by Blackwell Publishing Ltd, 9600 Garsington Road, Oxford OX4 2DQ, UK and 350 Main Street, Malden, MA 02148, USA

full employment, combined with redistributive taxation, buoyed by a grow-ing capitalist economy, to fund generous public services. However, as Ben Jackson has recently shown, this is to ignore the fact that the Revisionists also had their own agenda for ownership.[2] Crosland, along with sympathetic thinkers like Douglas Jay and James Meade, put forward a reforming agenda with the following basic elements.[3] They called for the more progressive taxation of wealth and wealth transfers (for example, inheritance tax),[4] and for measures to increase workers' participation in decision making within the firm.[5] They supported moves to enhance the role of the Co-operative move-ment.[6] Perhaps most intriguingly, they also advocated a new form of public ownership. Instead of taking over specific firms and industries, and then trying to manage them better than the private sector, they argued that the state should build up a portfolio of stocks and shares across the economy. In this way, the state could benefit from the appreciation of firms' assets during the economic boom, and would get a new source of revenue from the annual dividends on its shares.[7] The party's 1958 statement, *Industry and Society*, came out in favour of creating this new model of public ownership, though the idea ultimately had little impact on party policy.[8]

Similar ideas have featured in Liberal party debates. The Liberals have a history of thinking on these issues dating back at least as far as the 1928 *Yellow Book*, and they have poured much time and energy into developing their own agenda of 'Ownership for all' from the 1930s well into the postwar period.[9] The Liberal agenda included, as for Labour's Revisionists, the reform of wealth transfer taxation, plus a longstanding commitment to the taxation of land value. Liberals envisaged the introduction of profit-sharing and co-determination in firms and measures to support savers. In the 1970s and early 1980s the idea emerged of endowing all citizens as of right with some capital of their own.[10]

The Liberals were initially more sceptical of the Revisionist idea of developing state-owned share portfolios. However, in the 1980s, following the formation of the Social Democratic party (SDP), and the electoral alliance between the Liberals and the SDP, Revisionist and Liberal thinking began to converge. James Meade was a key figure here, serving formally as an economic advisor to the SDP while also being a respected informal adviser within Liberal circles. In this context, both the Liberals and the SDP sympathetically explored proposals for state-owned share portfolios and, related to this, policies for endowing all citizens with a claim on capital as of right.

In 1989 Paddy Ashdown, leader of the new Liberal Democrat party formed by the merger of the Liberals and the SDP, published *Citizens' Britain*, a book intended to give an ideological lead to the new party. Ashdown called for the Liberal Democrats to create a new 'citizens' capitalism' in which publicly owned share funds would be used to endow every citizen with a claim on the nation's capital: 'We could be much more radical about popular share ownership—we could give every citizen a stake in our economy. I would like to see a Citizens' Unit Trust or Universal Share Option Program (USOP) established in which every adult citizen has a stake'.[11] He broadly endorsed James Meade's plan to develop a 'Citizens' Share Ownership Unit Trust' holding, as a long-run goal, 10 per cent of the assets of 'all private sector enterprises over a certain size'.

In brief, the British centre-left has a distinctive and rich tradition of thinking about ownership, which calls for the taxation of wealth transfers; democratisation of firms so that workers participate in profits, capital and decision making; and the widening of wealth ownership and/or claims on wealth, possibly connected to the creation of publicly owned portfolios of stocks and shares.

New Labour and stakeholding

With this background in mind, let us now turn to New Labour. Ownership was in one way fundamental to New Labour's self-definition: New Labour defined itself as 'new' precisely by revising the famous clause four of the party's constitution. But this defined New Labour only negatively. It made clear what New Labour was *not* about. It did not offer an alternative positive account of where Labour ought to stand on the politics of ownership.

One powerful and attractive resource for positive redefinition was provided at this time by Will Hutton's theory of 'stakeholder capitalism' as set out in his hugely influential book *The State We're In*.[12] Hutton argued that the British economy suffers poor long-term performance because of the relatively high cost of capital. In contrast to the manufacturing companies of social market Germany, which can rely on long-term investment from the banks, Hutton argues that British companies are constrained to get external finance from a financial sector that demands high returns in the short run. This produces under-investment and a loss of competitiveness. Accordingly, Hutton argued for reform of the financial sector to cheapen the flow of finance to industry. He also argued that British firms are hampered by an authoritarian model of corporate governance which undermines the establishment of long-term trust and collaborative partnership within firms. Hutton advocated a new system of corporate governance involving German-style codetermination. Authority within the firm should not lie wholly with capital, but should be distributed in a balanced way amongst a range of 'stakeholders', including labour, long-term financial backers and the community.

Hutton's basic prescriptions were shared by a number of centre-left commentators at this time, including Paul Hirst, John Kay and David Marquand.[13] To a considerable extent, these ideas clearly echoed long-standing proposals on the centre-left, in particular for the democratisation of the firm. The shift from an authoritarian model of the firm (capital hires labour and has the right to tell it what to do) to a 'partnership' model in which the firm is seen as a collaborative community in which labour and capital are equals had been a staple of Liberal thinking since at least the 1920s and, as noted above, had also been adopted by Labour Revisionists such as Crosland in the 1950s. Hutton's book compellingly linked a long-standing centre-left commitment to a plausible account of Britain's economic malaise (and to an independently attractive account of the flaws in the political system).

In January 1996, Tony Blair gave a speech to the Singapore business community in which he spoke about the need for a 'stakeholder' economy. The speech was widely reported at the time and perceived as an endorsement of Hutton's approach. It was included in Blair's book *New Britain* in a section devoted to 'Stakeholder Britain'.[14] However, looking back at the text of this speech, it is clear that Blair was by no means endorsing the sort of reforms proposed by Hutton. Blair explicitly ruled out *legislating* for the introduction of new stakeholder models of corporate governance: 'We cannot by legislation guarantee that a company will behave in a way conducive to trust and long-term commitment, but it is surely time to assess how we shift the emphasis in corporate ethos from the company being a mere vehicle for the capital market . . . towards a vision of the company as a community or partnership in which each employee has a stake.'[15] Blair was using the rhetoric of stakeholding, but shifting its content.

In essence, New Labour moved from a 'collectivist' notion of stakeholding to an 'individualist' one.[16] On the Hutton view, stakeholding is a *relational* idea: it is centrally about how to structure relationships within productive groups. It denotes democratic partnership in a stable, long-term association. But on the individualist view, 'stakes' are understood as *individual holdings* of assets (human or financial capital) and 'stakeholding' is about widening people's entitlements to capital so as to enhance their ability to participate in a market economy. It is about empowered individuals negotiating their way through the 'rough and tumble' of the marketplace and, if need be, exiting associations when they are dissatisfied. Its emphasis is on 'exit' rather than 'voice'.

Proponents of individualist stakeholding, such as Charles Leadbeater and Geoff Mulgan of the think tank Demos, suggested that Hutton's prescriptions were unsuited to the United Kingdom's political economy.[17] David Soskice argued that Labour could not realistically hope to create the institutional architecture of an 'organised' capitalism on the German model, but should try to work with the grain of Britain's more 'liberal' capitalism. Stakeholding should accordingly be about developing and spreading individual assets, rather than reforming corporate governance or the financial sector.[18]

New Labour had made a core strategic judgement: a Labour government should seek to work with the grain of the United Kingdom's liberal market capitalism, including its lightly regulated financial sector. Some regarded this as necessary for Labour's 'economic credibility'. Certainly, it posed fewer institutional challenges than an attempt to try to reconstruct the British economy on the lines of 'stakeholder capitalism'.

From stakeholding to asset-based welfare

Any balanced assessment of New Labour must give it credit for taking this revised notion of stakeholder capitalism quite seriously in policy terms. This was not just empty rhetoric. As Rajiv Prabhakar argues, the individualistic notion of stakeholding found expression in one of New Labour's more interesting and innovative policy initiatives: 'asset-based welfare'.[19] The immediate intellectual impetus to the development of asset-based welfare came from the United States. Michael Sherraden, an academic in social policy, pioneered the idea of Individual Development Accounts (IDAs). In an IDA scheme, low-income households are eligible to set up special saving accounts. For every dollar they put in, a third party matches this with a dollar amount (depending on the exact matching ratio). Sherraden argues that IDAs not only help poor households to accumulate crucial financial assets, but also suggests that the saving process has a positive psychological effect. Poor people become less fatalistic and develop a stronger sense of agency, which enables them to get out of poverty.[20] Parallel to Sherraden, Bruce Ackerman and Anne Alstott, two lawyers at Yale University, published *The Stakeholder Society* in which they argued that all American citizens should get, as of right, a US$80,000 grant at the age of 21, financed from a tax on inherited wealth.[21] Only by universalising real capital ownership in this way, they argued, could the United States make good on its promise of freedom for all.

Both proposals fed into British think tank discussion (notably at the Institute for Public Policy Research and the Fabian Society) which, in turn, impacted upon policy.[22] One outcome was the Child Trust Fund (CTF). Under the CTF every child receives a sum at birth, which must be invested in an account on their behalf. The sum then accumulates as they grow up. Families may add to the account up to an annual ceiling. On reaching 18, the individual can use the accumulated funds as he or she likes. Thus, the CTF was an attempt to combine state action and family saving to create a universal capital entitlement. A second policy outcome was the Saving Gateway, a variant of Sherraden's Individual Development Account. While British governments have long offered citizens subsidies to assist asset accumulation—for instance, through tax relief for private pension saving—these policies have tended to benefit disproportionately the already asset rich.

The CTF and Saving Gateway were innovative in being either universal (as in the CTF) or else targeted at those with least assets (the Saving Gateway). On the other hand, commentators were right to point to the way in which the thinking behind the CTF gradually shifted from the idea of endowing all young adults with capital as a new right of citizenship to an emphasis on promoting a new 'savings culture'.[23] There was a related worry that the development of asset-based welfare might come at the expense of more conventional welfare benefits or public services, and thus be part of a project of individualising exposure to risk. The government, however, explicitly presented it as a new 'pillar of welfare' alongside, and complementary to, these conventional pillars.

Both the CTF and the Savings Gateway have been abolished under the Coalition government. This must be regarded as a major set-back for the centre-left, given its historic commitment to what Liberals once called 'Ownership for all'.

The new politics of inheritance

Asset-based welfare may have been innovative, but it was of limited scale compared to background inequalities of wealth and major developments in the economy. The National Equality Panel, reporting in 2010, found that inequality in wealth was much higher than inequality across other dimensions such as income, with some evidence of a long-term rise in wealth inequality in recent decades.[24] Income inequality rose under Labour, with changes in top incomes related closely to fluctuations in the stock market.[25] House prices almost trebled from 1997 through 2007, making it increasingly difficult for ordinary earners with no existing housing wealth to get a foothold in the housing market.[26]

These developments, particularly in the housing market, in turn impacted on the politics of ownership in a way that put Labour on the defensive. As more families saw their housing wealth nudge over the threshold for potential liability to inheritance tax, a media campaign emerged to reform or scrap inheritance tax. The campaign included newspapers such as the *Daily Express* and the *Daily Mail* and television programs such as the *Richard and Judy Show*. The Treasury's response was to emphasise how only a small proportion of households pay any inheritance tax. Little attempt was made to defend the principle of taxing the transfer of wealth across the generations. According to some commentators, this left the field open for critics of the tax to claim the moral high ground.[27]

The centre-left tradition of thinking about ownership has long accepted that there is a compelling case for the taxation of wealth transfers across the generations. In part, this reflects a distinction between deserved and undeserved wealth and a judgement that it is fairer to tax inheritances as largely undeserved wealth than wealth or income that an individual has earned through their own efforts.[28] It also reflects a judgement that unequal inheritances of wealth contribute to inequality of opportunity. Consistent with this view, there was a continuing interest in the progressive reform of the taxation of wealth transfers within and around New Labour. The 1994 report of the Borrie Commission on Social Justice recommended a shift to a capital receipts tax (where tax falls on the recipient of an inheritance, based on the amount he or she receives, rather than falling on the estate).[29] Peter Mandelson and Roger Liddle called in their 1996 book *The Blair Revolution* for a 'reformed inheritance tax' to be used to pay for a system of interest-free loans to help young married couples.[30] The Fabian Society's Commission on Taxation and

Citizenship, reporting in 2000, called for the existing inheritance tax to be replaced with a capital receipts tax as a better, more equitable way of taxing the transfer of wealth across the generations.[31] Subsequent think tank outputs repeated the call for reform.[32] Two recurring themes here were, first, the shift from a tax based on estates to one based on capital receipts; and, second, the idea of linking a reformed tax of wealth transfers to the creation of some form of universal capital grant: a *citizens' inheritance* system in which taxes on the wealth of one generation are used to secure wealth entitlements for all members of future generations. Some of the thinking behind the CTF was shaped by this perspective.[33]

However, at the Conservative party conference in October 2007, the then shadow Chancellor George Osborne announced that the Conservatives would, if elected, raise the threshold for inheritance tax to £1 million (from £300,000 at the time). The Conservatives got an immediate bounce in the polls and Labour was arguably persuaded by this not to go for a general election. In response to Osborne's move, the Labour government immediately announced a measure which in effect doubled the inheritance tax threshold for many families. With some justification, the Conservatives claimed that while they were still the Opposition, it was they who were now making government policy.

Labour's retreat on inheritance tax in 2007 was significant in a number of ways. First, it showed how the party was unable politically to articulate a strong moral case for the taxation of wealth transfers across generations, despite the deep roots of this idea in the centre-left tradition and the continuing plausibility of the underlying moral arguments.[34] Second, it marked a clear end to some of the radical possibilities implicit in asset-based welfare, in particular to any prospect of linking innovative policies such as the CTF with a progressive reform of inheritance tax.

After the crash: back to stakeholding?

New Labour's position had in effect evolved into that of a moderate left version of neoliberalism. The economy, deregulated in many areas, was left to get on with the task of creating wealth, with the financial sector particularly important in this regard. The tax dividend from growth was then channelled into public services, in-work benefits and modest schemes of asset-based welfare. For the most part, Labour took the neoliberal conception of the firm, as a profit-maximising entity with sovereign authority in the hands of capital, as a given. A partial, delimited exception to this was the interest in 'public interest companies' in public services (for example, Network Rail, foundation hospitals).[35]

This situation was apparently revolutionised by the banking crash of 2008. Immediately related to overly risky lending by major banks and other financial institutions, the causes of the crash were traced back in part to the deregulatory moves of the 1990s.[36] As a result, the intellectual dominance of neoliberalism was suddenly challenged. In response, ideas which had lost out in the struggle to define New Labour in the 1990s began to re-emerge. People started once again to ask questions about the structure of the financial system and its role in the British economy. Industrial policy moved swiftly from the lumber-room of anachronistic 1970s-style ideas to the cutting-edge of government thinking. And the crisis prompted a wider questioning of the neoliberal model of the firm and renewed interest in alternative models based on greater employee participation in profits, capital and decision making.

One work which encapsulates some of these themes is Will Davies' *Reinventing the Firm*.[37] Davies starts from the claim that the United Kingdom economy suffers from a banking crisis, a competitiveness crisis, a fiscal crisis and a 'moral crisis' related to rising inequality. He argues that the development of a new model of the firm, based on employee participation in profits, capital and authority, offers a way of responding to all four crises. Greater mutualisation would help to reduce systemic risk in the financial sector. Employee ownership and participation will help raise productivity and can thus form part of a competitiveness agenda. Mutuals—'societies, trusts or cooperatives that own assets and are run on behalf of their members'—might have a role to play, Davies argues, in a restructuring of public services to manage fiscal pressures. And democratisation of the firm can help to bear down on runaway remuneration at the top of companies—a factor driving increasing inequality. It would be misleading to characterise Davies' agenda as a straightforward return to Hutton-style 'stakeholder capitalism'. The emphasis is on the virtue of pluralism in ownership forms rather than to elevate one model of the firm, or one model of capitalism ('liberal' or 'coordinated'), over all others.[38] However, there is clearly a return to some of the concerns and insights of Hutton's work and, indeed, of the wider centre-left tradition of thinking about the firm which was largely occluded under New Labour.

Another interesting expression of post-Crash rethinking is the 'Blue Labour' perspective developed by Maurice Glasman.[39] For Glasman, Labour politics has a centrally conservative element. It is tied to the protection of common forms of life within which people find meaning and identity, and which are tied to where they live and how they work. Capital, seeking maximum profit wherever it can, has no interest in the conservation of these forms of life. Labour politics is about people organising themselves to hold down and temper capital's fluidity. This, in turn, calls for a politics of ownership. On the one hand, for example, it calls for a democratisation of the firm so that workers and capitalists share authority (though Glasman emphasises that this also requires trade unions to take more responsibility for the quality of work). This perspective also calls for measures to put assets and asset portfolios in the hands of local communities, subject to restrictions on how far communities can alienate their assets for immediate profit. Drawing on this idea, London Citizens, the citizen organising association, has argued that the government use a fraction of the payback from the bank bailouts of 2008 to set up new community-based investment funds. As Glasman puts it: 'The recapitalisation of local economies through an endowment cogoverned by the main institutions of civil society funded by 1 per cent of the bailout could keep the credit flow open to the poor at non-usurious rates and provide a basis for local, relational banking. It would entangle capital in local obligations and long-term relationships.'[40] A proposal along these lines was subsequently included in Labour's 2010 election manifesto.

Glasman's idea of 'Blue Labour' is, of course, in part a response to the idea of 'Red Toryism' floated by Philip Blond. Blond, too, has argued, post-Crash, for a revival of cooperativism, while situating the latter as part of a distinctively Conservative tradition of social critique and reform.[41] Another, related reflection of current rethinking is Labour's renewed interest in 'mutualism' in the final year of the Brown government, albeit an interest that was to some extent deflected into discussion of public service reform rather than reform of the wider economy.[42]

Again, it would be misleading to see Glasman's (or Blond's) ideas as merely a return to Hutton's ideas about 'stakeholder capitalism' (though Glasman shares a good deal of Hutton's enthusiasm for the German model). There is, however, a strong relational emphasis in these perspectives that is distinct from the individualistic conception of stakeholding which we have seen was so important to New Labour.

Conclusion: where next?

So where ought Labour—or the wider centre-left—to go next? What are the key elements of a future politics of ownership? Clearly, there are important challenges in relation to banking and finance and also the housing market. In conclusion, however, I want to flag up three specific questions that are amongst those that Labour and the wider centre-left will need to address. First, we need to ask what is Labour's/the centre-left's attitude to the taxation of wealth and wealth transfers. Can and should Labour seek to revive a critique of undeserved wealth and make a positive case for the taxation of wealth and/or wealth transfers? The future of inheritance tax remains one outstanding issue here. In the context of the debate over how to cut the budget deficit, some commentators have also argued for the contemporary relevance of a land value tax.[43]

Second, there is the question of how Labour and the wider centre-left should view asset-based welfare. Is this to be an experiment that falls by the historical wayside? Or should Labour return to the idea and commit itself to developing new policies akin to the CTF and the Saving Gateway? This question applies also to the Liberal Democrats. The Lib Dems have at times made a distinction between the CTF in particular (which they have opposed) and the broader idea of asset-based welfare (which they support).[44] However, they have not yet developed much in the way of concrete proposals for alternative forms of asset-based welfare to the CTF. Will the Liberal Democrats develop some proposals in the future?

Third, there is the question of Labour's and the wider centre-left's attitude to the firm. How far should Labour seek to promote a new model of the firm based on wider employee participation in profits, capital and authority? And what are the appropriate tools for promoting this?

Underpinning these specific questions is a deeper and wider question about the social obligations that surround wealth creation and the search for profit. As the banking crisis has led on to fiscal crisis and the Coalition government's agenda of rapid and deep public spending cuts, many have started to wonder if the basic social contract between business and society (and between the rich and the rest) has broken down. Citizen initiatives, such as UK Uncut, articulate this very vividly in their in-store protests against alleged tax avoidance by large firms and rich individuals.[45] Fixing the broken social contract will be enormously challenging for Labour and the wider centre-left, however. Some elements of a possible progressive new contract, such as a 'Robin Hood tax' on financial transactions, will be strongly resisted by the City. How can Labour create and sustain public support for a project of this sort? Can Labour learn new ways of doing politics, learning from a variety of sources, such as London Citizens and the best of the emerging anti-cuts movement? Can it learn to work in alliance with other parties, such as Liberal Democrats and/or Greens? These questions demand another discussion, but I suspect that only by learning a new politics with elements of strong, independent civic activism and party pluralism will Labour be able to make a break with the worst aspects of its recent past and reconnect to the vision set out so well by Anthony Crosland at the end of *The Future of Socialism*: 'The ideal . . . is a society in which ownership is thoroughly mixed-up—a society with a diverse, diffused, pluralist, and heterogeneous pattern of ownership, with the State, the nationalised industries, the Co-operatives, the Unions, Government financial institutions, pensions funds, foundations, and millions of private families all participating.'

Notes

1 A. Crosland, *The Future of Socialism*, London, Jonathan Chapman, 1956.
2 B. Jackson, 'Revisionism reconsidered: "property-owning democracy" and egalitarian strategy in post-war Britain', *Twentieth Century British History*, vol. 16, no. 4, 2005, pp. 416–40.
3 See D. Jay, *Socialism in the New Society*, London, Longmans, 1962; J. Meade, *Efficiency, Equality and the Ownership of Property*, London, Allen & Unwin, 1964.
4 Crosland, *Future of Socialism*, pp. 300–11.
5 Crosland, *Future of Socialism*, pp. 333–72.
6 Crosland, *Future of Socialism*, p. 494.
7 Labour party, *Industry and Society*, London, Labour party, 1958, pp. 56–7.
8 Labour party, *Industry and Society*, London, Labour party, 1958, pp. 56–7.

9 S. White, '"Revolutionary liberalism"? The philosophy and politics of ownership in the post-war Liberal party', *British Politics*, vol. 4, no. 2, 2009, pp. 164–87.

10 See, for example, S. Brittan and B. Riley, *A People's Stake in North Sea Oil: Unservile State Papers 26*, London, Liberal party, 1980.

11 P. Ashdown, *Citizen's Britain: A Radical Agenda for the 1990s*, London, Fourth Estate, 1989, p. 129.

12 W. Hutton, *The State We're In*, London, Jonathan Chapman, 1994.

13 See P. Hirst, *After Thatcher*, London, Collins, 1989, Chapters 4–6; P. Hirst, *Associative Democracy: New Forms of Economic and Social Governance*, Cambridge, Polity, 1994; J. Kay, *The Economics of Business*, Oxford, Oxford University Press, 1996; D. Marquand, *The New Reckoning: Capitalism, States and Citizens*, Cambridge, Polity, 1997.

14 See A. Blair, 'The stakeholder economy', in *New Britain: My Vision of a Young Country*, London, Fourth Estate, 1996, pp. 291–6.

15 Blair, 'The stakeholder economy', p. 295.

16 The distinction is introduced by the editors in G. Kelly, D. Kelly and A. Gamble, eds, *Stakeholder Capitalism*, Basingstoke, Macmillan, 1997, pp. 240–1. It is deployed comprehensively in R. Prabhakar, *Stakeholding and New Labour*, Basingstoke, Palgrave Macmillan, 2003.

17 See C. Leadbeater and G. Mulgan, *Mistakeholding*, London, Demos, 1996.

18 See D. Soskice, 'Stakeholding yes; the German model no', in Kelly et al., *Stakeholder Capitalism*, pp. 219–37.

19 See R. Prabhakar, *The Assets Agenda*, Basingstoke, Palgrave Macmillan, 2008.

20 M. Sherraden, *Assets and the Poor: A New American Welfare Policy*, New York, M. E. Sharpe, 1993.

21 B. Ackerman and A. Alstott, *The Stakeholder Society*, New Haven, CT, Yale University Press, 1999.

22 See G. Kelly and R. Lissauer, *Ownership for All*, London, Institute for Public Policy Research, 2000; D. Nissan and J. Le Grand, *A Capital Idea: Start-up Grants for Young People*, London, Fabian Society, 2000.

23 See A. Finlayson, 'Characterizing New Labour: the case of the Child Trust Fund', *Public Administration*, vol. 86, no. 1, 2007, pp. 95–110.

24 National Equality Panel, *An Anatomy of Economic Inequality in the UK: Report of the National Equality Panel*, London, Government Equalities Office/Centre for the Analysis of Social Exclusion, London School of Economics, 2010, pp. 56–60.

25 National Equality Panel, *An Anatomy of Economic Inequality*, pp. 34–48. However, Labour's tax and benefit reforms almost certainly prevented inequality growing by as much as it otherwise would. See M. Brewer, D. Philips and L. Sibieta, *Living Standards, Inequality and Poverty: Labour's Record*, London, Institute for Fiscal Studies, 2010.

26 The average house price for the United Kingdom (all dwellings) stood at £76,103 in 1997 and at £223,405 in 2007. This information is taken from http://www.communities.gov.uk/housing/housingresearch/housingstatistics/housingstatisticsby/housingmarket/livetables/, Table 513.

27 See K. Rowlingson, 'Is the death of inheritance tax inevitable? Lessons from America', *The Political Quarterly*, vol. 79, no. 2, 2008, pp. 153–61.

28 See, for example, R. H. Tawney, *The Acquisitive Society*, New York, Harcourt Brace Jovanovich, 1948 [1920].

29 Commission on Social Justice, *Social Justice: Strategies for National Renewal*, London, Vintage, 1994, pp. 390–1.

30 P. Mandelson and R. Liddle, *The Blair Revolution: Can New Labour Deliver?*, London, Faber & Faber, 1996, pp. 127–9.

31 Commission on Taxation and Citizenship, *Paying for Progress: A New Politics of Tax for Public Spending*, London, Fabian Society, 2000, pp. 271–89.

32 See M. Jacobs and R. Patrick, *Wealth's Fair Measure: The Reform of Inheritance Tax*, London, Fabian Society, 2003; W. Paxton and S. White, with D. Maxwell, eds, *The Citizen's Stake: Exploring the Future of Universal Asset Policies*, Bristol, Policy Press, 2006. The former called for a new capital receipts tax. The latter called for greater differentiation in rates of inheritance tax, taking less from smaller eligible estates and more from larger ones.

33 This was central to Ackerman and Alstott's model of stakeholding and found a clear echo in Nissan and Le Grand's proposal for a system of start-up grants paid for out of a reformed inheritance tax. The idea was also explored in Paxton et al., *The Citizen's Stake*.

34 See R. Prabhakar, K. Rowlingson and S. White, *How to Defend Inheritance Tax*, London, Fabian Society, 2008.

35 For a sympathetic discussion, see R. Prabhakar, 'Do public interest companies form a third way within public services?', *British Journal of Politics and International Relations*, vol. 6, 2004, pp. 353–69. For a critical view of Network Rail, see R. Jope, 'Public (interest) or private (gain)? The curious case of Network Rail's status', *Journal of Law and Society*, vol. 34, 2007, pp. 244–65.

36 See P. Mason, *Meltdown: The End of the Age of Greed*, London, Verso, 2009.

37 See W. Davies, *Reinventing the Firm*, London, Demos, 2009.

38 Davies, *Reinventing the Firm*, pp. 29, 37–58.

39 See M. Glasman, 'The common good', in P. Harrington and B. K. Burks, eds, *What Next for Labour? Ideas for the Progressive Left*, London, Demos, 2009, pp. 39–43; M. Glasman, 'An embedded economy', in J. Purnell and G. Cooke, eds, *We Mean Power: Ideas for the Future of the Left*, London, Demos, 2009, pp. 113–26.

40 Glasman, 'An embedded economy', pp. 122–3.

41 P. Blond, 'The rise of the red Tories', *Prospect*, no. 155, February 2009.

42 For helpful comment, see A. Painter, *How to Seize the Mutualism Moment*, http://www.nextleft.org/2009/12/how-to-seize-mutualism-moment.html

43 P. Legrain, 'There is an alternative to the VAT rise', *Guardian*, 3 January 2011, http://www.guardian.co.uk/commentisfree/2011/jan/03/public-sector-cuts-alternative-vat-tax

44 See P. Marshall, 'Introduction', in P. Marshall and D. Laws, eds, *The Orange Book: Reclaiming Liberalism*, London, Profile, 2004, p. 15; Liberal Democrats, *Poverty and Inequality: Federal Policy Consultation Paper 81*, London, Liberal Democrats, 2006, pp. 7–8.

45 See http://www.ukuncut.org.uk/.

The Death of Class-based Politics

PETER KELLNER

Introduction

SOME years ago Stephen Potter, a whimsical British satirist, proposed a way to deflate arrogant people who offered confident generalisations about different countries round the world, such as 'the French think sex matters more than food' or 'the Chinese are inherently superstitious'. Potter suggested a simple interjection: 'But not, I think, in the south.' This chapter could well provoke a similar reaction. It offers some sweeping propositions about the evolution of progressive politics over the past hundred years, and the bleak condition of social democracy today. To those who are tempted to respond 'it's more complex than that', you are right. Any attempt to paint a big picture in a single chapter is bound to omit many details of political life as it has evolved in recent decades. Equally, however, too much attention to detail and the short term is liable to miss a large and important truth about social democracy today: that it is in crisis, that the version that triumphed in Britain and other countries in the second half of the twentieth century is now bust, and that social democracy needs to reinvent itself if it is to survive, let alone flourish, in the twenty-first century. Although New Labour hinted at the revolution to come, it was in many ways a last hurrah for a dying doctrine.

Social democracy: versions one and two

Social democracy—or 'democratic socialism' as it used to be called—had two main versions in the twentieth century. Version one lasted until the Second World War. Its aim—though it was usually expressed as a distant goal rather than an immediate political programme—was to replace capitalism. In 1918 Labour agreed to a new clause four of its constitution, setting out the party's objectives:

To secure for the workers by hand or by brain the full fruits of their industry and the most equitable distribution thereof that may be possible upon the basis of the common ownership of the means of production, distribution and exchange, and the best obtainable system of popular administration and control of each industry or service.

It should be noted that this was never a cry for full-blooded state socialism. The call was for 'common ownership', not 'state ownership', and it wanted rewards distributed 'equitably' rather than 'equally'. Agreed by the Labour party barely three months after the Russian Revolution, it hankered for a broader, more democratic and dispersed system of economic control—not the import of Lenin's dictatorial methods. It was, in a sense, Labour's first

Published by Blackwell Publishing Ltd, 9600 Garsington Road, Oxford OX4 2DQ, UK and 350 Main Street, Malden, MA 02148, USA

'third way' exercise in triangulation—neither capitalist nor communist. It left no room for large, profit-seeking companies owned by private shareholders. Six years later, Britain had its first Labour Prime Minister, Ramsay MacDonald. The election manifesto on which Labour came to office said:

The Labour Programme of National Work includes the establishment of a National System of Electrical Power Supply, the development of Transport by road, rail and canal, and the improvement of national resources by Land Drainage, Reclamation, Afforestation, Town Planning and Housing Schemes. . . . The Labour Party proposes to restore to the people their lost rights in the Land, including Minerals. . . . The Labour Party is working for the creation of a Commonwealth Co-operative Service. It believes that so far only a beginning has been made in the scientific organisation of industry. It will apply in a practical spirit the principle of Public Ownership and Control to the Mines, the Railway Service and the Electrical Power Stations, and the development of Municipal Services. . . . It will place the Drink Traffic under popular control.

As with clause four, this fell short of promising a system of British soviets, but the direction of travel was clear. However, as Labour came nowhere near winning a majority, and Macdonald's government lasted less than a year, little progress was made.

The story of 1929–31 is similar: Labour's minority government lacked the support it needed to move Britain significantly to the left; and within two years it collapsed as it tried to fend off the great depression. The party's 1931 manifesto, proclaiming that 'the decay of capitalist civilisation brooks no delay', failed to rouse a worried electorate. During this phase one of social democracy, Labour never secured the votes it needed to kill capitalism. Its average vote share in general elections in the 1920s and 1930s was just 33 per cent.

By 1945, when Labour enjoyed enough support to rule with a clear majority, its priorities had changed. Without proclaiming a new set of long-term objectives, Clement Attlee effectively inaugurated version two of social democracy. Its emphasis (like that of Sweden's social democrats, who had pioneered this approach in the 1930s) was on government-funded services: free education of all children, unemployment benefits and pensions for all and, proudest of all, a new National Health Service in which everyone would have access to good quality medical care regardless of their means. Some industries were nationalised, such as the mines and the railways, and others regulated, but in the main Attlee's government sought to coexist with private capital, not to ban it.

Being a supreme pragmatist, Attlee never tried to repeal clause four of Labour's constitution. He saw no point in provoking the party's left wing. He simply ignored it. In Germany, the shift from version one to version two was more clear-cut. At a conference in Bad Godesberg in 1959, the Social Democratic Party (SPD) decided explicitly to turn its back on Marxist socialism:

Free choice of consumer goods and services, free choice of working place, freedom for employers to exercise their initiative as well as free competition are essential conditions of a Social Democratic economic policy. The autonomy of trade unions and employers' associations in collective bargaining is an important feature of a free society. Totalitarian control of the economy destroys freedom. The Social Democratic Party therefore favours a free market wherever free competition really exists. Where a market is dominated by individuals or groups, however, all manner of steps must be taken to protect freedom in the economic sphere. As much competition as possible—as much planning as necessary.

Shortly afterwards, Hugh Gaitskell sought a similar change for Britain's Labour party, using the incontrovertible argument that the party had in practice abandoned its dream of taking over every private business, so why not admit it and say so? He was defeated by a coalition of the trade unions and the left, who maintained their devotion to the religion of common ownership; so clause four remained unchanged until 1995 when Tony Blair finally persuaded the party to bring it up-to-date. In practice, however, every Labour government since 1945 has pursued broadly the same goals as Attlee (and Germany's and Sweden's social democrats): to use the power and resources of government to provide healthcare and education, to establish and sustain a range of universal insurance and welfare benefits, and to regulate rather than destroy the private sector.

Version two of social democracy proposed partially different means from version one, but radically different ends—and it proved to be far more popular than version one. Its adherents dominated Swedish politics for six decades; it produced four majority Labour governments in Britain (and might have produced more had the left not sought to return to version one in the 1980s); Germany's SPD, which had never won more than 35 per cent support before Bad Godesberg, never won *less* than 35 per cent in the four decades afterwards. Version two has also been adopted by the mainstream left in other European countries recovering from communist or fascist dictatorships. Indeed, such was its success that most centre-right parties have accepted most its reforms when they have won power back from the centre-left.

The paradoxical position of social democracy now

We ought, then, to be at a moment in political history when we can declare social democracy to be the winner of the ideological struggles of the twentieth century, having extruded from the major European democracies the appetite for both state socialism and laissez-faire capitalism. And the role of the banks in provoking the recent recession has produced demands in many countries for tougher government regulation—in other words, a social democratic response to a failure of capitalism. Yet if ours is an era when social democracy is triumphant, that is not how it feels. Within the last eighteen months, Germany's SPD has achieved its lowest share of the vote (just 23 per cent) since the Second World War, Britain's Labour Party has received its second-lowest share (30 per cent) since 1918, and Sweden's Social Democrats have lost a second consecutive election for the first time since the 1920s.

The stark truth is that social democracy became a victim of its own success. Socialised healthcare, free education and universal welfare proved so popular that voters wanted ever more of them. In economists' parlance they became 'superior goods'. Our demand for them has grown faster than national income. As we live longer, as increasing numbers of us want later schooling and higher education, as new and more expensive drugs and treatments became available and as we seek better living standards in retirement, social democracy becomes ever more expensive. In Britain, government spending on health, education and welfare has grown from £2 billion in the early 1950s to more than £400 billion today. If we strip out the effects of inflation, welfare spending has risen almost tenfold. In the same period, GDP has almost quadrupled. This is historically unprecedented. Expenditure on health, education and welfare has risen two-and-a-half times faster than GDP. The cumulative effect has been staggering. As a percentage of national income, spending on 'social democracy' has climbed from 11 to 28 per cent: from a modest and affordable figure that guaranteed its popularity to one that provokes sharp questions about whether its costs have outrun its benefits.

Almost half of this 17-point increase has been paid for by massive cumulative cuts in defence spending. The dismantling of empire, the withdrawal from East of Suez in the 1960s and the end of the Cold War have, altogether, enabled Britain to cut defence spending from 9 per cent of GDP in the early 1950s to 2 per cent today: a peace dividend of 7 per cent of GDP, worth £100 billion a year. A quarter of today's total social democracy spending is financed by that peace dividend.

Few people outside the defence community would regard that as anything other than an unalloyed blessing; and it is not the reason for today's agonies for the Labour party. The pain has been caused by the way the rest of the increase—around 10 per cent of GDP—has been financed. The money has come chiefly from higher taxation. And that explains a large part of the doctrinal crisis Labour now faces. The biggest beneficiaries of social democracy, Britain's working class, used to pay relatively little for it. Most people doing manual jobs—and they and their dependents comprised two-thirds of the electorate in the 1950s and 1960s—paid either no income tax or only small amounts. The great bulk of income tax was paid by the other one-third: Britain's middle and upper classes. This class divide was reflected in voting habits. In 1966, when Labour won a majority of almost 100, the party won thirteen million votes. While eleven million of these were working-class votes, just two million came from the middle class; 60 per cent of working-class voters backed Labour, compared with just 20 per cent of middle-class voters. That 40-point 'class gap' testified to social democracy's essential electoral appeal: that most of the costs were borne by the middle-class minority, and most of the benefits enjoyed by the working-class majority.

Today things are very different. In last May's general election, 8.6 million people voted Labour. YouGov found that they divided as follows: 4.4 million middle class, 4.2 million working class. For the first time ever, Labour's middle-class vote exceeded its working-class vote. The party received 33 per cent of the working-class vote and 27 per cent of the middle-class vote. The 'class gap' was just six points.

Many things changed between 1966 and 2010. Britain's middle class became a majority. The pattern of industry and the nature of manual work changed massively. Trade unionism largely disappeared from the traditional private sector. Had the cost of social democracy remained a constant share of GDP, Labour would still have faced large electoral problems as its class base shrunk and the culture of solidarity fractured. In the 1980s and early 1990s, it became fashionable to argue that Labour could never win again, precisely because the Labour-voting classes were shrinking, the Conservative-voting classes were expanding and voters in both classes were becoming more individualistic.

However, the rising cost of social democracy has also taken its toll. Taxes, and especially income tax, loom much larger in the lives of lower paid workers today than they did half a century ago. We still want good schools and hospitals and generous pensions, but we also want nice homes, reliable cars and all the benefits of modern technology. Labour could still say to its supporters: 'We believe in welfare and public services: we shall look after you and your family.' But, by 2010, this was no longer a clinching sales pitch when a reformed Conservative party could credibly argue: 'We, too, will look after you, but we shall run Britain's public services more efficiently and so leave you with more in your pocket for you to choose how to spend.' Labour found itself losing votes from millions of people who believed one or both of two things: that the party could no longer be trusted to run the economy well and spend money wisely, or that their taxes had risen too high and more of their earnings should be left in their own pockets. At a time when the immediate challenge is to reduce the government deficit, YouGov finds consistently that big majorities want spending cuts rather than tax rises to carry the brunt of the burden. We still want the benefits of social democracy, but increasingly we begrudge the bill.

In short, for most people social democracy has shifted from being the unambiguous good it was some decades ago to being a contingent blessing that depends on its benefits being seen to be bestowed in a fair, affordable and efficient manner. The recent recession and sharp rise in borrowing have brought matters to a head, but the long-term trends were already raising ever sharper dilemmas for version two of social democracy.

New Labour as version three?

Hence the need for a new form of social democracy: a version three. What should this look like? One obvious answer would be to learn from New Labour. Just five years after its 1992 election defeat and gloomy prognostications that the party could never win again, it achieved its biggest ever landslide. In many ways Tony Blair 'got' the political nature of Labour's task: to win as many middle-class votes as possible rather than just seek to win back its working-class base. It was a signal achievement to lift Labour's share of the middle-class vote from 22 per cent in 1992 to 36 per cent in 1997, while at the same time increasing its share of the working-class vote from 44 to 53 per cent. As an exercise in self-discipline, classless soft-focus appeal and 'policy-lite' professionalism, Labour's campaign to destroy a discredited Conservative government could scarcely be bettered.

However, that campaign had nothing to do with the task of reshaping social democracy for the twenty-first century. To see what lessons New Labour offers on this, we must examine how it used its power once it was elected. Its record was, in truth, mixed. On the credit side are three big achievements. First, it legislated for greater fairness, not only through equal rights laws but by introducing the national minimum wage—a law that YouGov consistently found to be Labour's most popular social reform. Second, it sought to reform the management of the public services, though whether its plans were bold enough or sufficiently thought through remain a matter for debate. Labour's third achievement was its most controversial— though, in decades to come it may come to be seen as its most important. It introduced a new system of fees and loans for university students. In so doing, Labour started to broaden the income base for social democracy spending, relieving general taxation of some of the burden and switching it to the beneficiaries.

With that important but single exception, New Labour declined to challenge version two of social democracy. Indeed, in many ways, the Blair and Brown administrations sought to buttress it. My Freedom Pass and winter fuel allowance provide grateful memories of the Labour years and the party's devotion to universal welfare. Overall, government spending on health, education and welfare grew faster between 1997 and 2010 than over any comparable period since 1945: by 60 per cent in real terms, and from 23 per cent of GDP to 28 per cent. The advantages are undeniable: smaller class sizes, shorter hospital waiting lists, better-off pensioners and so on. Only once, however, was the price made explicit: when Gordon Brown increased national insurance rates to help fund increased spending on the NHS in 2002. Otherwise, Labour rode a ten-year tide of a growing economy and buoyant tax revenues, supplemented by extra borrowing and what were, often inaccurately, labelled 'stealth taxes'.

The tide was always bound to recede one day and expose the long-term fragility of this strategy. Disaster struck in 2008 when recession hit and government borrowing soared to terrifying heights. Labour lost its reputation for economic competence. For ten years Labour had boasted that it had abolished 'boom and bust'. Suddenly this boast—and, by extension, all boasts about managing Britain's finances well—turned to dust. The question turned from who should benefit from Labour's largesse, to who should pay for its mistakes? Gratitude for the improvements of the previous decade gave way to fears that taxes would rise, public services would contract and ordinary working people would suffer. This in turn provoked a mounting sense of insecurity, one of whose outlets was a growing hostility to immigrants who were widely thought to be taking homes and jobs from British families.

In short, Labour lost power having failed on two fronts: the economy had crumbled on its watch, and its version of social democracy had run out of road. No matter how hard Brown pleaded, and with some justice, that the recession had been provoked by greedy bankers and American mortgage-lenders, and that he had led the world in making sure that recession did not morph into slump, voters had lost trust in him and his party. Many voters felt the pinch—and resented what they believed was the excessive help directed at the 'wrong' people, such as bankers and immigrants. Here is a selection of YouGov findings from the past two years:

- 62 per cent of Britons think 'Labour used to care about the concerns of people like me'; just 19 per cent think it still does.
- The two groups that voters think government should help most are 'ordinary working people' and pensioners. The two groups they think Labour actually wants to help most are immigrants and single-parent families.
- Just half the public think Britain's public services improved under Labour—and most of them think much of the money was wasted.
- Only 24 per cent trust Labour most to cut spending 'in a way that is fair for all'.

Plainly, if it is to return to power after such damning verdicts on its record, Labour needs to rebuild its reputation for both economic competence and fairness. It also needs to reconnect with an electorate that has become profoundly suspicious of politicians in general, and Labour politicians in particular. These are tough challenges: the record of Labour after its defeat in 1979 and of the Tories after 1997 is that it can take a decade or more for a party in opposition to regain the trust of voters who have rejected it so decisively. In addition—and it is arguably a precondition if Labour is to achieve those objectives—the party needs to accept that version two of social democracy has run its course, and that New Labour's attempts to fend off its demise ultimately failed.

Social democracy reconceived

What, then, is to be done? What will be the components of a viable version three of social democracy? Whereas the critical shift from version one to version two happened in terms of proclaimed ends (from the dream of replacing capitalism to acceptance of a market economy), the shift from version two to version three will largely concern means. The central challenge is to build a fairer society without imposing significantly higher taxes. This will not be easy. However much we dream of a perfect society in which greed is banished, solidarity trumps individualism and everyone pays taxes willingly, Labour's fortunes are more likely to revive if the party accepts the constraints that are likely to persist for any foreseeable future. These are some of them:

- The pressures on health, education and welfare spending will continue to increase. Even if the present government succeeds in achieving efficiency savings that last and manages to curb the rise in 'social democracy' spending in the short term, the underlying demographic pressures will soon reassert themselves.
- General rises in taxation will continue to be unpopular. That does not mean taxes cannot be raised in specific circumstances, such as Brown's rise in national insurance to help finance the NHS or this year's rise in VAT to help reduce government borrowing, but most future increases in 'social demo-cracy' spending must be found from sources other than taxation.
- Employment trends will continue to generate a more atomised, insecure workforce in which more and more people need qualifications to get jobs, more of those jobs are short term, and more and more time is spent working online, alone and often remotely. Solidarity of any kind, let alone class solidarity, will be in shorter and shorter supply. Even though there are many examples of widespread altruism and voluntary action (David Cameron's concept of a 'Big Society' should not be dismissed out of hand), the core of Labour's appeal must be that of individual benefit and security.
- Trust in politics, civil servants, senior public managers and the efficiency of public service has declined sharply. Unlike some of the other trends listed here, this could be reversed over time. But it will not happen quickly: Labour would be unwise to assume much change before the next election. This distrust, as well as cost, will limit the appeal of traditional, version-two social democratic measures.
- Globalisation will limit the freedom of individual countries to tax, or impose other restraints on, companies or rich individuals. Action must be coordinated with other governments. Social democracy has always con-tained a strong internationalist ethic; now, cooperation across borders is more vital than ever.

Alert readers will notice that this list contains some huge gaps: the danger of climate change is one, the threat from terrorism another. A third, and perhaps the trickiest in the short term, is the need to draw the poison from the interconnected issues of immigration, ethnicity and identity. These are of course massively important matters. Labour needs to get them right, but British politics as a whole needs to get themse right, just as it needs to find the most efficient way to deliver public services, involving the private sector where this can be done without harming equity. On these matters, social democrats should seek consensus across the mainstream of British politics, not turn them into dividing lines with the Conservatives and Liberal Demo-crats. A rough parallel may be drawn with the coalition that governed Britain from 1940 until 1945: the parties stood together to win the war against Hitler, but Labour prepared a distinctive, radical and, as it turned out, massively popular programme to win the peace that followed. Version three of social democracy, then, should not attempt to solve all the problems facing Britain and the world. It should concentrate on what can make social democracy distinctive in the twenty-first century, not what makes it merely enlightened.

One place where distinctiveness can be found is in the left's core values. Ever since the French Revolution, and arguably since the days of Britain's Levellers in the 1640s, the defining ambitions of progressive politics have been liberty, equality and solidarity. Down the centuries, the context for pursuing these ambitions has changed, and many battles won. We have universal suffrage, more-or-less free speech and, in principle if not always in practice, equality before the law. Discrimination on the grounds of race, gender and sexuality is now illegal. In each case issues remain: Should prisoners have voting rights? Have our laws on libel and contempt been drawn too tightly? Are the latest changes to legal aid skewing access to justice? Has discrimination really disappeared? Yet many of the goals for which previous generations of progressive activists strove have largely been achieved.

This puts social democrats in a historically new position—in some ways, as small-c conservatives defending the gains that have been secured. Historically the words 'progressive' and 'radical' were often used interchangeably because progressive demands invariably needed radical action. This is not always true today. Much of Labour's campaigning against the present government involves the quest to save the public services and preserve the welfare benefits that have been built up since 1945. Or consider the quest by civil libertarians to defend the human rights of terrorist suspects: what could be more proudly conservative than to seek to uphold the 332 year-old Habeas Corpus Act? This does not mean such stances are wrong, or that they are not progressive. Far from it. But if social democracy version three is to be an essentially defensive doctrine, then the consequences are profound. Labour will have to become very different kind of party and its campaigns will have an utterly different character.

However, we have only to look around us to see that much still needs to change. Inequalities of all kinds are rife: in wealth, income and power, but also in health, education, access to public amenities and the risk of being a victim of crime. Tony Blair's noble target of abolishing child poverty by 2020 looks certain to be missed. And the hold on power of the privileged elite shows few signs of slackening. Gordon Brown was the first university-educated prime minister for more than 240 years never to have attended Oxford or Cambridge. (The previous one was the Earl of Bute, who attended the Dutch university, Leiden, which was just as 'posh' as Oxbridge, but happened to be abroad.) There are no signs of this daring social experiment being repeated anytime soon: our current prime minister, deputy prime minister and opposition leader are all Oxbridge graduates.

That might not matter so much were Oxbridge's admissions systems fairer. At the last count, less than 1 per cent of their undergraduates had qualified for free school meals. In contrast, as a recent Sutton Trust report entitled *Responding to the New Landscape for University Access* pointed out, as many 15 per cent of new undergraduates at Harvard qualify for Pell grants (a federal system for supporting students from low-income American families). That is what happens when a university takes seriously its obligation to track down the brightest students, however weak their local school, promote a 'needs-blind' admissions policy to encourage such students to apply, and give added first-year support to students to make up for the deficiencies of their schooling.

As that example shows, the challenges of creating a more equal society remain formidable. Fifty years ago, in social democracy's heyday, the task seemed straightforward. Equalise incomes through an aggressively redistributive tax-and-benefits strategy, and equalise well-being and opportunity through well-funded public services, especially health and education. However, as this chapter has sought to demonstrate, that strategy has run its course. Voters won't elect a party that promises ever higher taxes on ordinary people to fund social democracy spending, and globalisation limits the taxes that can be imposed on profitable companies and rich individuals.

Social democracy 'version three' needs to square the circle, with a vision for equality whose price voters are willing to pay. In the manner of television newsreaders warning of flash photography and unpleasant scenes in the report coming up, I should warn readers that the three proposals that follow will upset progressives who brook no retreat from the principles of universal welfare and income equalisation.

Universal benefits—the state pension, child benefit, winter fuel allowance and so on—have been one of the glories of social democracy version two. They bind the country together. They give everyone a stake in society. They avoid the stigma and inefficiency of means-tests. They underpin a worthy set of social contracts: that working-age people have a responsibility towards the elderly, and workers without children should contribute to the costs borne by parents bringing up the next generation. Yet they are extremely, and increasingly, expensive. If a choice must be made between sustaining universal welfare and maintaining the quality of state schools and the NHS, universal services surely trump universal cash transfers. To those who disagree, here is a question: if Labour wins the next election, do you really think an early priority, when so many underfunded government services will be clamouring for extra cash, should be the restoration of child benefits for higher-rate taxpayers? The harsh truth is that universal welfare is now in conflict with the fight against poverty. If, say, all cash benefits were withdrawn from all higher-rate taxpayers, and the age for retirement benefits (pension, winter fuel allowance, Freedom Passes) raised to 70 for standard-rate taxpayers, then serious money would be available to support people with real need (including those in their sixties no longer able to work but not yet at retirement age).

Clearly it would help if such reforms could be implemented without expanding the role played by conventional means-tests. Ending benefits to higher-rate taxpayers would achieve this. We would then have a range of semi-universal benefits, available to all who pay no tax or the standard rate. And if the present government's plans for an integrated, universal benefits system are implemented in full, it should be possible to increase the benefits to the poorest households without increasing the use of means-tests.

Would this kill the contributory principle: the important notion that we all pay into the national pot, and should all be able to draw from it when we need to? The principle would arguably survive for two major reasons. The first is that our 'needs' are not purely financial. They include healthcare for us all when we fall ill and schools for our children when we are parents. It is central to the version of social democracy proposed here that these universal services should be sustained and properly funded. Second, while it is proposed that cash benefits should be curbed, everyone who falls on hard times would still have access to them. People would lose, say, child benefits when they are reasonably prosperous, but if circumstances change, the payments kick in— and, indeed, at a more generous level than is possible under a universal benefits system. It might be argued that this actually enhances the contributory principle that we all contribute according to our means and all have access to cash, education and healthcare when we truly need them.

Now to the second shocking proposal: to broaden the income base of public services so they are not as completely dependent on tax money as they are today. As we have seen, this has already happened with university education. A good case can be made for arguing that the coalition government has done too much too fast to shift from tax-funding to student loans, but, as with ending child benefit for higher taxpayers, no future Labour government is going to reverse what has happened. The challenge is to turn cofunding from a 'right-wing' cause, intended to cut taxes, into a progressive cause, designed to ensure that everyone has access to high quality public services. Charles Clarke has addressed this head-on in a report, sponsored by KPMG entitled *Achieving the Potential*.[1] He points out that, while the term 'cofunding' is recent, the practice is nothing new. It was the Attlee government that introduced prescription charges in 1951 to protect the funding of the NHS; and parents have to pay for many of the desirable add-ons provided by state schools, such as breakfast clubs and school trips. Cofunding, then, should not be regarded as an ideological taboo, but as a practical matter: how, and in what circumstances, can cofunding be used to expand collective provision for all?

Clarke puts forward a number of proposals. For example, schools should be encouraged to undertake many more 'non-core' activities in the early morning, evening and at weekends, to charge for them but make them available free for children who qualify for free school meals. Similarly, the NHS could distinguish between 'core' and 'non-core' activities, keeping core services free but competing with the private health sector to provide non-core services (such as some check-ups and non-essential treatments) for which those who can afford them must pay. By such means, social democracy version three can do more to fulfil the historic mission to make high-quality services available for all, but in an affordable way.

This leads to shocking proposition number three: that progressives need to view equality in a new way. The left normally views it solely, or predominantly, in terms of income. Seen through that prism, not only was the last Labour government a failure because income inequalities widened, but it is hard to see how any future government could narrow the gap significantly in an era of globalisation and international competition to attract investment and jobs. There are some on the left who say that precisely because of the constraints imposed by having an open economy, Britain should return to more autarkic ways, with strict controls on imports, investment and foreign exchange. This merits a detailed argument, but not here. This chapter assumes that, for the foreseeable future, the United Kingdom will remain an open economy and must live with the constraints that this imposes.

Given these constraints, it should be possible by applying the measures outlined above to end extreme poverty, but probably not to make Britain a generally more equal-income society. That, though, should not mean we give up on the dream of equality. Rather, we should work for a society in which well-being is not so intimately associated with income. The issue of university admissions is a case in point. It is not just Oxbridge, but virtually all the 'Russell Group' of top universities that have a terrible record in admitting pupils from poorer families. A combination of government pressure, shaming publicity and American-style initiatives to attract such pupils would be a big step towards greater equality of life-chances.

More widely, social democracy version three should aspire to a broader concept of universal *access*: access not just to high quality education and healthcare, but to neighbourhood streets free from muggers and drug-pushers; to dry, warm and affordable homes; to local parks where children can play safely; to chances to retrain when jobs disappear in the face of technological change; to local shops that sell fresh food at reasonable prices; to systems of part-public and part-private insurance that can guarantee reasonable living standards in hard times and old age; and so on. In short, social democracy should challenge the assumption, implicit in the ideology of the free market, that all that matters is money. Our goal should be a society in which money matters less. This vision of equality would ensure the social membership rights of a healthy society, alongside the political rights that previous generations struggled to secure, such as the rights to vote, to associate and to speak freely. It would be based on what R. H. Tawney advocated for the Labour party eighty years ago: 'a common view of the life proper to human beings'. This vision of social, rather than financial, equality is not one that all on the left will share, but it cannot be condemned as lacking in ambition.

In order to make this vision real, social democracy also needs to continue to challenge the 'right-wing' view that smaller government is better government. The (valid) cliché holds that we need smarter government, not larger government; the underlying principle asserts, as it always has, that individual effort cannot solve all our problems, and that collective action needs to combat the harmful side-effects of the free market. It is in this sense that the virtues of solidarity still need to be proclaimed, however atomised our daily lives become. It should also be stressed that this is not an 'anti-Big Society' argument, but the very opposite. The gains from voluntary action and local initiative cannot be fully realised unless they work in harness with public institutions within the framework of sensible laws. Progressives should insist that the minimum wage, lead-free petrol, the blood transfusion service, Sure Start centres and smoke-free pubs and restaurants are worthy elements of the Big Society—and we have them only because Parliament willed that we should. Version three of social democracy should reassert the importance of public action that enhances private initiative. It could do worse than revive the maxim of the Diet Pepsi advertisements from the 1980s: 'You can do it. We can help.'

Those proposals will not be easy to implement. They require policies as radical as anything dreamt by social democracy version one or implemented by social democracy version two. And there is, of course, plenty of room for argument about the principles outlined here, let alone the details. What is certain is that social democracy version two is dead, and Labour has little chance of refreshing and reviving itself unless it rises to the challenge of designing a new version three. *Pace* Stephen Potter, this needs to be done even, and perhaps especially, for the south.

Note

1 The full text is available at: http://charlesclarke.org/wp-content/uploads/2011/01/Achieving-the-Potential.pdf

Back to Class: Lessons for the Labour Party

ALAN FINLAYSON

Introduction

The Labour party, as everyone knows, was born from a class-based political movement. It was formed to represent in Parliament the interests of a section of society defined by its position in the division of labour and its exclusion from full political rights. A century later, as everyone also knows, New Labour sought to demonstrate that it had left behind what now seemed to be a narrow conception of political representation. In his 1999 speech to the Labour party conference, Tony Blair made the official announcement: 'The class war is over.' Upon this premise New Labour built both an electoral strategy and a governing philosophy. But the premise was flawed. It consisted of an inadequate understanding of class and the politics that derive from it.

New Labour's leaders had learned, for instance, from Giles Radice's influential pamphlet *Southern Discomfort*,[1] that Labour was identified by a key part of the electorate as a party primarily of the working class, and thus also of the past; they concluded—not unreasonably—that in order to win elections they had to convince people that this was not true. However, they further concluded that the way to overcome this perception was to step aside from too close an association with the industrial working class, that to look like a party which shared their interests would always be to look like a party interested in failures and losers, and that Labour had to be remade into a party for winners (or, at least, for those who imagined themselves to be so).

However, this analysis of electoral opportunities was confused by New Labour's leaders with an analysis of the actual politics of the nation. They convinced themselves that class is solely a matter of subjective perspective and cultural identity. But class is not subjective. It is about who has more power and who has less. Class politics concern the ways in which those with power seek to keep it, and those without it seek to take it. In forgetting this, New Labour became blind to the most important contemporary political dynamics, unable to see that the impact even of its best and cleverest policies would be limited. Instead of leading in the field of class politics, it became wholly driven by it.

All of this is now history. New Labour's 'project' is over. But if it is to be sure of what to do next, Labour has to understand what happened. And that means it has to relearn the politics of class.

Published by Blackwell Publishing Ltd, 9600 Garsington Road, Oxford OX4 2DQ, UK and 350 Main Street, Malden, MA 02148, USA

Interests

In 1999, addressing the Labour party conference in Bournemouth, Tony Blair uttered the line that, I believe, most succinctly captures his social, political and economic philosophy. He told the conference, in a bold declaration, that: 'The Future is People.' The meaning of this claim may not be apparent immediately. It occurred in between two fascinatingly unlikely partial citations of the radical tradition. The first of these—'A spectre haunts the world: technological revolution'—invoked *The Communist Manifesto* prior to a declaration of the impact and importance of computer technology and global currency markets. Such forces, Blair explained: 'Don't stop at national boundaries. Don't respect tradition. They wait for no one and no nation. They are universal.'[2] The country, he was saying, had no choice but to adapt and to do so it needed:

A knowledge-based economy. A strong civic society. A confident place in the world. Do that and a nation masters the future. Fail and it is the future's victim. The challenge is how? The answer is people. The future is people.[3]

What Blair meant was that future economic security would come from the talent of individuals. Their imagination, creativity and skills would be the driving force of economic development and security in the 'fast-forward future'. This entailed a politics characterised by the following demand: 'Not power to the people but power to each person to make the most of what is within them.' That led into Blair's second reference to the radical tradition: 'People are born with talent and everywhere it is in chains.' However, where Rousseau had meant to refer us to a natural condition of liberty which life in modern states had corrupted, Blair was pointing to an injustice that the state could and must resolve:

Fail to develop the talents of any one person, we fail Britain. Talent is 21st century wealth. Every person liberated to fulfill their potential adds to our wealth. Every person denied opportunity takes our wealth away. In the 18th century land was our resource. In the 19th and 20th century it was plant and capital. Today it is people.[4]

A vital task for the state, then, was to remove fetters on talent. And that meant that Labour had to free itself from its 'narrow' ideology representing 'the interests of an exploited workforce' and because of which: 'People were made to feel we wanted to hold them back, limit their aspirations, when in truth the very opposite was our goal.' In place of such class politics, Blair announced the birth of:

A New Britain where the extraordinary talent of the British people is liberated from the forces of conservatism that so long have held them back, to create a model 21st century nation, based not on privilege, class or background, but on the equal worth of all.[5]

This was why the class war was over: in order to prosper in the new global knowledge economy, the nation would need to maximise the potential, and draw on the talents, of all. According to Blairism, the economic necessity of a society of free talent contradicted our entrenched culture of 'snobbery and prejudice, ignorance and poverty, fear and injustice'. Consequently, social justice was no longer simply the cause of New Labour, but 'the nation's only hope and salvation'. The 'historic mission' of 'the new radicals' in the Labour party was: 'To liberate Britain from the old class divisions, old structures, old prejudices, old ways of working and of doing things, that will not do in this world of change.'

Looking back on these arguments one striking feature is the extent to which they are underpinned by a weirdly Marxian eschatology (perhaps this was the unconscious motivation for the homage to the *Manifesto*)—that is, they rely on an implicit claim about the necessary outcomes of a historical process driven by technological and economic forces; class division is not abolished by political reform or a moral crusade, but rendered redundant by the demands of global capitalist economics. Consequently, the policy challenge is construed as that of adaptation to necessity—as if there are no agents in any way responsible for driving or directing our great transformation, no specific interests in play, let alone contradictory ones, and so no need for the untidy politics of trying to mediate between them or supporting one over the other. There is only the historic 'mission' of the 'new radicals': enabling everyone to recognise their common interest and so bring the nation into harmony with necessity.

This was not just empty posturing. Labour really did seek to liberate talent as it understood it. For instance, the primary justification for public sector reform was not the reduction of costs, but the need to break down 'producer-led' services so that provision believed to keep people locked in a culture of deprivation and low aspiration could be replaced by services that were individualised and tailor-made to ensure that individuals would become able and willing to enter the labour market and make the most of themselves.[6] Labour also passed important legislation to prevent labour-market discrimination on the grounds of gender, age, disability, ethnicity and sexual orientation. But the fundamental policy goal of New Labour was to change people's sense of themselves. As Blair explained, he wanted to convert the 'traditional welfare state' into 'the opportunity society' where everyone has 'genuine opportunity to make the most of your talent'. He wanted to 'put middle-class aspirations in the hands of working class families and their children'.[7]

In retrospect, it may be that New Labour's most original contribution to the art of government in the United Kingdom was this: policy motivated not by aspirations or by the attempt to meet them, but that made aspiration itself the object and goal. The 'enabling', 'generative' 'social investment' state[8] would liberate people from their own counterproductive behaviours. It would help them to see that in the absence of land or plant they still possessed what was now the most important source of capital: a body and a mind. And once they saw themselves that way, it was thought, individuals would invest time, money and effort into enhancing the value of that capital. In the process—in a wholly virtuous cycle—they would reduce their cost to the state and increase their contribution to GDP.

A wide range of New Labour's policies can be understood in these terms. For instance, strategies for the policing of troubled communities (on-the-spot fines, anti-social behaviour orders [ASBOs], the linking of council house tenancy agreements to responsible behaviour, the imprisonment of parents whose children truant) have enabled the use of the criminal law in the regulation of socially unproductive or costly behaviours[9] and were developed and justified as a way of increasing social capital, challenging cultures of deprivation and low aspiration. Curriculum reforms across the Key Stages and the preschool Foundation Stage emphasised employability, the people-skills needed to flourish in the workplace and individual career ambitions as well as managing money, learning to save and invest. Innovations such as the Savings Gateway and the Child Trust Fund were not primarily redistributive measures, but ways of tackling resistance or incapacity that hindered participation in the banking, savings and investment industries.[10] Most importantly, housing became a mechanism to alter aspirations by encouraging a risk-taking orientation to the future, and creating a 'home-owning, wealth-owning, asset-owning demo-cracy'.[11] Home ownership was a contribution to the equalisation of life-chances,[12] an asset that would enable individuals to access funds to finance the fulfilment of their aspirations while taking responsibility for their own financial future and becoming long-term investors.[13]

This 'direction of travel' led New Labour to become greatly concerned with 'behaviour change'.[14] In a reversal of the social democratic emphasis on the governance of institutions in order to attain positive outcomes for individuals, New Labour decided that 'individuals need to change their own behaviour in order for government's wider goals for society to be achieved'.[15] Behaviour-change policies are now to be found across the national and local levels of government in the United Kingdom. They are an example of a New Labour policy approach that the Conservative-led Coalition has enthusiastically continued.[16] Government has embraced behavioural economics, evolutionary psychology and neuroscience in the effort to govern individuals' behaviours and ensure that they become appropriately aspirational citizens.

To the extent that New Labour had a core philosophy and policy frame-work, this was it. It is in no sense an outright abandonment of the classically social democratic conviction that the state can be positively employed to promote economic growth and social equality. But it is a major reformulation of the justifications and mechanisms for so doing. Rather than intervene in macroeconomic processes or seek to mediate between the demands of capital and labour, the New Labour state developed policies to make up for market failure on the supply side; it would provide the kinds of worker and consumer demanded by contemporary markets.

The limitations and biases of the approach are, especially now, very clear. First, the aspirations with which government was most concerned were those of the poor or working class. They refrained from addressing the aspirations of the very rich until it was too late. By then, excess, unrealistic aspirations and misunderstandings of risk at the top end of the income scale had contributed to a generalised crisis. Second, the aspirations on which government focused were limited: they were those that involved individual attainment in the workplace and fulfilment in the marketplace rather than those that directly enhanced collective security. New Labour promoted aspirations of the kind that most contributed to the intensification of a financialised economy which turned out to be dangerously unbalanced. Despite early interest in constitutional reform and bold talk from Gordon Brown about a new 'constitutional settlement', Labour was not greatly interested in the aspirations of people as citizens.[17] Third, the New Labour approach to aspiration and behaviour change was based upon a limited conception of the forces and processes responsible for engendering aspirations. This was indicative of New Labour's failure to understand power. In his now classic account, Steven Lukes outlined 'three faces of power': the first is the power to make and take decisions; the second is the power to set limits as to what can be a matter for decision; and the third is the cultural or ideological power to shape the desires that inform the decisions individuals make.[18] New Labour was hugely preoccupied by the first form of power, thinking that if it increased individuals' capacity for taking decisions it would thereby make them more powerful and free. And in pursuing this goal New Labour exercised the second form of power. The decisions it wanted to enhance were specifically those that concerned individual labour-market value and output, and debt-financed consumption. But it completely ignored Lukes' third face of power, and in so doing ensured that, however hard it tried to engender behaviour change, government would be only a very small voice in an ocean of insistent noise. To put the point bluntly: policies to improve attitudes and behaviour related to individual diet pale next to the attitudes and behaviour of those who actively and sometimes aggressively market bad food; the impact of exhortations to defer gratification and study for a job in middle management is limited within a celebrity culture that promotes instant gratification attainable from the magical touch of televisual fame.

New Labour acted as if government was the most influential power in the land, able to make things happen just by passing a law or amending a regulation. Yet it also acted as if the efforts of media corporations, supermarkets or credit card companies could not shape behaviour. New Labour seemed unaware of the possibility that these institutions might want to shape behaviour in the pursuit of their own private, rather than the public, interest and, across policy domains such as obesity and alcohol abuse, sexual behaviour, financial management and others, actively resisted opportunities to restrict the power of profit-seeking providers to influence individual behaviour.[19]

New Labour's fundamental intellectual error was a failure to understand the reality of collective interests and, especially, the reality of class interests. It could not see that one of the causes of poor people is rich people, and that sustaining a culture of low or misplaced aspirations is in the short-term interest of some. Because they did not include any significant challenge to the social and cultural power of corporate economic agents, the attempts of New Labour to cultivate economically valuable and socially responsible talents and attitudes could only ever have limited success. Indeed, ultimately, these efforts contributed to the expansion of a credit boom and the markedly uneven spread of risk for which the many and not the few must now pay.

Able to think only in terms of individuals' desires and *preferences*, and to see itself as having the role only of helping these be properly guided and then freely met, Labour forgot to think in terms of *interests*. It could not see the extent to which class interests in a nation might be in contradiction with each other, and that what was good for some might not be good for others. Unable to appreciate fully that one of the things that politics is, is the management, reformulation and cooptation of such interests, it was itself coopted. In contrast, the uneven impact of current austerity programmes, the way in which they are weakening public services for the least well off, while making education and healthcare available for private investment for profit, suggests that at least some in the Conservative party understand the politics of class interest perfectly.

Equality

Class, I have said, is more than a subjective attitude or identity. Inequities of power and action that derive from class continue to exist whether or not people consciously think in terms of class. But this does not mean that class has no effect on attitudes or identities, or that it lacks a subjective dimension. Indeed, one of the ways in which class domination is sustained and reproduced is through the ways in which it writes itself upon our bodies and minds.[20] The culture of class tells each of us that dignity and worth are not universal properties, but due only to some, and it encourages actions and attitudes that reinforce this belief. We assign value and status to all sorts of things (appearance, accent, possessions, postcode, holiday destinations, clothes) and then attempt to possess or display these things so that others may see them and grant us status. When Rousseau said that we were all in chains, he was not referring to talent but to an independence of spirit and mind that had been lost to *amour propre*, the need to live not according to our own inner motivations but in order to be seen, approved and admired by others in a society of unequals.

It is a contemporary commonplace that such a culture of class is a thing of the past. And, undoubtedly, such distinctions are no longer manifested and maintained in the way they were in Britain of the 1960s, 1970s or 1980s. The clarity and uniformity with which we might once have assigned rank and value to objects and attributes is a thing of the past. But this is not at all the same as the abolition of class. Our contemporary 'structure of feeling' is not one of easy going egalitarianism, but rather of nervous individualism, a sense of an entitlement to status matched by anxiety about all those waiting to take it away. The 'Blair Years' were in fact marked by intensified *ressentiment*, which manifested itself as ostentatious distaste and even disgust at those we could imagine to be beneath us and aggressive ridicule of those who could be shown to have been placed above us on false pretences—moods catered to effectively and profitably by some, perhaps all, of our national newspapers.

Two outstanding cultural phenomena of New Labour's time in office exemplify this. The first is the recasting of class as a kind of ethno-cultural identity most easily encapsulated, and dramatised, by the figure of the 'chav'. We were allowed—encouraged even—to despise the chav as the ultimate in low taste and misplaced aspiration while holding him or her responsible for all our social problems. In contrast, we knew that we at least had status and dignity. And the second example of our aggressive ridicule of those placed falsely above us? There are many but perhaps the most ironically emblematic is Cherie Blair. While declaring class to be a thing of the past, in its own conduct and the presentation of its own aspirations New Labour demonstrated the extent to which it remained enmeshed in the culture of class distinction and differentiation. And, in the level of its rhetoric and its policy, for all the promotion of classless aspiration New Labour reinforced the core of the cultural ideology of class: that only some are worthy of dignity and respect.

In 2009 Alan Milburn was asked by Gordon Brown to lead an investigation into social mobility and access to 'the professions'. This issued in a report entitled *Unleashing Aspirations: Fair Access to the Professions*.[21] In a widely reported press release, Milburn explained the findings: 'Frankly there are too many kids out there from average income families who are bright . . . and who want to go on to get a top professional career but haven't got the right connections, haven't necessarily gone to the right school, maybe haven't had the chance to go to university, and that has all got to change.' Milburn thus recognised some of the ways that those who already hold power, and have access to resources, use them to keep others down—something the report euphemistically and coyly called 'opportunity hoarding'. And yet that same report—in its framing and in its fundamental assumptions—was wholly committed to the distinctions that contributed to, and justified, such hoarding.

The paradox of the concept of mobility is that it invites us to measure equality in terms of the volume and speed of movement up and down a hierarchy—that is, it relies on the very thing it appears to be concerned to overcome. Consequently, the concept retains coherence only by ruling out any thought of equality of outcome and instead embracing a concept of equal opportunity that is really the opportunity to do better than others. This implication was spelled out perfectly by Milburn in a speech he made shortly after taking up an appointment with the Conservative-led government in 2010 (and published in the Labour party magazine *Progress*). Rather than try to correct market inequalities, he explained, public policy, should concentrate on the labour supplied to those markets ensuring that 'that those who have the aptitude and aspiration to do so get a fair opportunity to progress'—that is, the opportunity is available, but only some can qualify.[22] This is not policy for a world after the class war. It is an attempt to change the rules of engagement. It is a policy intended to create elites, but Platonic, rather than Burkean ones— that is, elites who hold their rank not because of tradition, prejudice or the trappings of prestige, but through training and expertise. As Milburn puts it: 'The goal we should be aiming for is to . . . prevent both social advantage and social disadvantage being inherited rather than earned.' And the implication of this is that if you haven't 'made it', then that is a position you have justly earned for yourself. But what does 'making it' entail? Milburn's report took its lead from a white paper on New Opportunities, which concerned itself with 'obstacles to careers in certain high status professions' thus affirming a given link between occupation and status. *Unleashing Aspiration* defined 'professional' jobs as those with entry requirements, codes of ethics, systems for self-regulation, sense of vocation and structures for professional development. That could be quite a lot of jobs so it is interesting how specific is the list of examples provided:

Doctors, dentists, nurses and vets . . . [l]egal professionals, such as judges, barristers, solicitors, paralegals and court officials . . . accountants, bankers, management consultants and business and finance advisers . . . such as journalists, publishers, designers, writers and artists . . . senior civil servants, managers in local government . . . armed forces officers and senior police officers . . . archaeologists, chemists, mathematicians and physicists . . . professors, lecturers, teachers and early-years specialists . . . architects, engineers, surveyors, town planners, urban designers and construction specialists.[23]

The definition of 'professional' is thus restricted to those forms of work which privilege mental over manual labour. The report, rather than seek to generate respect for all the skilled and difficult occupations, for all those forms of labour without which the country cannot function, reaffirmed a very traditional idea of 'good' jobs. It made clear that it is not good enough to be a police officer, you ought to be a senior officer; working for the council makes you less valuable than those who run it; plumbers, electricians or carpenters are not as important as the people who designed the building such labour actually makes possible. In short, the report seems concerned to promote equal chances to become one of the few worthy of respect. It does not presume that equal respect is due in the first place.

It would be churlish to reject everything in *Unleashing Aspiration*. Many of the recommendations on enabling people to access careers through a variety of routes are eminently sensible. Yet it is also indicative of the effects of New Labour's conversion of the ideal of equality into the ideal of equal access to the labour market while still believing that some forms of labour were more equal than others. It does not tackle class prejudice but promotes it and, in some ways, in an even more virulent form. Gone is the notion of dignity won through the collective organisation of labour and the pride of being part of a fundamental industry. One of the core ethical claims of socialist political philosophy has always been that people can and should be valued regardless—that equality is a starting presumption, that people are not to be valued and respected because they are or might become accountants. A national economy needs lots of other kinds of work to be done; not everybody has the same kinds of talent and not all talents lead to mental rather than manual labour. But all can be respected and all can be fairly rewarded. New Labour abandoned this perspective. Is it too much to say that some voters recognised that New Labour did not see them as of status, and that it only valued people who looked like itself? And is it too much to think that this gave rise to a resentment out of which others on the political spectrum made much capital?

One outcome of the Labour party's electoral defeat in 2010 has been a resurgence of explicit anxiety about class, and about the relationship of the party to it. In *Why did Labour Lose—and How Do We Win Again?* Liam Byrne drew attention to the collapse in support for Labour among C2 voters as well as among what he referred to as mid-range income families.[24] Ed Miliband, in his leadership campaign, made quite similar arguments, describing the collapse of Labour's vote among C1s and C2s as a 'crisis of working-class representation for Labour'.[25] Both affirmed the need to 'speak to aspiration'[26] and show how 'aspirational modest-income Britain' will 'get ahead' in the decade to come.[27]

However, the pollster Peter Kellner has insisted that 'social class is no longer the main determinant of voting'.[28] In the 2010 election, he showed, more middle-class than working-class people voted for Labour, a fact explained very simply: 'Today, middle-class Britain outnumbers working-class Britain by four-to-three.' Furthermore, 'people are far less inclined to vote along class lines than they used to'. In 1950 'the act of voting, and voting Labour, was of a piece with being a miner', but today, 'for the overwhelming majority of us, our shared experiences are not of pain, struggle or oppression, or of the collective institutions that helped people to survive and fight back— trade unions, working-men's clubs, the Co-op and, sometimes, churches. Today's shared experiences and irritations are of credit cards, Tesco, mobile phones, MoT tests, Sky, mortgage-lenders, commuting, the Internet and the X-Factor'.[29]

Although they differ, for all three of these contributors class remains a fundamental concern—but only inasmuch as it is a way of talking about electoral market segmentation. What is at issue between them is how best to infer from class, attitudes and tastes to which one can then appeal, not the ways in which interests that might be related to class or the ways in which political strategy might shape attitudes and tastes. There is no 'third face' of power here.

All three are concerned only with the working class and the middle class rather than with the intensification of wealth and power at the top end of the social scale. That top end is there, however, peeking at us from the margins of inference. Byrne, for instance, writing of the desire of the aspirant middle classes to better themselves, remarks that: 'Powerful forces in the global economy plus fiscal consolidation will mean it is harder than ever before.'[30] But he does not say what (or who) those forces are. And isn't Kellner's description of the end of class in fact an eloquent testament to its increased importance? Everyday life, he explains, is not shaped by an organic culture composed of historic and localised customs around food, religion, labour and entertainment, but by the massive power of private commercial institutions. He describes a 'post-class' consumer culture in which we are all 'irritated' by credit card companies, a massive supermarket chain, commercial television, telecoms companies and banks. Yet he writes as if these are not agents with interests and the power to further them, but merely background conditions like the weather or the availability of copper ore.

What Kellner means, of course, is that subjectively people do not think of themselves solely or primarily in class terms. But class, as we have seen, is not merely a matter of attitudes. Trapped within the illusion that it was, Labour was unable to understand the forms and sources of power with which, as a government, it had to contend. Nor did it understand the culture of status and distinction to which it then so singularly contributed.

Conclusion

Politics always involves a struggle to keep up with social change and be in tune with 'new times'. But that does not mean that one can learn nothing from the thoughts and feelings of the past. Three core propositions of socialist, social democratic and social liberal thought stand out as at things forgotten by New Labour and which, had it remembered them, might have been valuable. First, the proposition that sometimes there may be exploitation when participants do not themselves recognise it—that is, 'free choice' is not a sufficient criterion of judgement for the rightness of actions and the consumer is not always a King; often she or he is a subject. Second, people's choices entwine with each other, and not always harmoniously. A paradox of politics is that in order to enable aspiration and freedom there must also be limits. One person's right to aggressively market sweets to children is another person's early-onset diabetes. Setting such limits is always a matter of fine political judgement: these are the real 'hard choices' a good government is prepared to take. And third, aspirations can be collective as well as indi-vidual. For New Labour this might be the most important lesson of all.

In his autobiography Blair suggests that it was his feeling for aspiration that most distinguished him from the left. He writes of Ed Balls that 'he suffers from the bane of all left-leaning intellectuals. As I have remarked elsewhere, these guys never "get" aspiration.'[31] What can Blair mean? Did the people that risked imprisonment or transportation for organising unions lack aspiration? Were those who fought for universal suffrage failing to have ambitions for the future? Were the women who risked all to promote sex equality lacking in a 'forward vision'? Was the institution of systems to provide support to all members of our community 'from cradle to grave' an act lacking in 'go-getting' spirit? Are those who today seek to bring about a world unthreatened by environmental despoliation really failing to 'aspire'?

All political movements, across the political spectrum, have aspirations. What matters is not their presence/absence, but what they are. What matters more is that, inevitably, the aspirations of some contradict the aspirations of others. Labour has to learn the lessons of class power and class politics and reconsider its own aspirations. It cannot end class conflict simply by wishing it away. It has to choose which side it is on.

Notes

1 G. Radice, *Southern Discomfort*, London, Fabian Society, 1992.
2 A. Blair, Speech to the Labour party conference, Bournemouth, 1999, http://www.britishpoliticalspeech.org/speech-archive.htm?speech=205
3 Ibid.
4 Ibid.
5 Ibid.
6 D. Freud, *Reducing dependency, Increasing Opportunity: Options for the Future of Welfare to Work*, London, Department for Work and Pensions and HM Stationery Office, 2007; P. Gregg, *Realising Potential: A Vision for Personalised Conditionality and Support*, London, HM Stationery Office, 2008.
7 A. Blair, 'Reforming the Welfare State', speech in Beveridge Hall, 11 October 2004.
8 A. Giddens, *The Third Way*, Cambridge, Polity, 1998.
9 A. Crawford, 'Governing through anti-social behaviour: Regulatory challenges to criminal justice', *British Journal of Criminology*, vol. 49, 2009, pp. 810–31.
10 See A. Finlayson, 'Characterising New Labour: The case of the Child Trust Fund', *Public Administration*, vol. 86, no. 1, 2008, pp. 95–110; A. Finlayson, 'Financialisation, financial literacy and asset-based welfare', *British Journal of Politics and International Relations*, vol. 11, no. 3, 2009, pp. 400–21.
11 G. Brown, leadership acceptance speech, Manchester, 2007.
12 See Y. Cooper, 'Housing and Life Chances', speech to Fabian Society, 15 May 2007.
13 M. Watson, 'Constituting monetary conservatives via the "savings habit": New Labour and the British housing market bubble', *Comparative European Politics*, vol. 6, no. 3, 2008, pp. 285–304; M. Watson, 'Financialised economic agency and the housing market', *Planning Practice and Research*, vol. 24, no. 1, 2009, pp. 41–56; I. Ertürk, J. Froud, S. Solari, and K. Williams (2005) 'The reinvention of prudence: household savings, financialisation and forms of capitalism', CRESC Working Paper 11, Manchester, University of Manchester, 2005.
14 D. Halpern, C. Bates, G. Mulgan and S. Aldridge, with G. Beales and A. Heathfield, *Personal Responsibility and Changing Behavior: The State of Knowledge and Its Implications for Public Policy*, London, Prime Minister's Strategy Unit, Cabinet Office, 2004, http://www.cabinetoffice.gov.uk/media/cabinetoffice/strategy/assets/pr2.pdf; M. Taylor, 'Behavioural battleground', *Guardian*, 17 September 2008.
15 A. Darnton, *GSR Behaviour Change Knowledge Review: Overview of Behaviour Change Models and Their Uses, Briefing Note for Policy Makers*, London, Government Social Research Service, 2008, p. 1, http://www.gsr.gov.uk/downloads/resources/behaviour_change_review/policy_briefing.pdf
16 R. Litherland and C. Child, 'Why talk about behaviour change?', *Guardian Public*,

1 October 2009; K. Kerswell and S. Goss, eds, *Challenging Behaviour*, London, Society of Chief Executives of Local Authorities (SOLACE), 2008, http://www.solace.org.uk/library_documents/30_SFI_Challenging_Behaviour_October_2009.pdf

17 Brown, leadership acceptance speech, 2007; also see R. Lister, 'Investing in the citizen-workers of the future: transformations in citizenship and the state under New Labour', *Social Policy and Administration*, vol. 37, no. 5, 2003, pp. 427–43.

18 S. Lukes, *Power: A Radical View*, Basingstoke, Macmillan, 1974.

19 E. Shaw, 'New Labour: a party for whom? The case of obesity and alcohol misuse'. Paper presented at the annual meeting of the Political Studies Association, University of Swansea, 2008, http://www.psa.ac.uk/journals/pdf/5/2008/Shaw.pdf

20 See R. Sennett and J. Cobb, *The Hidden Injuries of Class*, New York, Vintage, 1973.

21 Panel on Fair Access to the Professions, *Unleashing Aspiration: The Final Report of the Panel on Fair Access to the Professions*, London, Cabinet Office, 2009.

22 A. Milburn, 'Social mobility in an age of austerity', speech to Progress and Helena Kennedy Foundation, House of Commons, 25 January 2011, http://www.pro-gressives.org.uk/articles/article.asp?a=7466

23 HM GovernmentG, *New Opportunities: Fair Cchances for the Ffuture*, Cm 7533, London, HM Stationery Office, Cm 7533, 2009, pp. 14—15.

24 L. Byrne, *Why did Labour Lose—and How do We Win Again?*, London, Progress, 2010.

25 E. Miliband, 'The Labour leadership', in D. Abbot, E. Balls, A. Burnham, D. Miliband and E. Miliband, *The Labour Leadership: How Important is it that the Party has a Distinctive Ideology*, London, Fabian Society, 2010, http://issuu.com/fabiansociety/docs/labour_leadership_essays?mode=embed&backgroundColor=FFFFFF&layout=http%3A%2F%2Fskin.issuu.com%2Fv%2Fcolor%2Flayout.xml&pageNumbe=65

26 Miliband, *The Labour Leadership*, p. 59.

27 Byrne, *Why did Labour Lose?*, p. 4.

28 P. Kellner, 'Labour is not just the party of the working class', *YouGov Commentaries*, 31 August 2010, http://today.yougov.co.uk/commentaries/peter-kellner/labour-not-just-party-working-class

29 Ibid.

30 Byrne, *Why did Labour Lose?*

31 A. Blair, *A Journey*, London, Hutchinson, 2010.

Why did Labour's Public Service Reforms Fail to Transform Communities?

JESSICA ASATO

Introduction

THERE are fifteen separate references to reform in Labour's 1997 manifesto, but not one reference to the reform of public services. From reforming the Bank of England to the reform of the Common Agricultural Policy, New Labour certainly had institutional change in mind, but public services were not its main priority when it came to power. Only when New Labour had experienced the frustrations of government, did the need to address public services become a pressing goal. By 2005, 'reform to achieve change in public services'[1] had become its principal obsession.

The pursuit of reform became an important tool to demonstrate New Labour's credentials as a party that was keen to renew in government and ensure it stayed ahead of the public's aspirations. The long years of opposition had left Labour's leadership acutely aware of the pitfalls of indulging in issues which tickled the underbelly of the party, but which were distrusted by the public. Reform, with its overtones of progress and competent management, helped to present the party as moving in line with the priorities of public opinion. This desire to use the public as a barometer for policy shifts was written into the heart of New Labour. The 1997 manifesto boldly stated: 'New Labour is the political arm of none other than the British people as a whole.'[2]

Reform as an expression of New Labour's commitment to staying on the side of the public was, however, fraught with difficulties. Over the years it led to 'initiativitis'—the constant announcement of new programmes of reforms, and the persistent rebranding of previous initiatives—which led to a sense that New Labour was reforming for the sake of it, not because it would make a tangible difference to people's lives. This led to claims that reform had become a value in itself, and that New Labour ended up judging itself by its reforming zeal, rather than by measuring itself against a set of higher aspirations such as improving quality of life, or creating greater equality.

Too often, local solutions to public service problems were ignored, even where there was proof that the public were content with services as they were provided at the time. The desire to move away from 'one-size-fits–all' sometimes morphed into 'another-size-fits-all'. The pace of change, which focused too much on dismantling structures rather than winning hearts and

Published by Blackwell Publishing Ltd, 9600 Garsington Road, Oxford OX4 2DQ, UK and 350 Main Street, Malden, MA 02148, USA

minds, left public servants and users confused about the ultimate purpose of Labour in government.

Reform also failed to address those anxieties that did not relate directly to public services, such as feelings of insecurity in the wake of immigration and societal change, or a sense that globalisation and the market was failing to increase people's happiness and quality of life. This is not to suggest that New Labour's public service reforms failed to change people's lives. They did this in many different areas. But too often the mechanistic, managerial language did not speak directly to people's lived experience.

The problems with New Labour's public service reforms were in some ways rooted in the nature of British government. Talking with the public has never been its strong point. Some good reforms, such as those proposed by the Darzi Review, were inhibited by being poorly communicated. The impartiality code of the Civil Service meant that the political aspirations informing reforms were often non-existent or watered down, leading to a sense that reform meant tinkering rather than transforming. And Tony Blair's strong sense of what middle England wanted and his drive to ensure New Labour reflected its aspirations, meant that choice and exit were sometimes prioritised above keeping services equitable for poorer groups. Finally, New Labour was adamant that left-wing critics in the party, unions or media would not throw it off course. Sometimes this meant that it failed to listen to genuine public unease—for example, about local Accident & Emergency (A&E) closures or the lack of social house-building.

This is not to say that New Labour was wrong to embark on public service reform. Its election successes speak for themselves in this respect. The two years of Gordon Brown's premiership have been widely seen as broadly representing a slowing down of reform and this may well have contributed to a sense that New Labour had nothing left to say for itself.

The journey to public service reform

New Labour's 'bible', *The Blair Revolution*, devotes three times the number of pages to Labour's vision for Europe than it does to the question of public services. Indeed, its original scepticism about the need for structural change in public services is illustrated by New Labour's opposition to the 'Conservative's public-service "reforms"'—note the inverted commas. In particular, Labour rejected market-driven reforms, particularly the internal market in the National Health Service (NHS) and compulsory competitive tendering at local authority level. The aim, according to the authors of *The Blair Revolution*, would be to 'articulate a vision for public services which motivates dedicated staff and at the same time spurs the whole system to greater consumer-responsiveness, efficiency and "value for money"'.[3]

Prior to 1997, the theory seemed to be that public services could be improved by raising the quality of public service professionals, introducing a small amount of performance management and avoiding the trap of 'privatisation for its own sake'.[4] Once in government, however, Tony Blair began to believe that a substantial restructuring of services was needed. In his memoir, *A Journey*, Blair wrote about his 'battle to change structure, to alter the "givens"'[5] of public services. He started to wonder whether Labour had been right to 'dismantle wholesale GP [general practitioner] commissioning in the NHS and grant-maintained schools in education'. By the postscript, the former Prime Minister suggested that progressives should aim to be 'getting value for money in services like healthcare, opening up competition in areas such as education, radically altering welfare'.[6] The overwhelming regret of Blair was that he was not radical enough in his first term in government, especially regarding public service reform.

New Labour still found plenty of reforms to drive through during Blair's time in office. The problem was that for all the rhetoric about putting the public in control of public services, its methods for achieving change were too restrictive, too directed by the centre and many of its reforms ended up impacting upon, not empowering, people without their understanding, or sometimes their consent.

NHS reforms

The NHS Plan 2000, represented Labour's first major assault on NHS structures. It combined increased investment in the health service with reform—a dual philosophy that became a leitmotif for reforms in other sectors. The argument ran thus: to win public consent for spending money after New Labour's commitment to maintain Conservative spending plans for two years after the 1997 election would require the government to demonstrate that the money was not simply being tipped into a black hole. Tony Blair wrote that when he spoke, he focused 'almost entirely on the overriding need to modernise, and in particular how we couldn't just be advocating more money in public services'.[7]

Eleven years later, it is clear that this strategy spectacularly failed. That Labour mismanaged public spending is the judgement of most of the public. Polls consistently show that people hold Labour to blame for the need to cut spending, rather than the current Coalition government.[8] How could its spending, and the many positive results it produced, become Labour's Achilles heel?

Combined with an increase in investment in the NHS by a third in real terms, the NHS Plan sought to create 7,000 extra beds in hospitals, over 100 new hospitals, the renewal of 3,000 GPs premises, 7,500 more consultants, 2,000 more GPs, and 20,000 extra nurses. This expansion was matched by redesigning the NHS 'around the needs of the patient' by introducing national standards including stronger maximum waiting times for appointments, and in A&E, as well as targets to reduce inequalities. There was no pretence that this was incremental reform. The Plan sought to tackle 'systematic problems' dating from the formation of the NHS in 1948. Not for the first time perhaps, Labour 'over-sold' what government had the capability to achieve from the centre.

The 2005 general election was fought ostensibly on whether Labour should be given a mandate to continue its investment and reforms and 'embed the new progressive consensus'.[9] Commitments included a maximum waiting time of eighteen weeks, with an average of 9–10 weeks from referral to operation; choice of hospital; expansion of the Expert Patients Programme and personalised budgets in social care. All of these pledges represented a significant policy shift from forcing the NHS to do better through targets, to involving patients more in choices about their healthcare.

That Labour's reforms led to huge progress in the NHS is undeniable. The NHS 'ran faster, smoother, more efficiently, its formerly shabby face scrubbed up, regaining self-confidence', Polly Toynbee and David Walker concluded.[10] The death rate fell by 17 per cent, particularly for circulatory diseases and eventually for most cancers. Waiting times were slashed, making Labour's 1997 pledge of simply reducing the numbers of people on waiting lists look unambitious by comparison.

Contrary to the current government's assertions about the state of the NHS, Labour can authoritatively say that it transformed the NHS and left people healthier. That Cameron felt he had to give assurances about protecting NHS spending in the run-up to the 2010 general election shows the extent to which Labour forced the Conservatives onto its territory. But at the same time, health inequalities rose: the poor continued to receive poor services, even if they were better than in 1997. Too often Labour sounded happy to accept inequality as long as services had moderately improved for the worst off. New Labour's hope was that in trying to tap middle-class aspirations for better public services, the poorest would benefit too. They sometimes did, but in the process New Labour seemed to forget that its priority was to improve the outcomes of the most disadvantaged in society.

Moreover, while Labour should be commended for using empirical evidence about what made health services better—for example, by moving money from acute services to those in the community and creating specialist centres of excellence—they often failed to win the support of the public. The clamour to oppose the closures of A&Es in the face of good clinical evidence led to a disconnection between the state, which felt it was acting in the public interest, and local people who felt their choices had been ignored.

And, finally, New Labour picked some fights where it might have behaved very differently. The debate around Foundation Hospitals is one such example. Alan Milburn promoted this policy on the basis that the best performing hospitals needed to be freed from direct Whitehall control. Instead, he might have linked the change to a return to the principles of mutualism. By arguing for Foundations on the basis that they would better engage the community with their local services, he could have helped to allay fears that this would create a two-tier NHS. There was mention of local empowerment of users in the new model, but making so much of the focus on the need for diversity of provision in the NHS made the concept impenetrable for ordinary people. Once again this looked like reform for reform's sake, rather than because New Labour believed that there was value in people being involved in decisions about their local services.

Education reforms

While Labour's reforms in the area of health generated mixed results, in the field of education its reforms did contribute to lifting the most disadvantaged out of poverty. It is in education where there is the clearest evidence that Labour helped to transform the lives of communities. The initial programme of cutting class sizes and implementation of the literacy and numeracy programmes were top down in their method, but also successful. Teaching professionals may have disliked the specific nature of the literacy and numeracy targets, but they helped to focus the leadership of schools on raising attainment.

Specialist schools, started under the previous Conservative government, were allowed to grow under Labour until almost 90 per cent of schools enjoyed this status by 2008. Looked upon with suspicion by supporters of comprehensive schools, the new status simply helped to develop an ethos in schools and lever in extra support from the community. Similarly, academies were hugely opposed by Labour's left and the education establishment, but have surprised many by their ability to turn around failing schools. By mimicking the ethos, discipline and unwavering concentration on standards seen in the best state and private schools, not for the middle class, but for pupils in failing schools, Labour was trying to show that the poorest also deserve the best educational opportunities. By contrast, the current government's approach, which consists of encouraging the best performing schools to become Academies, undercuts the importance of bringing in fresh approaches to poorly performing schools. The battle over Academies became a sterile debate about 'structures versus standards' precisely because the defenders of the model hailed it as one of New Labour's most important innovations in education policy. The advocates of choice as a mechanism claimed that the power of user exit from substandard public services would have a greater effect on standards than either user voice or state control.

Mechanisms that promote 'voice', such as patient complaint systems, school governing boards and local community forums, have been criticised as empowering middle-class complainers who have greater educational and financial resources to skew public services to work to their advantage. Greater choice over providers—for example, of hospitals or schools—on the other hand, has been promoted as providing a more even playing field, enabling the poorest to have as broad a range of good choices as the middle classes.

I was a strong advocate of choice—for instance, the 'choose-and-book' system in healthcare and in increasing diversity of school education—in the hope that the strong incentive to attract patients and pupils with the funding that followed them, would help to push up standards in all public services. As the Public Administration Select Committee found in its report in 2005,[11] however, there are a number of factors which in practice limit the equitable consequences of choice-based mechanisms.

The need for extra capacity to allow for good providers to expand and the resultant closure of poor services means that extra money is constantly needed to keep services functioning at an adequate level for all service users. In addition, choice in healthcare, where health professionals can be more mobile to respond to demand for services, may be more appropriate than choice in education, where the rapid turnover of staff can have a detrimental effect on a well-performing school.

The Public Administration Select Committee concluded that public service reform should combine elements of choice and voice, but that without planning, particularly at the local government level, both elements have their downsides. Research into the performance of academies suggests that it was the strong leadership of these schools, as well as their well-paid, motivated staff and a clear ethos that made them successful that lay behind their success. It should be no surprise that educational standards in non-Academy schools have risen where all of these factors are present too. The extra money going into education cannot be ignored either. Increasing the number of teaching assistants, who have liberated teachers to get on with their job, would not have been possible without the injection of funding to schools.

As the government pursues further choice in health and education, research on the impacts of choice versus voice will illuminate the argument as to which is the more powerful method for driving public service reform without reducing equity.

Welfare reform

Welfare was the key area selected for reform by Labour before 1997. Tackling the consequences of mass unemployment associated with the Thatcher era was a key objective, particularly in relation to the young unemployed. Labour developed a proposal to pay for this without breaking its spending commitments via a windfall tax on the privatised utilities. The New Deal was initially successful, as the economy grew, and it provided tailored support to help not just young people, but also lone parents, the disabled and even musicians. Problems arose when the programme had found work for the easily employed and started to deal with people who were labelled 'retreads'. Here, too, New Labour's language imprisoned its decent ambitions for people's welfare.

Its rhetoric started out by emphasising 'welfare to work' and ended up with a stress upon 'rights and responsibilities' in a bid to appease the right-wing press who were suspicious of New Labour's credentials. The idea of a 'something for something' society emerged, but the language was targeted solely upon the poorest on benefits, not the richest in society. Tony Blair is surprisingly candid in his book on this point: '[E]emotionally I shared the view that some of the top earnings were unjustified, but rationally I thought this was the way of the world in a globalised economy, and there was more harm than good in trying to stop it.'[12] What Labour failed to realise, until too late, was that the nature of work in the United Kingdom—low paid and insecure—meant that many of the people who were on benefits were not long-term scroungers, but casualties of the low-end jobs market.

By the end of New Labour's time in government, the notion of payment by results had started to take hold, combined with private and voluntary-sector welfare-to-work organisations looking holistically at the person in front of them. But the damage had been done: public attitudes shifted decisively towards the idea that being on benefits made you a blight to society. It then became difficult to win any argument with the left that conditionality in benefits need not be a punishment, but part of a better contract between individuals and the state. What started as a very progressive programme to support and help people to get over the most difficult barriers to work became an aspect of the dog-whistle politics in which New Labour indulged too often.

The trouble with reform

So where did Labour go wrong? Part of the problem was the sense that New Labour instinctively disliked public servants. Tony Blair felt that he had to show that he was not prepared to be owned by the producers of services, or fall prey to the claim that Labour was in the clutches of the unions; hence the significance of his claim that two years of public sector reform had left 'scars on his back' in a speech given to the British Venture Capitalists Association. Yes, the public sector enjoyed pay increases, improved terms and conditions and new career options, but its workers were not invited to be partners in many of these reforms. Of course there were conservative forces in the public sector: social workers who opposed giving users the right to spend individual budgets, and GPs who fought against patients' rights groups wanting more access to information about their care. While it was important for New Labour to stand against these voices, it engaged with voluntary sector and campaign groups too little, and used the language of 'private versus public' too much.

It was absolutely right for New Labour to get away from being seen as a party that only represented the public sector, but since so much of what it wanted to achieve had to be delivered by public servants, it made little sense to alienate and confuse these workers at the moment they were expected to do more heavy lifting. The truth is that professional standards in most areas of the public sector have risen substantially: public servants are not as opposed to change as they once were. To characterise this whole group in such a negative way belittles the innovation and pockets of excellence that exist in what continues to be a beleaguered sector.

Blair recognised that the sheer pace of change could impact on the success of public service reform. Writing in his memoirs about the early years of the first government, he acknowledged a desire to 'drive through reform, but not to a depth or at a pace that overwhelmed people, that disorientated or destabilised them'.[13] But this ambition was set aside pretty quickly. In fact, Blair seemed to relish the idea of divide and rule in relation to public services. He frequently defined himself against the Labour party, against the public sector and against the forces of conservatism. Sometimes this was not his fault: union opposition to many of New Labour's sensible public sector reforms was just as pig-headed in its opposition. But it contributed to a sense that New Labour did not really care about 'stakeholder engagement'. In Blair's words: '[C]onsensus is wonderful, but not if it is part of a delusion that making real change with real impact is going to please everyone. It isn't. And in these circumstances the "consensus" can be a sign that the reform isn't really biting, in which case it probably isn't going to fulfil its purpose.'[14]

The inability of New Labour to communicate its successes in government, or the rationale for its reforms, was so frequently raised in seminar discussions that it became something of a cliche. Blair firmly laid the blame at the door of the media. 'The basic design of a modern set of services was being debated repeatedly in the government,' he wrote, 'but this was at points so hidden from view that the public had no idea about it and therefore, sadly, no real chance to participate in the debate.'[15] Labour tried to compensate for this by launching the Big Conversation in 2003, the brainchild of Matthew Taylor. It was, according to Taylor, successful in making politicians shift away from giving speeches to engaging with the public, even if it failed to develop detailed policy recommendations.[16] But the real failure was that the exercise was seen as a way of trying to fixing Labour's message at the top, rather than giving the public the tools to fix their communities themselves.

Labour came to the idea that the public should be put in control of services far too late. Cooperative schools were promoted by Ed Balls in 2008 as an alternative to the idea that schools had to compete to raise standards in education. The idea of the 'new mutualism' was first flirted with by New Labour in the late 1990s. In the preface to a book by Peter Kellner on mutualism, Tony Blair wrote: 'The debate around the "Third Way" is about achieving outcomes that truly benefit the many and not the few. It is about the development of ideas which break from the traditional public versus private battles.'[17] But there was little specific commitment to mutualism in the public sector. And this represented a missed opportunity to realise the benefits of public sector reform, without losing public support along the way. In spite of New Labour being the advocate of the notion that 'what counts is what works', it ended up being overly dogmatic, believing there was too much merit in using the private sector and failing to recognise that not everyone who opposed change was a conservative.

Conclusions

The major problem in terms of New Labour's reforms to public services concerns how it approached it, and how it narrated what it did. Targets were necessary to raise standards in services quickly, but they left Labour open to the accusation of being overly statist and top-down in style. The perverse incentives these initiatives could create and the stifling of innovation stemmed from policies that impacted upon public servants rather than enlisting their help. The overly managerial way in which New Labour governed in its first two terms, haunted its third. The government did try and change tack: innovations such as individual budgets and the expert patient programme reflected the recognition that steering not rowing was indeed the best way of governing. But by then it was too late. All further change in public services was seen as government meddling because the legitimacy of reform had not been established. Indeed, by the end of Tony Blair's time in office, he declared that 'consensus' in these areas was not desirable in any case.

Finally, New Labour failed its own test of pragmatism. With Academies, NHS providers and private finance initiatives (PFIs) there was too much sense that the private sector represented the 'silver bullet' rather than simply seeing private sector forces as part of the mix needed to deliver public goods. It is inaccurate to see New Labour as simply continuing the Thatcherite market-isation of public services. But at times key figures in New Labour evangelised about the importance of choice and competition when standards in services often improved through much more mundane factors, such as good leader-ship. New Labour needed a different narrative to bind people in their communities to public service change. Despite these failings, it would be hard to deny that many communities have changed for the better since 1997 because of New Labour's public service reforms. To what extent that will be totally obliterated by the Coalition remains to be seen.

There are several lessons for Labour to take from this period, now that it is in opposition. First, that the party and wider Labour movement should have a stake in reform from the outset. Academies, Foundation Hospitals and personal budgets were all measures that had a progressive purpose, but were not widely understood. Labour's current policy review needs to address the issue of how to ensure that communities and unions 'own' policies in these areas.

The second lesson of this period is that language matters. Pursuing mutuals instead of Foundation Hospitals, or private sector assistance in delivering public services, denote a commitment to the ethos of public service that sometimes seemed lacking in New Labour's lexicon. The very word 'reform' has become devalued and associated with endless change and reorganisation. It, too, might need to be replaced.

Third, Labour needs to be more content that different communities will choose different solutions to challenges in relation to services. The Coalition government may be overstating its localist credentials, but if it leaves office at the next election, Labour will have to deal with local governments that have become used to providing more direction over services than previously. This is an opportunity Labour should seize rather than reject.

Finally, Labour should remember that just because the evidence for a policy change is compelling, this does not mean that the public is convinced. It must campaign for change on the ground if it wishes to implement it in practice. This may slow down the process of reform, but it might help bind the public to changes that will protect the legacy of future policies.

Notes

1 Labour party, *Manifesto: Britain Forward not Back*, London, Labour party, 2005, p. 6.
2 Labour party, *Manifesto: New Labour Because Britain Deserves Better*, London, Labour party, 1997.
3 P. Mandelson and R. Liddle, *The Blair Revolution: Can New Labour Deliver?*, London, Faber & Faber, 1996, p. 151.
4 Ibid., p. 153.
5 T. Blair, *A Journey*, London, Hutchinson, 2010, p. 273.
6 Ibid., p. 669.
7 Ibid., p. 209.
8 In the YouGov Economy Tracker, 6–7 March 2011, 40 per cent of respondents agreed that Labour was the most to blame for the current spending cuts compared to 27 per cent who nominated the Con–Lib Coalition.
9 Labour party *Manifesto 2005*, p. 8.
10 P. Toynbee and D. Walker, *The Verdict: Did Labour Change Britain?* London, Granta Books, 2010.
11 Public Administration Select Committee, *Choice, Voice and Public Services: Fourth Report of Session, 2004–2005*, http://www.publications.parliament.uk/pa/cm200405/cmselect/cmpubadm/49/49i.pdf
12 Blair, *A Journey*, p. 587.
13 Ibid., p. 210.
14 Ibid., p. 586.
15 Ibid., p. 589.
16 'It's good to talk', Matthew Taylor's Blog, 24 February 2009.
17 P. Kellner, *New Mutualism: The Third Way*, London, Co-operative party, 1998.

Shirley Williams in Conversation with Tony Wright

Church House, Westminster, 9 September 2010

Tony Wright It is my enormous pleasure to preside over this session with Shirley Williams.

Shirley Williams Thank you very much. First of all thank you for letting me come—if I am not a fly on the wall, I am a wasp on the wall waiting to see who I can sting. It is also very kind of you to let somebody like me come along and be part of this discussion. If I may say so, it has been an extremely high quality discussion and if I make one or two critical remarks, which I am about to do, it does not take away from that. The sheer professional quality of the debate and discussion has been very considerable indeed.

Let me just say, first of all, something about the history and then something about the gaps. First the history. It is quite important to remember, and the constitutional session was very good indeed, that virtually every one of the major constitutional reforms that were adopted by Labour in its first term grew out of the so-called 'Cook–McLennan discussions'. In other words, they came out of what was a pre-coalition approach to the issue. I remember in 1976 when I was a member of the Cabinet, Roy Jenkins came to the Cabinet and proposed four things, with my support. The first of them was that there should be a Human Rights Act, the second was that there should be freedom of information, the third was that there should be proportional representation and the fourth was that there should be devolution for Scotland and Wales. Every single one of those propositions was voted down by a huge majority of the then Labour Cabinet. The only one where Roy and I were able to get additional support from members of the Cabinet was freedom of information where we were able to attract the support of Tony Benn. That is just an historical fact, and that means therefore that the impact of the move towards something of a coalition discussion—at a time when Paddy Ashdown thought that the Liberal Democrats were likely to become part of a left-of-centre coalition—was absolutely crucial in Labour taking on those constitutional reforms. Once the first term of Tony Blair had gone away, there were virtually no further significant reforms. They all came within that first term, and I think that is not without significance.

The second point that will shock you even more is that I remember perfectly well that both the Liberal Democrat party and the Labour party were totally opposed to the minimum wage in 1991. I know because I campaigned along with Chris Pond, who was head of the Low Pay Unit, to persuade both parties to adopt the idea of the minimum wage. Both were

Published by Blackwell Publishing Ltd, 9600 Garsington Road, Oxford OX4 2DQ, UK and 350 Main Street, Malden, MA 02148, USA

strongly against it, as all their economic advice was that it would lead to massive unemployment. That is to say there would be huge unemployment at the bottom end of the wage scale. I remember that we managed to persuade the Liberal Democrats, despite the almost complete opposition of the whole of the parliamentary party, to vote down their policy which was against the minimum wage. They rather liked voting down the parliamentary party and instinctively supported the principle of a minimum wage.

Labour was shocked by the fact that the Liberal Democrats had now bought into the minimum wage, and rapidly followed. But all of the advice that both parties drew on emphasised the inevitable fact of higher unemployment that would result from the minimum wage. So we ran our campaign on the basis of Senator Kennedy's analysis that the minimum wage in the United States, far from adding to unemployment, had actually reduced it because of the increased propensity to consume among those entitled to the minimum wage. It is a piece of history which most people are happy to forget.

In a very good discussion earlier, we still left out one of the most important issues which relates to why the Liberal Democrats have ended up in a coalition with the Conservatives: that was the very depressing record of Labour on everything to do with civil liberties. Whether you look at the prison population, detention without trial, the attitude towards extraordinary rendition, Labour's record was very bad indeed. One of the things that those of you who are going to rebuild the Labour party have simply got to ask is why that happened. And ask yourselves how it could possibly be the case that we had, year after year after year, the biggest prison population in the whole of Europe with the single exception, if you want to include Russia as the whole of Europe, of Russia.

Thirdly, if you look again at the record and at the recent tsunami of books about the Blair administration, it is significant that time after time after time, all our examples of which way to go come from the United States. Schools, welfare systems, attitudes towards imprisonment, they all come from America. Yet in case after case, the more progressive and appropriate example would have come from Europe.

That brings me to two other gaps apart from civil liberties. One very important discussion we had relates to Will Hutton's notion of looking again at the attitude towards ownership. This is fundamental in changing to a system we can all live with and not just the capitalist system—which incidentally has shown almost as serious failures as the old state communist system. I agree we must seek to develop a new economic model. It is hard to see how this can emerge unless we address the issue of ownership—not only individual ownership of capital, but more significantly the failure and dysfunctional effect of the shareholder system. This means the issue of accountability in the whole of the private sector is now central and Labour has got to think about it. Labour's role here is very important, but the scale of change has to be even greater than most of the people so far in this audience have recognised.

This brings me to another gap in the discussions which is very close to my heart. We talked a lot about the failure to address the issue of the 40 per cent of kids who don't go on to university. It is actually more like 43 per cent that we have shown very little interest in historically, including for much of the previous Labour government's period in office. One reason for this, quite frankly, is that the radical proposals put forward by Mike Tomlinson in 2004 to have a credit-accumulation system where those undertaking vocational courses and those undertaking academic courses would be part of an overall umbrella system of qualifications which allowed for mobility between the two sectors were rejected by the Blair government. All that was proposed brilliantly, radically and excitingly by Tomlinson, and was rejected by the then Prime Minister on the grounds that it would put at risk the gold standard—the A-level system. Yet the A-level system is basically shot. More and more very good state schools as well as many very good private schools are moving towards the international baccalaureate. They perceive that the A level has become the victim of the Internet because it is all about memorising and copying and setting down again what you are expected to, and has very little to do with either imagination or innovation. It is the system in which we have allowed ourselves to be imprisoned, with the result that people on the vocational track are still in this country, unlike Scotland, regarded as having failed to make it and having failed to succeed.

A final point about devolution. Somebody said that devolution should not be to countries but to people and this is absolutely vital. Labour has been very autocratic and many see it in that way, not having devolved power to individuals in the delivery of public services, for example. The other point about devolution is that it is increasingly leading to the Celtic countries going in one direction and England in the other. We see now that the Celtic countries over and over again revert to 'old' Labour, pre-Blair. And that is also because there is effectively no Conservative party in either country. Meanwhile England goes sweetly on its way and is likely to become more 'right wing'. You need to look further at the question of whether the United Kingdom can still hold together, unless we think very carefully about what I term 'clasping' policies: policy that brings the cultures of the UK together rather than splitting them apart.

TW So how can we best explain the basis of Labour's failures in office—is there a thread that connects all of these together?

SW They are not discrete failures. They all flow from the fact that essentially Tony Blair, who was a brilliant politician and communicator, was a Christian Democrat and not a Social Democrat.

TW That leads me on to my second question: it seems to me that one of the really big questions going beyond the discussion that we have had so far is this. I always see you as quintessentially a Social Democrat and you left the

Labour party in a way that I could not because I was tribal Labour and my parents wouldn't have allowed me to leave! You inhabited a broad progressive tradition which I think made you more able to move in a way you felt stayed with that tradition. It seems to me that the dilemma we are confronting now is not just the dilemma of the Labour party in this country, the dilemma, is that of social democracy itself. This is a generalised problem across all social democratic countries. There you are, a fully paid-up life-time Social Democrat and yes you can identify the particular failures of Labour in power, but what about this question of what an earth has social democracy itself got to say now about some of the big issues confronting us. Does it provide the basis for a social movement in the way that it did a hundred years ago when it started? Can it get a purchase on some of these issues that really can get some public resonance? Is it yesterday's tradition? Or tomorrow's?

SW That is a huge question. I think social democracy is for yesterday and tomorrow, but not today. Why do I take that easy way out? Because tomorrow will bring us the terribly harsh facts of environmental warming, of resource scarcity, of growing ageing in the West, and effective competition steadily going up the value chain from the newly emerging countries. This means that we are beginning to move from a period of plenty to a period once again of scarcity. The question then will be in the rich but 'illusion-hugging' West how we can deal with that in a way that will actually enable us to avoid authoritarian regimes and sustain the concept of democracy. In that context, first of all, equality will come back with a bang and I think the sense of outrage, and not just unfairness, but outrage, at the share of resources that go to a very small proportion of the population will become much greater than it is today. I can see that emerging in the next few years. There will be a lot of pressure to pursue more intense regulation of the banks and financial interests. That will only work if we are willing to accept the role of the EU: it is not going to work at the national level. We have to think about how we square the concept of fairness and equality with what is going to be a scarcity of resources to share among ourselves. We are entering a phase of austerity; I don't know if this age of austerity is going to end anytime soon.

TW That is a really interesting answer because you might realistically expect that the collapse of financial capitalism would have meant a real opening to the left right across Europe; but it has had the reverse effect—people huddle for cover and the movement has been rightwards and not leftwards. If you look historically, isn't it the case that social democracy has done best when capitalism has done best? As long as the economy was doing its business, as long as the City was pumping out money, we could invest in hospitals and rebuild schools. When capitalism doesn't deliver the goods, we are in deep trouble.

SW I'd like to dispute that: I don't think what it did was to produce social democracy. It produced a very successful Labour private-sector capitalist government. Labour in government almost completely failed to narrow the gap between rich and poor. It did less badly than the Conservatives, but not much. It did not address the issue of wealth taxation and what it did was to produce a wonderful period of prosperity, which, to be fair to the Labour government, kept it away from further deterioration which happened in the United States. I remember the ratio of executive pay to average working pay under the Labour government was under roughly ten times where it was in 1964 when I first became an MP and the ratio was about 9:1. It is now 60:1 in the United Kingdom, and more like 110:1 in the United States. Now, everybody did fine because the rising tide did lift all boats, but it did almost nothing to reduce the differences between the boats. So everyone was happy until the chill came. And when the chill came those who thought they had done relatively well in those years become much more conscious of the 10 per cent at the top. That may be even truer of Europe than it is of the United States. What has happened in the United States is a rounding on government itself. One of the things that struck me on my recent visit to the US was that we were in a way a fortunate country in having a coalition. When you saw what happened when the political parties were unable to work together at all, you then see a period of very real difficulty. I think we are going to get through the difficulties and no doubt the Liberal Democrats and the Conservatives will be bashed around and no doubt that is perfectly fair. But there is a real question in the United States as to whether they can get through this. That is because of the level of tribalism which has become even more acute as a result of what is seen as the failure of democratic government in continuing to deliver prosperity to most of the American people.

The New Labour Government's Place in History

BRIAN BRIVATI

THE YEARS 1997 to 2010 will be seen as a seminal era of profound change and challenge for the United Kingdom. As a 45 year-old, it is tempting to see the period in which one comes to maturity as generally defining because it frames so much of your own self-image. However, objectively speaking, the period in which Labour held power was one of the most turbulent in geopolitical and socio-economic terms of any period since the end of the Second World War. While judgements on the performance of the New Labour governments must, by definition, be partial and limited this close to events, the current dominant view of these administrations as generally unsuccessful and disappointing needs to be challenged. Though the verdict is mixed, in terms of British history these years will come to be seen in a much more positive light than they are at present.

It was the combination of challenges running simultaneously through this period and unexpected events changing the course of policies and priorities that made this such a seminal epoch. Britain faced a much greater strategic and human challenge between 1939 and 1945. But there is no other period in modern British history during which governments simultaneously faced a systemic global financial crisis, major international conflicts, which meant that our armed forces were engaged in two separate foreign wars, and such fundamental changes to our polity and society. The very nature of the nation-state was questioned, reformed and remains debated to a greater extent than at any time since the beginning of the twentieth century. In sociological terms, this was also a period of profound generational change and one in which the impact of digital technologies became embedded in the lives and experiences of an overwhelming majority of British citizens.

At the same time, what J. K. Galbraith termed the 'Culture of Contentment' became palpable in the concentration of long-term poverty geographically and socially in some communities of the United Kingdom, while the bulk enjoyed a decade of sustained affluence. The multicultural nature of British society was challenged, and the nature of British identity and citizenship questioned. The ability of government to influence and shape events in such a period was limited. But how well did Labour do?

There are broadly three ways in which history might judge the Blair–Brown governments in terms of their response to these combinations of challenges and events. Each depends on the perspective from which you are looking and the balance of the judgement is different in each.

Published by Blackwell Publishing Ltd, 9600 Garsington Road, Oxford OX4 2DQ, UK and 350 Main Street, Malden, MA 02148, USA

The angles from which we might judge these governments, I would suggest are as follows:

- The Blair–Brown governments in comparison with other administrations facing similar challenges in terms of the geopolitical and socio-economic context, and also their performance in comparison with past governments.
- The Blair–Brown governments in comparison with other progressive governments in British history set out an ambitious programme of change and reform, but how did they perform as reforming administrations?
- The Blair–Brown governments might be understood in terms of a broader reading of contemporary British history, but what difference did they make to the course of British history?

This chapter suggests how this era of contemporary British history might now be judged, and offers a view on these governments with particular reference to the changing place of consensus since 1945. It focuses on the issue of 'consensus' because of the central role this concept plays in the evaluation of governing performance. Governments since 1945 can be broken down into consensus breakers/makers, and consensus managers. How one views Britain's performance over this period is largely determined by how one views governments in relation to the polity they inherited, and the polity they left behind.

Historical comparisons

Although these administrations are identified by the names of the two prime ministers who ran them, it is a mistake to evaluate them purely in terms of the personalities of the two leaders. Moreover, the Blair premiership was in many ways a joint premiership because of the dominant and critical role that Gordon Brown played as Chancellor. Though Blair goes out of his way in his memoirs to present his administration as presidential, it was in fact collegial in many respects with Brown, Peter Mandelson and Deputy Prime Minister John Prescott all playing key roles. It was not a conventional cabinet government, but then conventional cabinet governments have rarely existed since the 1960s.

In terms of comparison, the governments that New Labour will come to be seen as resembling most are the Conservative governments of the period 1951–1963—although the context in which Blair–Brown operated was even more challenging in many respects. Churchill, Eden and Macmillan inherited a new political and economic settlement created by the postwar Attlee government and based on the mixed-economy welfare state. Beginning with Churchill, these administrations were set on pursuing a fundamentally different path, which would undermine and ossify the welfare state by failing to extend and develop it, while at the same time failing to reform it in the direction of the free market deregulation they favoured. In other words, these governments became trapped early on by a commitment to fulfil the terms of the settlement outlined by Attlee, and therefore did much less than they had hoped in moving the country in their own direction. They were hampered in their ambition for change by the advent of a series of small conflicts and one large one: Suez. They faced profound sociological change driven by new technology in the form of the affluent society. They could not move far to the right because of the electoral constraint of the consensus that supported the Attlee settlement, and they faced a profound challenge in terms of redefining the place of the United Kingdom in the world as the British Empire continued being dismantled and the strategic basis for the withdrawal from East of Suez was laid. While not wishing to carry the comparison too far, we can see that there are similarities with New Labour era.

The Blair–Brown government inherited a political economy that was founded on the Thatcherite consensus and enshrined the status of the free market, the degradation of the public and the lionisation of the private. Central to this consensus was the proposition that Labour could not win if it proposed increases in direct taxation, a radical defence policy, the re-nationalisation of utilities or industry in general, or a withdrawal from the European Union (EU). This new political economy was operating in the context of a profoundly changing geopolitical context with the rise of new economic superpowers and a deep shift in the nature of the security threats to United Kingdom citizens. These combined to create, in the last years of the Major government, a crisis of identity in British culture. However, like Churchill, the Blair–Brown governments inherited a sound financial situation and a ready-made economic model based on an Atlantic version of capitalism.

In some ways, the Blair–Brown governments were more successful at remaking the consensus they inherited than the Churchill–Eden governments had been because while they firmly endorsed the free market model, they placed public services back at the heart of the governing mission of United Kingdom politics. Macmillan utilised the new affluence to drive his electoral success in 1959, and made a virtue of his governing through consensus. New Labour won in 2001 and 2005 because they delivered the domestic economic goods that were required.

In terms of foreign policy challenges the record of these two governments can also be compared. The New Labour project initially had no foreign policy. The Chicago speech was Blair's intellectual justification and rationalisation of decisions already made. It was not an ideology worked out on the basis of social democratic principles. Even if it was one that basically fulfilled the fundamental principles on which the Labour party had been founded—representation for all—it was also one of the finest post-hoc rationalisations ever penned by a serving prime minster. It was certainly needed. The place of these governments in British history has become deeply intertwined with the Iraq War. These earlier Conservative administrations oversaw the end of the British Empire and launched a final bid to maintain power beyond economic means through the Suez Crisis. The terms of United Kingdom policy were set by events and the response was forced, reluctant and contingent on a final reckoning with reality. The post-hoc rationalisation was then offered by Macmillan in his famous 'winds of change' speech.

Though they shared a taste for fine rhetoric, the situation faced by the two governments was markedly different. Faced with the shock attack that happened on 9/11, the Blair government, and Blair personally, consciously and intuitively, embarked on a new strategic direction. In part, this was in defence of the United Kingdom, but it was also heavily influenced by internationalism and the responsibility to protect. The liberal interventions in Kosovo, Afghanistan and Iraq established a new basis for British foreign policy and a new articulation of the exercise of British power abroad. This new basis is, at the time of writing, being continued by the Coalition government in Libya.

Overall, the comparison between the New Labour government and a previous government that faced similar challenges can be seen as a positive one. What then of other reforming governments? The great reforming administrations of the twentieth century were not only social democratic and progressive in their political self-image. The Thatcher governments of 1979–1991 made significant changes to the political economy of Britain. However, for the purposes of this section, we are attempting to compare like with like—that is, governments that were identified or self-identified with a social democratic and liberal approach while setting out a significant reform agenda. Two administrations fit this bill: the Liberal government elected in 1906, and the Labour government elected in 1945. How does New Labour compare?

Such an evaluation of the New Labour governments needs to distinguish between the periods before and after the financial crisis. The 1906 and the 1945 governments changed the terms of political discourse and articulated a lasting consensus on the approach of the state to the management of welfare and the running of the economy. Before 2008, the New Labour governments were, aside from in the public sector, moving within the Thatcherite consensus and did not change it significantly. This judgement is based on a comparison of the political economy Labour advocated at the 1979, 1983 and 1987 general elections and the political economy articulated in the 1997, 2001 and 2005 general elections. The former were based on nationalisation and then the renationalisation of leading industries, direct government planning of significant aspects of the economy, withdrawal from the EU because it was seen as a capitalist club, the development of welfare provision and radical views on defence policy. The latter manifestoes signalled the abandonment of these ideas and the embrace of the market economy in which the state had no role in industry but was confined to the delivery of public services. Many have argued, not least from within the administrations themselves, that while they endorsed much of the Thatcher governments' reform agenda, Labour moved Britain's political economy in new directions. Assessing such claims requires judgement about what constitutes an appropriate benchmark against which to judge the basis of the political economy of a political party. Historically, New Labour moved significantly away from a theory of the state that promoted an active role in the economy to one that denied such a role. While it maintained a distinct view about the delivery of public goods in health, education and welfare, in contrast to Thatcherism, it is nevertheless the case that in its own terms the Labour party rewrote its own benchmarks in these years.

In other words, compared to these other two greatest left-of-centre reforming governments, New Labour's record, despite the minimum wage, Sure Start, devolution and so on, remains that of an administration operating within terms set by previous administrations, rather than defining those terms itself. Moreover, the broad basis of welfare reforms and constitutional reform were not devised by the New Labour leadership. The entire constitutional and welfare agenda had been developed during the leadership of John Smith and articulated by his Social Justice Commission. When the reform agenda outlined in that document was exhausted, the New Labour governments ran out of steam and ideas.

A shift away from the endorsement of the Thatcher consensus came only in the final phase of these governments, after the financial crisis. Then the rules of the political economy established by Thatcher were ripped to shreds by Gordon Brown. The level, nature and structure of the intervention organised by Brown reopened the entire debate on the nature of British capitalism, on the divide between public and private, on state ownership of enterprises, and on the ability of the state to regulate. However, even here this was not a return to the agenda of the 1980s. Companies were nationalised with the intention of privatising them again, regulation was limited, and there was no resort to income tax rises to pay off the deficit generated by the rescue packages. Though forced by events rather than grounded in a planned and implemented project, New Labour remade the Thatcherite consensus in the last two years of power as the Conservatives rejected the approach taken and presented a significantly different way forward.

Consensus

Tony Blair's expressed intention when he became prime minister was to change Britain forever. His personal concerns changed drastically during his time in office as he became much more focused on security and international policy. His successor, Gordon Brown, also came to be more concerned with global issues, but this was in part by necessity rather than choice. Together, however, they reshaped the direction of travel for the United Kingdom. How then are we to attempt to fit the New Labour governments into British history? In earlier work on this theme, I have suggested that a key dynamic of British history over this period has been consensus. I suggested a periodisation of the postwar era in terms of:

- Consensus construction: From the point at which reconstruction began to be considered in the Second World War—that is after Stalingrad—through to after the main body of Labour's legislative programme and the major structures of the Cold War were established, around 1949–50.
- Consensus operation: From then until around the time of the 1959 election this consensus basically operated with one major challenge—the Suez crisis of 1956—and an on-going debate about the status of sterling in the world economy. Suez caused a massive trauma about Britain's relative position but did not alter or challenge other elements in the operation of the consensus. The pound inspired the first major work in the decline debate, Andrew Shonfield's analysis of the position of the currency published in 1957. Thereafter the consensus was assaulted from both left and right, in political analysis and cultural commentary, as Britain's problems piled up.
- Non-consensus politics: Britain then entered a prolonged period of ideological instability. This lasted until 1979 when the debate was simplified in terms of support for or opposition to Thatcherism. In this period the consensus did not operate. The number of major questions about British politics and culture that were profoundly contested outweighed the number of issues on which there was a broad agreement, or at least a dominant view. The idea that suggesting radical alternatives or diametrically opposed sets of policies would be electorally costly was jettisoned. For the first time since 1951, Edward Heath's actual programme in 1970 and Harold Wilson's manifesto in 1974 offered starkly different programmes.
- Consensus construction and operation: Non-consensus politics lasted until after the 1992 election. There then began the construction of a new consensus based on the broad parameters of the Thatcher settlement. This was translated into a conventional wisdom about what was deemed electorally viable. It is difficult to date this before 1992 because Labour remained committed to withdrawal from the European Community, unilateral nuclear disarmament, increasing direct taxation to fund public expenditure and re-nationalisation of a gradually reducing list of industries. The initial shifts signalled in the 1992 election were stabilised by 1997 with the positive embrace of the market economy, the EU and even nuclear weapons.

This analysis suggests the following set of chronological demarcations:

- 1943–1950: Consensus formation
- 1950–1959: Consensus operation
- 1959–1979: Consensus breakdown, developing sense of political instability
- 1979–1992: Non-consensus politics ending in consensus formation
- 1992–2008: Consensus operation

Up until 2008, New Labour had come to terms with the political economy of Thatcherism and thereafter deepened and extended it. New Labour in power merged the two major critiques of British political economy by advocating an individualism that was tempered by improved public services and greater social responsibility. They shifted the Thatcherite consensus by making the need to improve public service delivery by any means available a key political priority rather than an afterthought. They extended the Thatcher consensus by the systematic abandonment of universalism in welfare provision which has permitted the perpetuation of an underclass, despite commitments to poverty reduction. They were able to do these things because they were the Labour party. In turn, because they were the Labour party they placed a much greater emphasis on public services and increased taxes to provide the expenditure needed in these areas, but they have not stopped the process of reforming the relationship between public services and the market. In terms of world power they endorsed the Thatcherite emphasis on Atlanticism. However, and in marked contrast, they have pursued a sustained attempt at moral leadership through debt reduction and have not abandoned the EU in favour of the United States on any major social or economic question, but only on security and defence issues.

In terms of British identity there has also been a striking endorsement of two contradictory impulses. On the one hand, New Labour was determinedly multiculturalist in its symbolism, appointments and ethos. On the other, it was overtly Powellite in its immigration and asylum policy and, in the main, on law and order. In terms of the constituencies a government must address, this combination of policies was broadly consensual. It was, with the exception of the liberation of Iraq, generally popular and tended to minimise the room for political opposition from both the left and the right. But more than this, it became in more instances than not, the generally accepted means of delivering.

Between 1997 and 2008 New Labour operated an inherited consensus in political economy—by the historical standards of what social democracy had meant since 1945 its deviation from that consensus, though important in mitigating aspects of inequality—represented little more than tinkering. Faced with challenges and events, the government did reshape aspects of that consensus, pushed its boundaries and redefined elements of it, but they did not abandon the main outlines and constraints to action that they had inherited from Thatcher. At times they even celebrated their embrace of these constraints.

For many in the Labour movement this proved unpalatable and party membership declined, party activism fell away and the very meaning of social democracy became open to serious question. To an extent the shift away from traditional party political activism and identity was a generational one, and the volatility of the electorate reinforced this shift. However, this is not to argue that the impact of New Labour was to deepen the depoliticisation of contemporary society. While the Labour movement and the Labour party have steadily declined, the level and intensity of political participation has increased in terms of environmental and anti-globalisation activism. Because Labour was in government and operating within the terms of reference of the consensus, it was unable and in many cases unwilling to engage with this politics. For much of the period in power this did not represent a problem for the party but historically it signals a profound change, and in terms of its ability to win power from opposition by mobilising those opposed to the direction of the coalition, it is an important challenge.

After 2008, the final period of New Labour in power saw the breakdown of this consensus which has ushered in a new period of non-consensus politics. There was a combination of factors at work in the shift away from the Thatcher consensus. The response of the government to the financial crisis was, of course, the most important. However, the repercussions of the expenses scandal should not be underestimated in terms of the demand for political reform. In broader historical terms, the impact of the expenses scandal will come to be seen as profound. Yet the breakdown in the consensus was driven more by a clear division between the two main political parties on the response that was necessary to the deficit and the extent of action that was needed to ameliorate, or indeed, reverse, the negative impact of the recession. To a significant extent the gulf between the two parties in terms of headline political economy priorities has again been exposed.

Ownership is a part of this renewed breach to be sure, but this should not be overstated. Rather it is the issue that proved so divisive the 1980s that has again emerged as a faultline: unemployment. Once again politicians are debating whether unemployment is a price worth paying for a return to economic competitiveness. This is now expressed as the speed and volume of deficit reduction, the level and intensity of cuts and the broad acceptability of a return to unemployment. Labour has returned to a tradition which places employment at the centre of its critique, expressed both as a defence of the public sector and a different model of economic management. The Coalition has elevated deficit reduction above all other considerations of political economy. The argument is clearer today than it has been since 1994.

Conclusions

At the beginning of this chapter, I suggested three ways in which we might view New Labour's place in history:

- The Blair–Brown governments in comparison with other administrations facing similar situations in terms of the geopolitical and socio-economic context; how did they do compared to past governments?
- The Blair–Brown governments in comparison with other progressive governments in British history that set out an ambitious programme of change and reform; how did they fare as reforming governments?
- The Blair–Brown governments in terms of a broader reading of contemporary British history; what difference did they make to the course of British history?

In conclusion, I want to suggest a much more balanced and positive appraisal of these governments than is currently the conventional wisdom. Compared to past administrations dealing with rapid changes in geopolitical realities, the necessity of foreign conflict and technologically driven social change, New Labour in power was responsive, imaginative and provided moral leadership underpinned by a clear sense of purpose and role. This contrasts very positively with the years 1951–1963, when Conservative governments were incapable of articulating a real alternative to Empire, and dealt with affluence by freezing the welfare state in its least developmental stage. The arid Churchill years were superseded by the wild adventurism of Eden and the complacent stagnation of Macmillan and Home.

In contrast, the benchmark moments of the years since 1997 represented attempts, however imperfect, to respond to the challenges associated with profound changes with policies that was driven by evidence and flexibility rather than ideology. The paradigmatic instance of that flexibility was the response by Gordon Brown to the financial crisis and the ripping up of the Thatcher consensus when it was no longer fit for purpose. However, the extent to which this governing performance was in a profound sense reforming or radical was also defined by the relationship between these governments and the Thatcher consensus. The Atlantic model of capitalism was only finally abandoned in response to events, rather than design. Compared to the governments of 1906 and 1945, these were not, in domestic terms, agenda-setting administrations in most respects. Rather they were followers of the Thatcher reform agenda. They spent a decade tinkering with a political economy that was failing. There was a profound lack of vision and courage in government: that was understandable in electoral terms, but leaves even the first Blair government a mere shadow of its predecessors in 1906 and 1945.

I would argue that the exception to this mixed view of the New Labour's place in history was in the field of foreign policy—a judgement which is far from a popular one currently. The radical nature of New Labour's foreign policy does set it apart from previous Labour administrations and may eventually come to be seen as its most positive and important global legacy. For the first time since the end of Empire, British governments had a firm foundation and a clear sense of purpose in terms of their engagement with the world. The purpose can be summed up as the 'Responsibility to Protect'. From Kurdish Iraq, to Sierra Leone, through the nations of the former Yugoslavia and in many other parts of the most challenging places in the world, the exercise of soft and hard power by the United Kingdom has been utilised in defence of this principle. From debt relief to regime change in Iraq, British foreign policy has rarely had finer hours in term of the development of sustained and ethically coherent foreign policy.

What difference did these governments make to the course of British history? I argue that they finally abandoned the Thatcher consensus and have left Britain in a state of non-consensus politics in terms of political economy, but in a consensus that they created and defined on foreign policy, as is apparent from the current Libyan crisis. More than this, they ended the idea that Britain was a country in decline and lacked a coherent role in the world. It was the United Kingdom that led the global response to the financial crisis, and is currently playing a central role in supporting the remaking of the Middle East and North Africa. Labour was made electable and will come back into power again. When it does, it will look back on a mixed legacy from these years, but one that can serve as the basis for a new agenda for reform and governance based securely on social democratic principles.

Afterword
Future Directions for Labour

PATRICK DIAMOND and MIKE KENNY

THE VARIOUS contributors to this volume highlight significant public policy challenges where Labour needs to draw important, sometimes even painful, lessons from its experience in government. The aim is ultimately to develop a resonant and forward-looking agenda for a future left-of-centre government in the progressive tradition. Here, we highlight several key strategic themes, and elaborate their broader significance for a revitalised conception of British social democracy.

The first concerns developing a new politics of social justice, combined with a stronger accent on innovation and growth. For this to be viable, Labour has to discard its reputation for excessive reliance on traditional forms of state provision that engender dependency and passivity, neglecting the enormous appetite for self-organising, community-orientated approaches. It means returning to the argument for a wider diffusion of property and asset ownership that addresses widening inequalities of wealth and economic power in British society. This emphasises the imperative of building more affordable social housing, broadening the basis of home ownership, strengthening regulation in the rental sector to promote security of tenure, and ensuring people on middle and lower incomes have access to more secure finance.

Labour must also develop concrete proposals to address the steady erosion of living standards among hard-pressed families above the cut-off point for tax credits, whose desertion of Labour was a key factor in its spectacularly poor performance in the Midlands and the South of England in the 2010 general election. This should include proposals to improve take-home pay for low- and middle-income households through a comprehensive reform of the tax system, shifting the onus from income tax to inheritance, property, unearned income and environmental 'bads'. The long-term aim should be to tilt the United Kingdom economy away from the low-wage, low-skilled, low-productivity syndrome that has historically characterised British capitalism through a proactive industrial strategy, accepting that the future lies as much in high-value services and knowledge-based industries as traditional heavy manufacturing.

Nonetheless, Labour will struggle to gain real momentum unless it rebuilds the party's reputation for economic competence. No centre-left party in the industrialised world will attain office unless it is trusted to manage the economy fairly and efficiently. Labour has to regain its credentials for prudent and sound economic management. It must start by emphasising that the objectives of economic stability and economic reform are intimately con-

Published by Blackwell Publishing Ltd, 9600 Garsington Road, Oxford OX4 2DQ, UK and 350 Main Street, Malden, MA 02148, USA

nected. Structural reform of Britain's economic base is needed in order to correct macroeconomic imbalances, ensuring that the British economy is less dependent on financial services. There will be no long-term stability in the United Kingdom economy without fundamental reform of financial regulation, the banking sector, and capital and credit markets, as well as stronger international regulatory oversight and cooperation between countries at the global level.

The second theme concerns the contraction of the public domain, and Labour's relationship with the British state. New Labour restricted its room for manoeuvre by being too much in thrall to the doctrines of the New Public Management that had been introduced in the 1980s and 1990s by its Conservative predecessor. It is far from clear that marketisation and competition provide the answer to all of the challenges besetting Britain's public services. The emphasis on efficiency and value for money has threatened to negate the importance of quality and experience rooted in the transactional relationship between professionals and the citizen. The introduction of quasi-market mechanisms led to fragmented delivery across major areas of the public sector, eroding confidence in public services despite historic levels of investment in hospitals, schools and policing. Labour has to develop a new conception of the state allied to an enhanced and strengthened notion of the public realm. This means developing delivery models for public services that are neither exclusively market-based nor statist. It should learn the lessons of coproduction and mutualisation, but rather than favouring any particular model, the accent should be on greater plurality and hybridity in the structures of delivery and public management. The state in Britain has to be fundamentally reinvented, but the answer will not be found in central planning driven top-down from the centre.

A final theme concerns Labour's patchy and inconsistent record on constitutional and political reform. The party urgently needs to put together a new prospectus for democratic change in the United Kingdom. It needs to convince sceptics that it has the will and determination to see through far-reaching reform of Britain's institutions, even where vested interests attempt to veto change. That means framing a compelling argument about the inability of the anachronistic Westminster model to deliver the responsive and effective governance that the United Kingdom needs. Setting aside partisan tribalism and working with the Liberal Democrats on vitally important issues such as House of Lords reform is important as an initial step to repositioning Labour as the party of radical constitutional reform. In this volume we do not consider foreign and European policy, but Labour also needs to think beyond the nation-state given the global and international nature of today's challenges and the ever-more insistent implications of greater interdependence.

The scale of the task facing Labour in the coming years is hard to overstate, as several contributors to this volume make painfully clear. Shaping a credible strategy not only for winning elections, but successfully governing Britain depends on facing up to the new strategic context, exercising leadership that is sufficiently brave to pursue long-term ambitions, as well as dealing with the pressures and tactical opportunities of the 'here-and-now'. Labour's policy review has to address the most pressing and urgent dimensions of change that Britain will confront in the period ahead, while not being afraid to draw on the lessons of New Labour's record in a non-doctrinaire fashion. More generally, Labour needs to accept that we are in a period when social democracy is at perilously low ebb across Europe. This does not necessarily make it an ideological lineage that belongs only to the past. Faced with the cluster of issues that are likely to dominate the political agenda of the next decade—the growth deficit, the continuing fallout of the financial crisis, the demand for equalising the costs and burdens of global economic restructuring, climate change, an ageing society, the sustainability of pensions and public provision of social care—new collective solutions and a commitment to reclaiming the public interest may well rise in salience once again.

As a prerequisite, the argument of this collection is that Labour has to re-engage with the last thirteen years in government. This will not guarantee success by any means, but ignoring the lessons of the party's record in government means discarding an immensely valuable resource. The danger is always that Labour once again reverts to the status of the natural party of opposition, preferring doctrinal purity over the dilemmas and hard choices of governing in a tough and demanding world. Instead, it must plot a path back to power by assuming the mantle of an accomplished and trusted party of government in British politics, firmly anchored in the progressive tradition from which it can continue to draw inspiration.

Index

Note: page numbers in italics refer to tables and diagrams; alphabetical arrangement is word-by-word.